ENDORSEMENTS

Fr. Peter Sanders presents the healing ministry in a powerful new way using a simple but comprehensive approach. Traumatic events of recent years have crushed people spiritually and psychologically. Healing is desperately sought as many are broken and depressed. Jesus gives the answer. "Come to me, all you who labor and are burdened, and I will give you rest" (Matthew 11:28, NAB). Congratulations to Fr. Peter for creating a unique, solid new healing guide useful to all who respond to Jesus' call. May we become an instrument of healing love for one another.

—*Fr. Robert DeGrandis, S.S.J.,*
noted author and speaker
in the healing ministry

Reading this book cleared my mind and made me feel as if I had attended a whole course on the healing ministry. As I read, I was struck by the clear wisdom which dispelled many weak, unclear, or inadequate teachings. It was truly a powerful experience. *Healing in the Spirit of Jesus* is simply the best "equipping for the work of service" I have seen and that we have desperately needed in this area. Seminarians, priests, leaders, and lay people alike will reap great benefits from Fr Peter's work.

—*Linda Schubert,*
author and international conference speaker
in the healing ministry

What an excellent healing manual for both the sick and those in ministry! I find it to be very provocative for both the Catholic and Protestant mind. I know that it has challenged me and changed my perspective regarding some areas of healing. We both have found that many of the experiences that we have walked through to be in agreement with his writings.

—*Revs. Don and Debby Boles,*
Pastors of Family Worship Center
(International Foursquare Church)
Exeter, CA

Fr Peter outlines the heart of the liturgical church for the ministry of healing. He draws a critical distinction in portraying healing as a dimension of our relationship with Jesus. This book will be a valuable tool not only for those interested in pursuing this calling but those who want a deeper personal relationship with Jesus and to be empowered by the Holy Spirit. Fr Peter shares much insight and wisdom from his experience in the healing ministry.

—*Carolyn Suty,*
U.S. Director,
Aglow International

HEALING
in the
SPIRIT of
JESUS

A
PRACTICAL
GUIDE
TO THE
MINISTRY

FR. PETER SANDERS, C.O.

*To Ann,
Many healing ...*
Fr. Peter

WINEPRESS WP PUBLISHING

ISBN 1-59721-520-3
Library of Congress Catalog Card Number: 2002114857

CONTENTS

ACKNOWLEDGMENTS

Give encouragement to each other, and keep strengthening one another (1 Thess. 5:11). Without words that gave me strength, this work would have never been started. Thank you to all who moved me along and encouraged me through many months.

Beyond words are deeds that were crucial to producing a coherent and orderly book. First in line is Rose Payán, who generously carried the work along with many hard hours of research, planning, and tedious editing. She worked with Susan Allardyce, who had the monumental task of transcribing the original tapes.

Second, thanks go to Father Thomas Kieffer and Father Michael Drury, beloved confreres in my Oratorian Congregation who demonstrated patience and offered wise advice. Chapter 13 on the Catholic Church's teaching was essentially inspired by Fr. Michael.

The members of a covenant group to which I belong, Fire of Pentecost, faithfully read and offered many revisions, challenges, and corrections, for which I am grateful. These are Nora Merlo, Rose Payán, Linda Schubert, Chip Sundstrom, Carolyn Suty, and Ernie VonEmster. God bless all of you for your fruitful efforts.

Finally, I thank the team of WinePress Publishing for thoughtful and professional collaboration.

INTRODUCTION

WHY ANOTHER BOOK ON HEALING?

There is little doubt that the ministry of healing, mainly as an expression of the movement of the Spirit of God in the twentieth century, has had an immense impact on the whole Body of Christ, in almost all Christian denominations. In most places there is at least a tacit acceptance that the Lord Jesus Christ continues to heal his people through the power of his Spirit.

Through the years many books on Christian healing have been published. Some are practical in that they offer help; others answer questions and doubts; still others relate testimonies. One thing they all have in common is that they reflect the current state of healing ministry when they were written. Many works are simply out of date, representing ideas and understandings that have seen better days. There is a "graying" of the charismatic renewal and other renewal movements. Most individuals involved in healing ministry are of that first generation of the renewal. They have learned a lot and have taught us much and we owe them a deep debt of gratitude.

The new generation in renewal, its ministries, and specifically the healing ministry, needs fresh, concrete guidance to grow into fullness. We need the collective wisdom of the successes and failures of the past generation. We also need fresh teaching that will inspire, empower, and equip a new generation of healing ministers. This book, together with the volumes that will follow, are purposed to put updated, comprehensive, and easily accessible teaching into the Body of Christ. They are meant to bring the operation of the gifts of the Spirit into a new maturity.

During the years 1997 to 2000, I was privileged to direct the Institute for the Healing Ministry in the Catholic dioceses of San Jose, San Francisco, Oakland, and Monterey. Conducted both in English and Spanish, more than five hundred people went through the year-long process of teaching, study, workshops, and anointed prayer. These institutes provided a time of great grace and refreshment for the charismatic renewal in Northern California—they were truly a surprise from the Spirit of God. Theresa Heather, who, with her husband Rod, co-leads the Bread of Life prayer community at St. Justin's parish in the "Silicon Valley" of California, has been in the Catholic Charismatic Renewal in Northern California for more than twenty years. Recently she summed up what the Institute, with its teaching of the Word and its worship, meant for her:

> During the years at the Healing Institute, those hours spent, those Saturday afternoons spent driving to both the Santa Clara site and the Palo Alto site, were life-changing for many of us . . . We came into a whole new way of thinking. We sobered up. Many of us came into an understanding of Jesus' mind-set regarding healing. I believe it was a bridge for many of us from the old to the new.

The teaching contained in these pages and in the volumes to follow represents the fruit of both the curriculum presented at the

Institutes and the marvelous ways in which the Spirit so sovereignly led and taught us. I invite you to participate.

FOR WHOM IS THIS BOOK WRITTEN?

For Those Who Pray for Healing

I strongly believe that anyone in the Christian walk at some time or another will be called upon by the Lord to pray for healing. Several months back, I went to hear the Bible teacher Joyce Meyer in San Jose, California. Of many memorable moments, the one that stands out for me is when she challenged the thousands gathered by saying that parents take care of their children physically when they are sick, but how many actually pray with them for healing? That is just one example of literally hundreds of opportunities to pray for God's healing.

These pages are designed to give you ample practical help to know what to do—and what to avoid—when you are called upon to pray for healing. It is a book for *all* people who believe in the healing power of Jesus Christ, be they Catholic, Protestant, Orthodox, Charismatic, Pentecostal, "mainline," or Evangelical: all will find it upbuilding, encouraging, and reassuring (Cf. 1 Cor. 14:3). To this end, many authors and sources from a wide range of Christian traditions are reflected.

Because I am a Roman Catholic priest, I come from and am faithful to that particular tradition. However, I have tried to avoid polemical topics and to maintain in balance the great body of teaching and experience that all of us Christians hold in common. My references to the *Catechism of the Catholic Church* are not meant to force anything on non-Catholics. I suspect they will be pleasantly surprised by its insights. The use of the *Catechism*, beyond the rich source of material it affords, seeks to place the healing ministry for Catholics squarely in the mainstream of our Church.

For Those Who Wonder if They Are Called to a Healing Ministry

The premise of this book is that God's will is to heal. Therefore the book is first of all for those who believe that truth and wish to be instruments of his healing power in some way. In addition, it is for those who are called to be established in a regular healing ministry. These are individuals whom others can call upon and turn to with confidence for healing prayer. To that end, the book will provide practical ways to know if healing ministry might be the will of God for you. This is called discernment.

For Those in Healing Ministry Who Want to Improve and Update

This book aims to sharpen the skills of those who are already in some kind of healing ministry. A great many "veterans" of healing prayer faithfully attended the Institute for the Healing Ministry. They offered the kind of encouragement that is described in the Bible. I was also edified to see how these veterans responded and learned new things the Spirit would teach. If you are a veteran of healing prayer, I invite you to bring your insights into dialogue with the teaching in this book. Let God's Spirit speak afresh, confirm and give you new insights and help concerning the healing ministry.

For Those Already in Healing Ministry Who Question Whether They Belong There

It is my hope that these people will be affirmed in the gifts God has purposed for their lives and the places he has put them in the Body of Christ, the Church. My prayer is that by the time they finish this book, they will have a keener awareness of where God would point them in terms of ministry, even if it is to know that it is *not* in healing ministry. If this is the case, you—together with the whole Church—will have gained immensely. In the Institute, by the end of the first of three courses, those who stayed discerned the call to persist in healing ministry. Those who came with different reasons drifted off, knowing that God was most likely calling them elsewhere.

For Church Leaders, Lay and Clergy

If you are in a pastoral position and are apprehensive about healing ministry in your communities or parishes, this teaching will do three things:

1. It will help you to understand from a solid base what is involved in healing ministry.
2. It will give you a tool to guide those under your pastoral influence who practice healing prayer and need help to develop a strong foundation.
3. It might even encourage you to incorporate healing prayer in your own pastoral ministry!

THE PLAN

In this, the first of three volumes, you will learn that it was by virtue of the Anointing of the Holy Spirit that Jesus Christ accomplished his healing ministry. Biblical principles about how the Anointing works will be explored.

A critical issue for Christians is to know where they fit in the Church. That is, to what ministry they are called. Ministry is not just a matter

This book helps the reader go through the process of discerning if he or she is called to the healing ministry.

of choosing what "looks good" to a Christian believer; it is about seeking God's will and how Christ would have one serve in the Kingdom of God. This book not only discusses what the healing ministry is but also helps the reader go through the process of discerning if he or she is called to the healing ministry.

I believe that the healing ministry calls a believer in Christ to a unique pattern of spiritual life. The dimensions of the special way that ministers of healing prayer approach their relationship with God will be explored. This will be of great help to serve God's people with greater grace.

Finally, this volume will examine the principles of how to prepare for and accomplish healing events and flow with the Holy Spirit's power. These foundational principles apply to praying for physical healing and enable the minister of healing prayer to grow to heal as Jesus healed. The same principles also form the basis for the volumes that will follow on further areas of healing ministry. The teaching is cumulative. That is, one section builds upon and includes the previous sections.

Volume two will discuss the healing of the inner self—those areas of emotional and psychological brokenness that alienate us from God or are in disorder. Volume Three will concern the healing of the human spirit and its liberation from those things that can enslave it, namely curses, strongholds, and demonic powers.

If you are a believer, committed to serving Jesus Christ with your whole heart, I invite you to the exciting journey of healing prayer.

Part I

Healing, Ministry, and the Holy Trinity

Chapter 1

THE WELLSPRING OF HEALING

Have you ever felt yourself longing from a wounded place deep within to be whole and in God's presence? True and lasting healing starts with a yearning desire for the presence of God. Our heavenly Father is the Wellspring of all wholeness. He provides a stream of life-giving water to satisfy our longing. Ignatius, a first-century holy bishop from Antioch, Syria, said it this way:

> My earthly love has been crucified and in me there is no more fire for material things, but rather a living water that murmurs within me and says to me: "Come to the Father!"

It was an echo of Jesus' own words to a broken woman of Samaria:

> "If you knew what God is offering
> and who it is that is saying to you,
> 'Give me something to drink,'
> you would have been the one to ask,
> and he would have given you living water . . .

The water I shall give him
will become in him a spring of water, welling up for eternal life.
(Jn. 4:10,14, NJB)

She did receive the living water and consequently became a worshiper of the Father in spirit and in truth. Her life was changed around; her outlook was transformed. She declared to her townsfolk, "Come see a man who told me everything I have done" (Jn. 4:29, NJB). The living waters of God's healing Spirit are still with us today, as we seek to worship the Father in his Holy Spirit and in his truth, Jesus Christ. God's healing and the ministry of healing are not just about the relief of pain but, more importantly, wholeness in a relationship with the Father, Son, and the Holy Spirit.

SHEILA'S RE-MISSION

The hospital room had become sacred by Sheila's presence. As I entered, her family introduced themselves in a reverent hush. I had driven an hour and a half that New Years' Sunday afternoon to be with them in what could have

The real healing started: reconciliation within the family, a return to the Church to receive and be nourished by the body and blood of Christ, and experience of an inner peace and joy she had never known in her whole life.

been the final moments of her life, after a battle with cancer. I felt connected with her family; there was not only peace, but a saturation of the spiritual atmosphere with the presence of God. At the end of the Last Rites I asked for Sheila's blessing and put my head in her hand. Not only did she pray for me and my ministry, but gave me a word in prayer that has sustained me in many of long hours of spiritual battles.

More than two years earlier Sheila had been in a spiritual life-and-death crisis of faith, after the sudden, tragic death of her nine-

18

year-old daughter and major family problems had left her with almost nothing regarding a relationship with God. She was full of bitterness, anger, alienation . . . and cancer! The physicians said this was the last stage. Long since, she had stopped going to church. But she was willing to try prayer as a last resort. Two sisters in Christ from Gilroy, California were determined to get her to someone who would pray for healing. They got her to me. As we entered into relationship and prayer, we not only prayed for the issues involving terminal cancer, but also for the wounds that alienated her from God and her family.

Two months later, she drove to see me and declared, "Father, I'm in remission and feel great!" That's when the real healing started to take place: reconciliation in the family, a return to receive and be nourished by the Body and the Blood of Christ in a Church and an inner peace and joy that she had never known in her whole life. Sheila now enjoyed a dynamic prayer life that God used mightily. Beyond that, Sheila became an "evangelist" in her own way, bringing people the good news of Jesus' love for them and the promise of wholeness.

After a year the cancer manifested itself again. This time she conquered all the temptations to despair. She continued to serve God to the end and died a very happy woman. God had healed her in the ultimate way by the resurrection, but not before she had been healed to fulfill his purpose to serve the Kingdom of God.

Someone questioned, "Why didn't God heal Sheila?" He did! She was healed both in this life and in her coming home to him. The best anyone dealing with brokenness this side of heaven can do is to "go into remission" until God calls him or her to that final healing. Healing is always a "re-mission." When God intervenes for wholeness in our lives he gives us a new or renewed mission to serve him. Healing is about coming into God's purpose for our lives.

I want to propose to you a deeper way of looking at healing and healing ministry. Let us seek God's mind and heart about this life-giving aspect of a Christian's life. I invite you to look in a new way at the healing ministry so that you can be a more transparent minister of God's grace, and your ministry will be filled with his almighty power. *We need his way of looking at things so we can heal the way Jesus healed.*

I invite you to pray with me to the Father, the Wellspring of all healing, as you begin this journey.

> *Heavenly Father, you are a good and merciful God. You sent your Son Jesus, who revealed that if we saw him, we would see you, for he is your image. Take me, Lord, beyond my complaints and symptoms; move me into deeper relationship of healing with you. Let your Living Water flow in me! Amen.*

Chapter 2

JESUS CHRIST, THE HEALER

JESUS REVEALS WHAT HEALING IS

One of the most urgent questions for wounded people today is, What does it mean to be healed? When people you have prayed for say they were "healed," what are they talking about? Let's begin by focusing directly on the healing ministry of Jesus Christ.

> Begin by focusing directly on the healing ministry of Jesus Christ.

Surely one of the most dramatic stories about the healing ministry of Jesus is the woman with hemorrhages in Luke 8:43–48. She suffered twelve years from this affliction that had drained her strength and power to cope. She approached Jesus from behind, hoping to just touch the border of his garment. She was healed of the flow of blood. Jesus felt power go out from him and wanted to know who had touched him. Finally, the woman came forward and explained everything. Jesus declared, "My daughter, your faith has saved you. Go in peace."

This woman had suffered long years with hemorrhages and now, hoping for an intervention from God, came to Jesus in her pain. Besides the physical affliction, you can imagine the emotional and psychological pain. She pressed through the crowd and touched the hem of his garment. The connection she made with Jesus caused a flow of healing power that came from the Son of God. It dried the flow of blood and the flow of confused emotions that had blocked her destiny. She approached Jesus with a need; she left with a relationship with the Father.

The noted scholar Bargil Pixner maintains that the woman was a pagan from Caesarea Philippi.[1] The church historian Eusebius (c. 265–340) reports that in that area there was a house with an ancient statue to commemorate this miracle. It belonged to the woman who was healed and demonstrates that her miracle had a permanent effect—that of a relationship with God to which she was proud to bear witness.

Most people seeking healing are not usually looking for great spiritual growth, nor for great purposes in their lives—at least at first. They just want relief, a solution to a problem. We have our agendas, just like this woman had hers. She wanted relief from her suffering of twelve years. The Gospel of Mark, in the same parallel story (Mk. 5:25–34) says that after long and painful treatment under various doctors, she had spent all she had without being any the better for it; in fact she was getting worse! The woman with the hemorrhages also had emotional brokenness to deal with because her treatment with the doctors had left her traumatized on all levels: she was discouraged, broken, and resentful.

This account shows us how Jesus healed. As Jesus did, we too have to go to the deeper meaning of healing. If you ask them what healing is, most people would say, "I have been healed because my pain is gone." Jesus does something deeper. He said to the woman with hemorrhages, "Your faith has *saved* you." It is absurd to believe in a God who does not heal. Salvation is a relationship with God and that is what Jesus proclaimed throughout his whole ministry. More than relief from suffering, salvation unites us to the power of Jesus' resurrection. When there has been healing it is because the power of Christ's Resurrection has shone through.

Our "Agendas" and God's Purposes

Like the woman in the gospel passage, we want to touch Jesus, but many times it is with our own agendas. He respects our reasons for approaching him and he respects our pain. Jesus had a wonderful compassion for people in pain. However, he always went to the root cause and didn't stop simply at the relief of discomfort. He went to the spiritual problem and the spiritual hunger innate in all human beings. Even if they didn't realize it, he used people's pain and their desire for healing to go to a deeper level and more complete wholeness. Fr. Peter McCall maintains that the word "healing" can be deceptive. "It can be used to describe a situation where a person experiences a temporary relief or removal of obvious symptoms. Many people claim a healing when physical or emotional symptoms disappear. While such a relief from pain or oppression may be welcomed, the removal of symptoms alone does not necessarily show that healing has taken place."[2]

We are created on three different levels. God created us on the bodily/material level. Many who are seeking healing don't go beyond that. There is also the psychological, or soul, level. This is the realm of healing of memories—emotional and psychological healing. Still deeper is the spiritual dimension that God touches most intimately. Healing takes place when any dimension of us is put into relationship with God's grace. That is why Jesus said to the woman, "Your faith has *saved* you." Fr. Robert DeGrandis writes,

As we think of healing, the focus of our attention is automatically on the physical, but we have already ascertained that there is no such thing as only physical healing. It is the healing of the whole person—mind, body and spirit.[3]

Healing Is a Relationship

Now to our question: "What is healing?" Healing takes place when, after we have exposed our brokenness to him, Jesus, through the Holy Spirit, puts every level of our being into relationship with him and the Father. When people go into the healing ministry, the temptation is to pray only to relieve symptoms, to direct the healing prayer only to the pain. Jesus goes to the *root cause* and would have us do the same. He respects the symptoms, yet goes to the root cause and beyond that he puts all levels of our being into a relationship with him. Now, that is true healing! Regardless of whether people seeking healing are aware of God's care for the whole of us, that kind of care needs to be the orientation and the mind-set of the minister of healing prayer, because it was the way Jesus thought and acted.

> He respects the symptoms, yet goes to the root cause, and beyond that he puts all the levels of our being into a relationship with God.

Have you ever wondered if your prayer made a real difference for someone for whom you prayed? You will *know* healing has occurred when that person is able to say, "My relationship with God has gotten so much better since you prayed for me." Healing takes place so that a person can fulfill God's purpose for his or her life. Both Sheila and the woman with hemorrhages had something in common: there was a remission of the disease so they could be re-missioned in God's cause and used for his Kingdom. He will do the same for you as you expose your brokenness to him. Through you he will do likewise for those that come seeking healing.

Healing Is a Communion

The Apostle Paul draws the connection between sickness and those who partake of Holy Communion in an unworthy way: "Everyone is to examine himself and only then eat of the bread and drink from the cup; because a person who eats and drinks without recognizing the body is eating and drinking his own condemnation. That is why many of you are weak and ill and a good number have died" (1 Cor. 11:28–29, NJB). Jesus said, "Whoever eats my flesh and drinks my blood lives in me and I live in that person" (Jn. 6:56, NJB). The more fully we remain in the presence of the Lord, the more healing we receive. It is when we exclude God from the varied dimensions of our lives that we become wounded and ill. "Recognizing the body" is an acknowledgment and respect for his presence—both in the Eucharist and in his Body the Church.

To be in communion with someone starts with friendship with that person. When we live in friendship with God, we live in wholeness, because by grace through God's glory and goodness we "partake of the divine nature" (2 Pt. 1:4, NJB). God's "goodness" means that we share his grace; his "glory" means we share his presence. But it is not only the "vertical" relationship that makes us whole; the "horizontal" relationships with others need also to come into wholeness through the mighty power of the Holy Spirit. We have "holy communion" with each other. To the degree that our relationships become more holy (God-filled), we become healed. Sheila became spiritually and emotionally whole as she, after many years, went back to receiving the Eucharist, and her relationships started to have a God-dimension to them. Even though she passed into eternal life because the cancer later came back, we were able to celebrate her victory in Christ over death. She died living in communion. That was healing!

In the healing ministry, an awareness and deep appreciation of communion is essential to being his transparent instrument. This awareness is a grace that sets our goals straight for the ministry. Leo Thomas writes,

> God's friendship with us will do what any friendship will do. It will transform us *to the extent* that we receive it. As with all friendships, we are free to accept or reject the offer, and we can accept it to different degrees . . . *Health is the wholeness of God*, a wholeness we are called to when we become sharers in the divine nature. We grow *into* God's own health as we allow his friendship to transform our patterns of human behavior at every level of our being—mind, will, emotion, and even body functions.[4]

HEALING MINISTRY IS A WORK OF EVANGELIZATION

Sharing the Good News of Jesus Christ

Jesus proclaimed this passage when he did his first act of public preaching:

> The spirit of the LORD God is upon me,
>   because the LORD has anointed me;
>   He has sent me to bring glad tidings to the lowly,
>   to heal the brokenhearted,
> To proclaim liberty to the captives
> and release to the prisoners,
> To announce a year of favor from the LORD
> and a day of vindication by our God,
> to comfort all who mourn;

To place on those who mourn in Zion a diadem instead of ashes,
To give them oil of gladness in place of mourning,
a glorious mantle instead of a listless spirit. (Is. 61:1–3, NAB)

He proclaimed this word from Isaiah when he came to the synagogue of his hometown of Nazareth, after his Anointing near the Jordan River. This empowering of the Spirit of the Lord has come upon you and me because the Lord has anointed us with the same Spirit. There has been a divine bestowal of his power that we share with Jesus. Notice the first things said about the Anointing: *To bring good news to the afflicted.*

Whatever the affliction our supplicants (those who seek healing prayer) have, when the Anointing is present, there is something that must be announced to them that is good, uplifting, and positive. The phrase "preach the good news" in Greek means "to evangelize." One of the deepest meanings of the Anointing is that the good news is preached to those who are poor and in need. The healing ministry should be an integral part of evangelism. People are evangelized when healing takes place.

Often at healing events, we will take several testimonies at the end. One of the components of testimony is that it is "good news." A testimony to God's power says, "I trusted in God for healing. If I can do it, so can you: keep on believing that he will touch you." Good news opens us up to a walk of faith which God transforms into a living relationship with him.

Evangelism at its heart means that people come into a relationship with a living God, who is Father, Son, and Holy Spirit. It means putting one's life in relationship with the Word of God. When the Anointing of the Holy Spirit is manifest, Jesus is proclaimed as Lord, lives are transformed, the brokenhearted are healed, the captives are set free, those who are in prison are released and there is a proclamation of a year of favor from the Lord. That is the essence of the healing ministry of Jesus. It is ours too, because we all share the same Spirit in his Body the Church.

God's Covenant Draws Us Into Healing and Abundant Life

There are privileges that come with being baptized and living in covenant relationship with God. For Christians, baptism formalizes the beginning of that covenant with God. A covenant with God simply means that life is lived receiving God's grace of blessing and habitually letting it flow through you to others and back to God.

Being a child of God and living under the covenant means that you have a right to draw from the Anointing for your own personal healing, provided you live as a child of the covenant. When God was teaching his people about remaining in the covenant he spoke to Moses:

> If you listen carefully to the voice of Yahweh your God and do what he regards as right, if you pay attention to his commandments and keep all his laws, I shall never inflict on you any of the diseases that I inflicted on the Egyptians, for I am Yahweh your Healer." (Ex 15:26, NJB)

It also means that you, in turn, are a person who has the potential for the healing Anointing as well. Every level of your being has a right to enjoy the Anointing of God and to walk toward healing. Every part of you has a covenant privilege to be brought into that relationship with God that would enable you to sustain the Anointing.

The Lord Jesus says, "The thief comes to only to steal, and kill and destroy. I have come so that they may have life and have it to the full" (Jn. 10:10, NJB). In my own healing ministry every day I see people who have had their rightful things stolen—things like reputation, dignity, health. Part of them is often lifeless—in their marriages, work, spiritual lives. The list is long!

The One who gives life to the full is the Anointed One—Jesus, who bestows his Anointing and reclaims what was lost, brings to life that which was dead, and restores what was destroyed. That is why his message is followed by signs and wonders. We are reduced to an institution of silly, lifeless rituals when burdens are not lifted by them, nor are yokes destroyed.

> The message of abundant life was confirmed with healing, restoration, and resurrection power. Without this power, the Church's credibility is lost.

The pattern of God's Anointing hasn't changed. We see the same awesome power of God at work in the healing ministry of today when God confirms the message of his word with the manifestation of his power. Peoples' lives are changed, they are healed and brought into relationship with him who gives abundant life.

Edith

Edith is the mother of several grown children who have had their share of hardship. The most critical was her son Joe, trying to make his way in the world, unable to hold a job and exhibiting signs of anti-social behavior. He was increasingly violent and threatening members of the family with hateful violence. He had taken over his sister's house and was becoming increasingly depressed. Unexplained violent noises around the house were now terrorizing them.

There had been a stream of social workers and healthcare givers but Joe was not responding. The family considered a restraining order. In desperation for relief, they even turned to the occult. Chip Sundstrom, one of my partners in ministry, and I were called to the houses for prayer. We discerned and prayed for several issues, but there was only minimal relief. God has his own time and way. Edith had suffered for years with fibromyalgia and was now sleeping very little. Just moving about for her was a painful and laborious task.

Several months later, at a healing mass that I was celebrating Edith was there, as always begging the Lord to heal and deliver her son Joe. At that time I was teaching about the importance of letting God have his way and was leading congregations in the prayer of surrender to the will of God. Edith followed the prayer and God took her seriously. Suddenly, during the mass, she heard the distinct voice of the Lord in her heart saying, "You are healed." As she tells it, "I told the Lord, 'I don't want to be healed if Joe isn't.' I heard over and over, even as I left the mass, 'You are healed!'" Four days later, it occurred to Edith to walk up some stairs—something unthinkable for many months because of her fibromyalgia. No pain, no stiffness. Two days after that, her doctor announced, "You have a new body!"

Subsequently, Edith gave powerful testimonies that encouraged and inspired many people to seek God in their lives. As we continued to pray for Joe, he was able to find and hold a job and to be freed from demonic oppression. He no longer threatens harm and his mother gives thanks at every opportunity. The Anointing was manifested powerfully in Edith and in her family as a sign to hundreds of people, offering hope in the power of seeking a true relationship with their God.

"Be Not Like Horse or Mule"

It may be that you have been laboring under mistaken notions of God's healing, pursuing a relief of suffering more than a genuine relationship with him. If you have a strong self-will, his almighty Anointing can change you; it can change the way you think about him, others, and yourself. The Lord will not change you, however, without your consent. I am convinced that many of our persistent problems—the most difficult personal ones— are *allowed* by the Lord so that he can do the work he needs to do in us. Only then can Anointing increase and bear fruit in a ministry in the Body of Christ. It's a matter of being a disciple. The manifestation of the Anointing depends upon our surrender to God's way of thinking and his way of doing. The psalmist says,

> Do not be like the horse or the mule, which have no under-standing but must be controlled by bit and bridle or they will not come to you. (Ps. 32:9, NIV)

Through our surrender to his will, he will not only provide us with the Anointing for our personal healing, but will make us the instruments of his love and care for our loved ones and the people he places in our lives needing ministry. Take a moment now to cen-ter yourself on the Heavenly Father and in the name of Jesus, ask for the Holy Spirit and his Anointing. Surren-der yourself to his will—whatever he wants for you and your loved ones. Say, "I bind my will to God's will and I bind my life and ministry to God's highest and best pur-pose."

> Through our surrender to his will, he will not only provide us with the Anoint-ing for our personal healing, but will make us the instruments of his love and care for our loved ones.

To help, here is a prayer of surrender by St. Ignatius of Loyola:

Lord Jesus Christ, take all my freedom, my memory, my understanding, and my will. All that I have and cherish you have given me. I surrender it all to be guided by your will. Your grace and your love are wealth enough for me. Give me these, Lord Jesus, and I ask for nothing more.[5]

---

[1] Pixner, Bargil, O.S.B., *With Jesus Through Galilee*, Rosh Pina, Israel, Corazin Publishing, 1992, p. 47.

[2] McCall, Fr. Peter and Lacy, Maryanne, *An Invitation to Healing*, Bronx, NY, House of Peace, 1985, p. 23.

[3] DeGrandis, Fr. Robert, *Layperson's Manual for The Healing Ministry*, 1985, p. 11.

[4] Thomas, Leo and Alkire, Jan, *Healing as a Parish Ministry: Mending Body, Mind and Spirit*, Notre Dame, IN, Ave Maria Press, 1992, p. 44.

[5] St. Ignatius of Loyola, *Spiritual Exercises*, #234.

Chapter 3

THE ANOINTING

The Two Hands of God

One of the great fathers of the Church, St. Irenaeus of Lyons, gave us a marvelous way of thinking about the Holy Trinity in relation to us:

Now man is a mixed organization of soul and flesh, who was formed after the likeness of God, and molded by His hands, that is, by the Son and Holy Spirit, to whom also He said, "Let Us make man."[1]

God always works in creation through his two hands, Jesus and the Holy Spirit. The purpose of the Anointing is so that the power of God can accomplish certain and determined things in the supernatural dimension that could not be done in the natural. The way he works through the healing ministry is no different. Let us now focus on the "hand" that is the Person of the Spirit.

In his encounter with the woman with hemorrhages Jesus said he felt power go out from him. There was an impartation of power, *Holy Spirit power*. The flow of the power of God is the Anointing of the Holy Spirit. It produces signs and wonders in God's plan for the world, so that you and I can come into communion with the Holy Trinity. The word "Christ" means "the Anointed One." It is also what the word "Messiah" means in the Old Testament. St. Irenaeus puts it this way:

> The name "Christ" implies "he who anointed," "he who was anointed" and "the very anointing with which he was anointed." The one who anointed is the Father, the one who was anointed is the Son, and he was anointed with the Spirit, who is the Anointing.[2]

Healing took place by virtue of the Anointing of the Holy Spirit, who was constantly with Jesus and manifested himself in his ministry. The Holy Spirit filled Christ and the Spirit's power went out from him in healing and for salvation.[3]

The Power of the Lord Was with Him to Heal

In order to heal as Jesus healed, it is necessary to understand the Anointing and let it flow through us as it did through Jesus the day he met the woman with hemorrhages. In order to see it even more clearly let's look at another revealing story from the gospels:

> One day as Jesus was teaching, Pharisees and teachers of the law were sitting there who had come from every village of Galilee and Judea and Jerusalem, *and the power of the Lord was with him for healing*. And some men brought on a stretcher a man who was paralyzed; they were trying to bring him in and set [him] in his presence. But not finding a way to bring him in because of the crowd, they went up on the roof and lowered him on the

stretcher through the tiles into the middle in front of Jesus. When he saw their faith, he said, "As for you, your sins are forgiven." Then the scribes and Pharisees began to ask themselves, "Who is this who speaks blasphemies? Who but God alone can forgive sins?" Jesus knew their thoughts and said to them in reply, "What are you thinking in your hearts? Which is easier, to say, 'Your sins are forgiven,' or to say, 'Rise and walk'? But that you may know that the Son of Man has authority on earth to forgive sins"—he said to the man who was paralyzed, "I say to you, rise, pick up your stretcher, and go home." He stood up immediately before them, picked up what he had been lying on, and went home, glorifying God. (Lk. 5:17–25, NAB, italics added)

This incident is in many ways similar to that of the women with the hemorrhages, but in this case the afflicted one had four faithful friends. The thought at the time of Jesus was that disabled people were suffering the consequences of their own or their ancestors' sin (see Jn. 9:2). It was the duty of leaders to maintain this status quo. The man who was paralyzed was most likely abused and rejected by the prevailing religious dignitaries; but he at least had his friends. And what friends to have, who stopped at nothing to make sure he was placed in the presence of Jesus, placed under the Anointing!

When Sheila, the woman mentioned in Chapter 1, first came to me she was brought by her two friends, who knew the power of the Anointing. She was alienated from the Body of Christ. To go to meet a priest was a daunting prospect. I, in turn, was called on to befriend her. Friendship means you trust someone. By building a trust relationship with Sheila, the three of us could take her to the Anointing and place those broken places of her in God's presence. It is his presence that heals.

Luke 5:18 says that the power of the Lord was with Jesus so that he could heal. The phrase, "power of the Lord" represents the Holy Spirit, under the form of the Anointing. The Anointing is the presence and *manifest* power of the Holy Spirit, to do in the supernatural that which cannot be done in the natural, ultimately so that we can be brought into the life of the Holy Trinity. We can't understand how the Holy Spirit

> The Anointing is the presence and *manifest* power of the Holy Spirit, to do in the supernatural that which cannot be done in the natural.

works through us unless we see how the Holy Spirit worked through Jesus. He is the same Holy Spirit, and enables us to heal as Jesus healed—through the Anointing sent by the Father.

In the gospel account of the healing of the paralyzed man, Jesus could have talked all day about how good it was for this man to be healed or his sins to be forgiven, but if the power of God was not present, the man was neither going to be forgiven nor cured from his paralysis. So the Anointing is the controlling factor in this gospel story: "The *power* of the Lord was with him for healing."

The passage indicates that Jesus was engaged in a teaching ministry. There was a special moment God was preparing so that the manifestation of healing should take place. We can pray for healing at any time on the basis of our own feelings, and it would be a prayer of our own desires out of our own nature. But there are moments—God's moments—of the Anointing, which God has purposed for times and for places, that healing should occur. At those special opportunities the different levels of people's beings are placed in relationship with God the Father, Son, and Holy Spirit. That which was alienated now comes into relationship. That which was fallen down, now is raised up. Burdens of disease are lifted, yokes of bondage are destroyed. This is the effect of the Anointing.

THE ANOINTED ONE AND HIS ANOINTING

The Prophesies

The Word of God has much to say about the Anointing, especially by the prophet Isaiah. Jesus made these prophesies his own. Isaiah was a prophet who had a clear prophetic view through the Holy Spirit of that which was to come. God spoke through him with such precision that through these prophecies the world could recognize when the Anointed One and his Anointing would come.

> When that day comes, his burden will fall from your shoulder, and his yoke from your neck and the yoke will be destroyed . . .
> (Is. 10:27, NJB)

This prophesy was a foretelling of the greatest anointing that would take place through the Anointed One, Jesus, and the power of the Holy Spirit. In some of the earliest manuscripts of the Book of Isaiah, there is another phrase that follows in the Hebrew language: ". . . before the fat," which does not seem to make sense. Because the phrase didn't seem to flow, many editors have taken it out of the Bible altogether. In the *New Jerusalem Bible*, there are three dots to indicate that there is something unclear that followed, with the footnote, ". . . before the fat."[4] In this case, "fat" can also mean "oil"—that which is used to symbolize the presence and action of the Holy Spirit, or the Anointing.

Some translations explicitly say, the yoke will be destroyed "because of the Anointing." In other words, when the Anointing of the Spirit of God reaches out to burdens and lifts them; it stands up in front of unholy, oppressive yokes and destroys them. When God's Spirit is poured forth in power, it is then that mighty things happen!

Healing Ministry: A Result of the Anointing

Christians who, in faith, have received baptism are in relationship with Jesus, the Anointed One. His mighty Anointing is ready to be manifested or shown forth. Catholics, Orthodox, and other liturgical Christians receive an anointing with the chrism (perfumed oil consecrated by the bishop for this purpose). It signifies that the Holy Spirit has come to dwell within and rest upon those who are united with Christ.

Catholic thinking has traditionally put the emphasis on the permanent effect that the Spirit has in a person's life when one lives out one's life in Christ and his Church. St. Augustine declares:

> Not only has our Head been anointed, but we ourselves too, who are his body . . . We are all the body of Christ because we all share in the Anointing and in him, we are all Christ's and Christ, since in a certain way the whole Christ consists in both Head and Body.[5]

There is a permanency of the Anointing that keeps us in the Body of Christ and in relationship as sons and daughters of the Father—a very deep topic that we can't go into here. But there are times in which the Anointing becomes actively manifest, and is "put on display," so to speak. One category of manifestation is the celebration in faith of the sacraments. The other, complementary, side is when the charismatic gifts of the Spirit are manifest. At these times in the Church, as in the times that Jesus healed, preached, and freed people, the Holy Spirit is poured out in order to "lift the burdens and break the yokes" and build up the Body of Christ. They are moments of glory.

Evangelical Christians often put emphasis on these moments of special grace and call them moments of anointing. Benny Hinn in his book *The Anointing* states it this way:

I want you to understand: The presence of God the Holy Spirit leads to the Anointing of the Spirit, which is the power of God, and the power of God brings forth the manifestation of the presence. The Anointing itself—and anointing of the Holy Spirit—cannot be seen, but the power, its manifestations, its effects, can and should be seen. That is why I call it "the tangible anointing."[6]

What happens when the Anointing of the Holy Spirit is manifest? In the case of the immediate fulfillment of Isaiah's prophecy in his time, there was an oppression that had taken place because of the Assyrians. People were shackled on different levels of their being: social, bodily, emotional, and spiritual levels. As human beings we can relate to that. Oppression is something that pushes us down, bends us over, and often puts us flat on our face. This can take place on a very personal level but it also can take place on a family level, in the workplace, in friendships and it can take place on a social, national, or even international level. It can also take place in the Church. Those of us in the healing ministry constantly see the oppression of illness and spiritual bondage. Through prayer and worship, the Anointing deals with this and becomes for us a point of contact with the Holy Trinity that is healing and life-changing.

A Future of Wholeness

Later on in the book of Isaiah, we find this prophecy:

That day the deaf will hear the words of the book and, delivered from shadow and darkness, the eyes of the blind will see. The lowly will find ever more joy in Yahweh and the poorest of people will delight in the Holy One of Israel. (Is. 29:18–19, NJB)

Isn't this a beautiful passage about the messianic time? We can ask, What day is he referring to? These things would happen on the "Day" of God's visitation in his Anointed One, Jesus. It is a day when there would be a heavenly manifestation on earth of the Person of the Word of God. When the Messiah came, he showed by his teaching and healing that there would be a *future of wholeness* for God's people. On Pentecost, that day in history became our day. We are the "messianic people"—that is the anointed people— because Body and Head share the same power of God! Ever since, the Church has proclaimed that because of what Jesus did by shedding his blood in a sacrificial death, his glorious resurrection, and by pouring out the Holy Spirit, we can possess this future of wholeness. Signs and wonders have taken place throughout the centuries in order to manifest this aspect of the Kingdom of God. In God's kingdom, the future breaks into the present. This the particular work of God's Spirit.

In Catholic worship there is a powerful prayer of thanksgiving affirming the ministry of healing:

> Father, all-powerful and ever-living God,
> we do well always and everywhere to give you thanks,
> for you have revealed to us in Christ the healer
> your unfailing power and steadfast compassion.
> In the splendor of his rising
> your Son conquered suffering and death
> and bequeathed to us his promise
> of a new and glorious world,
> where no bodily pain will afflict us
> and no anguish of spirit.
> Through your gift of the Spirit,
> you bless us, even now,
> with comfort and healing,
> strength and hope,
> forgiveness and peace.

In this supreme sacrament of your love
you give us the risen body of your Son:
a pattern of what we shall become
when he returns at the end of time.[7]

The Deaf Will Hear!

When he opened ears they not only literally heard, it also meant they would be able to hear the Word of God with spiritual "ears" that connect with

When Jesus performed miraculous actions, they were signs having to do with people's future in God.

the heart. This fact will become increasingly important in your healing ministry: we don't go looking or praying for healing just so it will relieve pain. Rather, healing is a *sign* of something much deeper than the relief of symptoms: it is a communication and relationship with God himself. Because of this, the healing ministry has a *prophetic* dimension.

Isaiah's same word in 29:18 of the deaf hearing is represented as a prophetic act in the baptismal celebration of the Catholic Church. After someone is baptized and anointed, the priest makes the sign of the cross over the person's lips and ears and says, "*Ephphatha*," repeating the same words and gestures when Jesus opened the ears of the deaf and made the dumb speak. He said, "*Ephphatha*," meaning "be opened" (Mk. 7:34). This is a *sign* that he came to open people's reality to the Word of God.

Sometimes when we are feeling oppressed and pushed down, we are not able to understand the Word of God. Because of confusion, illness, or weariness we can't even hear it. When the Anointing is manifest, things are opened up. "*Ephphatha*"—"be opened!"—is a prophetic declaration by the one who baptizes that the Messiah is here with his Holy Spirit. God grants us the Anointing to hear his word and to speak it in due time.

The Anointing of Joy

The "eyes of the blind will see. The lowly will find ever more joy in the Lord." When there is anointing manifested in a person, there is joy! The oil is that of gladness. Anyone who gets into the presence of the Lord delights in him and can receive the oil of gladness (Ps. 45:7). This is the meaning of the gospel accounts of Jesus opening the ears of the deaf, even casting out oppressive deaf and mute spirits (Mt. 9:32–33).

Physical manifestations of a visitation from God have enormous spiritual consequences.

The prophet Isaiah declares,

> then will the eyes of the blind be opened, the ears of the deaf be cleared; then will the lame leap like a stag, then the tongue of the dumb will sing. (Is 35:5–6, NAB)

Physical manifestations of a visitation from God have enormous spiritual consequences. They are signposts that point to something deeper. When a physical healing takes place, a calling to a deeper relationship with God is also being signaled.

Journal Questions for the Anointing

1. How has your concept of what it means to be "healed" changed?
2. Have you experienced the power of God's anointing? When, in a supernatural way, has God lifted burdens, destroyed yokes, and brought you life in abundance?
3. How has your prayer of ministry with others conveyed to them the *Good News*?

[1] Irenaeaus, Adversus Hereses, 4, Pref., 4. Translated by the Rev. Alexander Roberts and James Donaldson. Excerpted from Volume 1 of The Ante-Nicene Fathers (Rev. Alexander Roberts and James Donaldson, editors); American Edition copyright © 1885. Electronic version copyright © 1996 by New Advent, Inc.

[2] Irenaeaus, Adversus Hereses, 3,18,3.

[3] *Catechism of the Catholic Church*-English Translation, Washington, DC, United States Catholic Conference, Liberia Editrice Vaticana, 1994, #695.

[4] See The New Jerusalem Bible, Garden City, NY Doubleday & Company, 1985, footnote "j", p. 1207.

[5] St. Augustine, Commentary on the Psalms 26:2 (CCL 38, p. 155).

[6] Hinn, Benny, the Anointing, Nashville, TN, Thomas Nelson Publishers, 1992, p. 74.

[7] Preface for the mass of the Anointing of the Sick from Pastoral Care of the Sick: Rites of Anointing and Viaticum, New York, Catholic Book Publishing, 1983, #143.

Part II

Readiness for Ministry

Chapter 4

STARTING THE JOURNEY: DISCERNING THE CALL TO THE HEALING MINISTRY

In the first section of this book we reflected on the meaning of healing, together with the healing ministry as a manifestation of the Holy Trinity. Apart from the plan of the Father, Jesus and his messianic anointing of the Holy Spirit, it is impossible to understand either God's healing or healing ministry. We saw how the Holy Spirit's anointing on Jesus gave him direction and power for his ministry as he sought the Father's will. Now, I invite you to look into whether this ministry is for you.

A PLAN OF DISCERNMENT

Entering upon a plan of discernment will enable you to face some important questions about the direction of your ministry and your place in the Body of Christ. It puts under the light of the Holy Spirit:

- what is from God and what is from your "flesh"
- what are the charisms, or spiritual gifts, God has given to you

- what place you are called to in the Body of Christ

The first point will be explored in this chapter. The second two will be discussed in later chapters. As you read, I invite you also to write down a prayer to the Father for heavenly wisdom in seeking the answer to these vital questions for the healing ministry. Have confidence! If you seek him, you will surely come into his direction for your life. Ben Sirach exhorts,

> Trust him and he will uphold you, follow a straight path and hope in him . . .
> Look at the generations of old and see: Who ever trusted in the Lord and was put to shame?
> Or who ever, steadfastly fearing him, was forsaken?
> Or whoever called to him and was ignored? (Sirach 2:6,10–12, NJB)

A MAN CALLED SIMON

Ministry and Magic

There is a story in the Acts of the Apostles 8:9–25 that talks about a person who attempted to be involved in ministry, but was unprepared. It relates a story about a man named Simon, who had extensive involvement with the occult and practiced witchcraft. He had obtained a great stature and was acclaimed by ordinary and important people alike, who called him "the divine power that is called Great." When Philip came on the scene, the people of Samaria came to believe in Jesus, be converted and be baptized. Simon himself became a believer and started following Philip around, dazzled by the miracles he was performing. When the Samaritans' conversion came to the attention of the apostles in Jerusalem, they sent Peter and John so that they could receive the Holy Spirit.

> When Simon saw that the Spirit was given through the laying on of the apostles' hands, he offered them money, with the words, "Give me the same power so that anyone I lay hands on will receive the Holy Spirit." Peter answered: "May your silver be lost forever, and you with it, for thinking that money could buy what God has given for nothing! You have no share, no part, in this: God can see how your heart is warped. Repent of this wickedness of yours and pray to the Lord that this scheme of yours may be forgiven; it is plain to me that you are held in the bitterness of gall and the chains of sin." Simon replied, "Pray to the Lord for me yourself so that none of these things you have spoken about may happen to me." (Acts 8:18–24, NJB)

Simon the magician was a man who God was likely calling to great things, like many people who are in the ministry. But he was misdirected. That misdirection came from what he was involved in before, namely witchcraft and the magic arts. This involvement set up ways of thinking in his mind and ways of acting in his life that led him to think that even the gift of God could be a part of his schemes. Simon's case is a lesson for the whole Christian community.

Gifts and ministries that are bestowed by God sometimes are misdirected by the enemy, often before the gift of God is manifested. God has a certain purpose as he guides us to our destiny. When God's purpose gets detoured, it often takes the form of scheming and even wickedness. This is what Peter saw when Simon the magician wanted to get money and power. This account about Simon is an important lesson for our discernment. It speaks to us about persons coming into their own ministry with broken or misdirected motivations. We must be careful that the ministry is done under the true Anointing of the Holy Spirit.

Danger! Occult-Contaminated Ministry

Whether you are coming into ministry or continuing in it, it is essential to have the attitude that you can be corrected and even repent of those things that have been discerned to be misdirected in your life. Each of us carries a certain amount of "baggage" from the past. This baggage can come from things we have placed ourselves into, either voluntarily or involuntary. Many people innocently become involved and even entrapped in a variety of movements that will then discolor their service to God.

One example of "baggage" is those who have been involved in the Masonic Lodge and have taken Masonic oaths. Often they go to Christian churches but their spiritual bonding remains with the Lodge. Masons are spiritually compromised because Masonic oaths most often involve occult or pagan practices. Every grade of the Masonic Lodge represents a deeper commitment, a greater misdirection of one's life.

Another example of "baggage" that will interfere with ministry is the New Age movement, with its blasphemous and twisted concepts of the grace of God. People sometimes use these ideas in the healing ministry. Many people have come to me who think they have special powers because their pantheistic ideas make them think they have to get in touch with "the god within," which is themselves. They believe they are able to direct and channel those powers. The New Age movement has taken them away from the true gospel of Christ.

In Latino, Oriental, and other cultures, witch doctors often use Christian venues. They might perform their "healing arts" with a Bible open and even read from it! They might have crosses or Christian and Catholic objects like holy water and statues of saints that they use in their "healing" practices. The underlying objective of these "healers" is to get money by manipulating people. This was Simon's problem in the Acts reading.

"Don't Say That to Anyone! Even the Pope!"

Recently, Mathilda, a woman whom I know to practice witchcraft, came to our chapel in Monterey. She brought another woman and her son, who was having some emotional and spiritual troubles. When they found out that we were about to celebrate mass, they seemed anxious to attend. During the mass, Mathilda cried and externalized devotion and emotion. They were looking for help from me because the young man, in spite of Mathilda's "prayers," continued to feel oppressed.

Years ago I had learned that Mathilda had the practice of inviting emotionally needy people to her house to perform witchcraft rituals over them, and then charged them money for her "services." After talking with and ministering to the young man, who told me the occult rituals she had done with him, I called her in and talked privately, asking her if these things were true. Tears filled her eyes as she insisted that they were lies and that she was with the Lord. Then I asked her point by point about the rituals she had performed on the young man. She responded by changing the subject at every turn. I exhorted her, telling her that if what people were saying was true, then she needed to repent, go to reconciliation with God (confession), renounce all witchcraft and resolve never to do this again. She cried as she emphatically denied everything. It was all a show.

The next day, the young man's mother came to the chapel, afraid because Mathilda the witch, upon leaving the chapel with them, had scolded her son, saying, "What you said to Fr. Peter, you don't say to anyone, not even to the pope!"

The Problem

If there is witchcraft in your past, or even a desire to "change people's fortune" by religious practices, paganism, or superstitions such as astrology, then true discernment of the call to the healing ministry without a complete repentance and renunciation of these

51

practices will be impossible. This may sound radical to some, but the stakes are too high not to attend to this issue. Even "Christian" devotions and prayer can be abused in an attempt to manipulate people. This kind of person is in danger of becoming a charlatan and discrediting Christianity. The danger for the Body of Christ is a loss of spiritual effectiveness for the Kingdom of God, a deviation of the Church from her mission.

In the last chapter I indicated that the healing ministry has a strong prophetic dimension: it is unto the purpose and destiny of God in the supplicant's life. Spirit-led prayer, as we will see, also has a prophetic dimension. Because of this there is a lot at stake for individuals and for the Body of Christ as a whole—and therefore a lot of room for deception from the evil one. It is crucial that our prayer be free from contamination, vanity, self-service and self-will, and manipulation.

Sin and Iniquity

There are two sources of spiritual contamination in prayer, discernment, and ministry:

> *personal sin and iniquity*—that which we ourselves have chosen to do against God's word;
> *generational sin and iniquity*—that which has been handed on to us by our previous generations.

Sin is rebellion against God's law in thoughts, words, or actions. It produces immediate guilt and responsibility we carry before God. The guilt is taken care of through repentance and receiving of forgiveness by the blood of Christ. *Iniquity* is the brokenness or wickedness that was produced by the sin. In the healing ministry the distinction between the two is vitally important. As we will see later on, *sin has to be forgiven; iniquity needs to be healed.* We Christians are called to rid our lives of spiritual contamination. But when there is unrepentant and unforgiven sin, then true and lasting healing is all but impossible. When there is the bruising of iniquity, healing is necessary to come to a true discernment of God's will and purpose. Cindy Jacobs, an evangelical teacher of intercessory prayer, has identified sins and iniquities that impede us from knowing God's will:

- occult involvement and witchcraft, even "white magic"
- secret societies like the Masons or Eastern Star
- robbing and defrauding God by not giving to him what is due in service, worship, and material goods
- bondages or diabolical attachments to sin[1]

Ministering with the True Heart of God

If we have false motives, we will inevitably falsify the spiritual gifts and the word of God. We can become like Simon, wanting to control and channel power of our own will rather than being genuine instruments of God's power. We need to look at the circumstances of our lives. Simon, like Mathilda, had a problem with the circumstances of his life: people were being deceived

> If we have false motives, we will inevitably falsify the spiritual gifts and the word of God.

by the occult power he wielded. Simon's life circumstances were such that he built up his own little world around a system that, in the end, was false, even perverse.

When Simon became a believer, many of his ideas, attitudes, and passions—in short, his *strongholds*[2]—carried over into the way that he thought that he could serve the Lord. This goes for us as well. The way we have thought or worked in the past does not necessarily mean we are going to think or work in that same way after we come into ministry. I have found that it is decidedly different.

Simon had another problem: People saw him work his magic arts and adulated him. Prominent and ordinary citizens alike said, "He is the divine power that is called Great" (Acts 8:10). This did something to him interiorly. When he became a Christian believer, the need to be adulated stuck with him from his past activity in the occult: it was a disordered passion—a *stronghold*—of vanity. For whatever reason, Simon was desperate to have people think highly of him. He wanted to perform signs and wonders, even if he had to falsify them. He wanted to have the power of God and control it in his own broken way.

How to Clear the Air

Coming to a true discernment of God's purpose is a wonderfully freeing experience, but it demands being totally honest with yourself and with God. There are some concrete things you can do that will set you on the right track. Further on you will have a chance to reflect on your own ongoing need for healing. As you approach discernment about whether the healing ministry is for you, the task at hand is to provide the foundation for hearing God's voice correctly. This means that *now* is the time to take care of the areas that would contaminate your hearing his voice. I recommend the following steps:

> *Identify your own personal sins, sinful patterns and those of your ancestors.* In Jesus' name, ask the Father to send the Spirit of Truth to convict you of the worldly places of sin in your life and to illuminate the sins of your ancestors.
>
> *Repent, ask for and receive the forgiveness* of your sins. The Bible says, "If we acknowledge our sins, he is trustworthy and upright, so that he will forgive our sins and will cleanse us from all evil" (1 Jn. 1:9). If you are Catholic

or Orthodox, make arrangements to receive the Sacrament of Reconciliation.

Ask God for healing of the iniquity that has been in your generational lines. Ask for healing of the iniquity that lies within you.

Renounce by name all involvement in occult, the New Age movement or other superstitious practices.

Break and cancel in the name of Jesus any curses that may have been incurred by idolatrous practices on your part and any generational curses resulting from your ancestors' actions.

Ask God to heal the damage caused by curses and seal your ancestral lines spiritually in the blood of Jesus.

Ask God to heal those wounds in you and seal yourself with the blood of Jesus.

If you are a Christian in a "liturgical" church, it is strongly recommended to attend the Holy Eucharist, prayerfully reflecting in mind and heart on the above indications. As you receive communion, let the power of the body and blood of Christ, cleanse, heal, and free you and seal these wounds.

FROM DISCIPLE TO APOSTLE

The purification described above is part of the basics of being a disciple of Jesus Christ. After the Anointing bestowed at Pentecost, the disciples entered into a permanent ministry situation that shifted their basic orientation from discipleship to apostleship, that is, from following to being sent. The fact of being a disciple of Jesus remains, however, a spiritual baseline for the rest of their lives, even as they are continually sent as his apostles. Let's consider a time in the ministry of the disciples-turned-apostles, Peter and John, freshly filled with the Holy Spirit. Here is a beautiful story about the fruits of discipleship.

> One day Peter and John were going up to the temple at the time of prayer—at three in the afternoon. Now a man crippled from birth was being carried to the temple gate called Beautiful, where he was put every day to beg from those going into the temple courts. When he saw Peter and John about to enter, he asked them for money. Peter looked straight at him, as did John. Then Peter said, "Look at us!" So the man gave them his attention, expecting to get something from them. Then Peter said, "Silver or gold I do not have, but what I have I give you. In the name of Jesus Christ of Nazareth, walk." Taking him by the right hand, he helped him up, and instantly the man's feet and ankles became strong. He jumped to his feet and began to walk. Then he went with them into the temple courts, walking and jumping, and praising God. When all the people saw him walking and praising God, they recognized him as the same man who used to sit begging at the temple gate called Beautiful, and they were filled with wonder and amazement at what had happened to him. (Acts 3:1–10, NIV)

The Look of Ministry: Face to Face with Jesus

The *disciple* Peter had allowed his ministry to be discerned and to be purified by the Lord. Now the *apostle* Peter is able to say to this handicapped man, "Look at us!" and through the word of faith instilled by Peter, the man was healed and able to go into the temple area and not just wait at the gate for alms. For the Jews, going into the temple meant going into relationship with God. This healing was facilitated by the fact that Peter was a purified disciple and therefore a powerfully anointed apostle.

There is a change in Peter's look, for Jesus had dealt victoriously with his strongholds of fear and self-will. First he invites the crippled man, saying, "Look at us!" Remember during the Passion when Peter denied Jesus, the cock crowed and Jesus and Peter exchanged a *look* (Lk. 22:60)? Peter's was a cowardly, self-centered, and guilt-ridden look of shame; he went out and wept bitterly. The look was one of sinfulness and iniquity and it caused soul-pain. He had spiritual work to do, even as Jesus underwent his passion. Peter was not fully restored until after the resurrection, when he went to Galilee and was face to face again with the risen Jesus. He worked it through with the Lord! Jesus not only restored him, but gave him a prophetic view into his future as the head of the apostles, *co-missioning* Peter for the care of Jesus' sheep.

At that time, Jesus said to him again as at his first calling, "Follow me!" (Jn. 21:19). The apostolate in Christ's Church, no matter what possessions or dignity one has, operates only on the basis of following Jesus and walking in the Anointing.

Now at the Beautiful Gate of the Temple, with that mission deep in his spirit, Peter is able to say with confidence and love to a cripple, "Look at us!" Peter's look now reflects the look of Jesus himself. Together with the name of Jesus, it heals.

> The apostolate in Christ's Church, no matter what possessions or dignity one has, operates only on the basis of following Jesus and walking in the Anointing.

Fellow Christian in the healing ministry, when you *look* at those who come for prayer, will it be:

- A look of a clear conscience, forgiven of your personal sins?
- A look that is purified of iniquity and the damage left by personal wounds and the wounding of generations past?
- A look that is transparent, full of the brightness of God?
- A look that transmits the compassionate love and healing of the Savior himself?

Peter had to experience being brought low—even humiliated—many times in order to be the Lord's transparent vessel and to walk in his ministry. Jean-Baptiste Chautard, a popular spiritual writer of the past century, states, "The apostle has got to cultivate humility (and only the interior life will show him how) to the point of effacing himself and disappearing from view until those who look at him see right through him to God, so to speak."[3]

The Power of Ministry: The Name of Jesus

We will see later on how Jesus has given us the supreme privilege to speak in his name. In discerning the call to a healing ministry we need to look at the way in which we use his sacred name. In ministry, it is accompanied by a declaration or word in prayer, just like Peter said to the crippled man, "In the name of Jesus the Nazarene, get up and walk." It is as if Jesus himself had said it because he was manifesting himself and his Anointing through Peter and John, who had become his transparent instruments.

In ministering in his name, like Peter and John, we can empower the broken and weak to "get up and walk"—into the temple of a healed relationship with the Father and abundant life in Jesus Christ. When we accompany the sacred name with declaration and prayer, let it be a word that is uncontaminated, not spoken through our owns needs and personal agendas. It will be a word—unlike Simon the magician's—that is purified from manipulation, falsification, self-righteousness, and self-glorification. It will be a word that we know Jesus himself would speak, and therefore we can invoke his name on it with confidence.

> When we accompany the sacred name with declaration and prayer, let it be a word that is uncontaminated, not spoken through our owns needs and personal agendas.

Peter's faith and word were so strong, that his actions were no longer done in the name of Peter but in the name of Jesus the Nazarene. He knew that Jesus had given him permission to use his name for he had heard the Master say,

> It was not you who chose me, but I who chose you and appointed you to go and bear fruit that will remain, so that whatever you ask the Father in my name he may give you. (Jn. 15:16, NAB)

In restoring the crippled man to God's temple by healing his ankles, Peter was putting faith in Jesus' name into action and bearing good fruit. Through being a disciple, Peter had come to experience the reality that Paul describes:

> I have been crucified with Christ yet I am alive; yet it is no longer I, but Christ living in me. The life that I am now living, subject to the limitation of human nature, I am living in faith, faith in the Son of God who loved me and gave himself for me. (Gal 2:20, NJB)

When we use the name of Jesus, we invoke the great *I AM* revealed to Moses and the patriarchs, for Jesus' name means, "Yahweh saves." The *Catechism of the Catholic Church* puts it this way:

> He is the faithful and compassionate God who remembers [the Patriarchs] and his promises; he comes to free their descendants from slavery. He is the God who, from beyond space and time, can do this, and wills to do it, the God who will put his almighty power to work for this plan.[4]

Peter's journey is your journey—to be the vessel of the Lord's compassionate healing love that is waiting to flow through you. It is the long journey of faith and discipleship. Peter's journey is one of a disciple who had to spend a long time searching, discerning, humbly accepting correction, changing, and letting God's excellence shine through him. With every successive trial, the Anointing was sustained—and was given in greater measure!

Being a person in the healing ministry means that you have to be willing—like Peter—to face your own pain, brokenness, your rebellion and your own opaqueness, so that God can shine through you with his glory. Only those who are willing to take that journey should be in the healing ministry. To discern where God would call you demands a consent on your part to let him expose these areas so that your ministry will be pure, so that you can heal as Jesus healed.

Journal Questions for the Spiritual Work of Discernment

1. Study, discern, research (if necessary), and pray the steps outlined in the section "Clearing the Air."
2. What are one or two key moments in your personal walk with Christ where you have been called to change your ideas or thinking? How were you changed?

---

[1] Jacobs, Cindy, *The Voice of God*, Ventura, CA, Regal Books, 1995, pp. 65–67.
[2] The subject of "strongholds" (2 Cor. 8:12) will be extensively treated in another volume of this series. Liberty Savard gives a succinct and handy definition of them as wrong attitudes, ideas, or passions that impede us from the knowledge of God or obedience to Christ. Dutch Sheets gives a more technical treatment of strongholds in *Intercessory Prayer*, pp. 172–177. Francis Frangipane also gives very helpful guidance throughout his book, *The Three Battlegrounds*.
[3] Chautard, Jean-Baptiste, O.C.S.O. *The Soul of the Apostolate*, New York: Image Books, 1961, p. 132.
[4] *Catechism of the Catholic Church*, # 205.

Chapter 5

READINESS FOR MINISTRY I: A SPIRITUAL INVENTORY FOR LIVING

THE CALL TO MINISTRY

There are two crucial issues that a Christian must deal with when considering the healing ministry:

- Am I really called to it?
- How do I know when I am ready for it?

A *ministry* is a service activity to the Body of Christ that is in some way regular, recognized, and habitual. It is a particular position in the Church. Some ministries—depending on the discernment by Church leadership—are formal and commissioned service, while others are based more on a person's normal service to Christ's Body.

Every true ministry is based on natural and supernatural gifts (charisms). A ministry is a conduit for the use of those talents and spiritual gifts. The fact that someone occasionally uses a particular charism does not mean that that person is in a ministry. Central to the healing ministry are what I call "threshold issues"—they get you in the door to see more clearly. The issues presented in this

61

chapter provide a discernment for entering, continuing, or deepening this service to the Body of Christ.

Reading this chapter and doing the suggested spiritual work will set you squarely on the road to seeking God's will about the two important questions noted above. Addressing the issues discussed below will enable you to be in a position to better hear the voice of God. It is a call to spend some serious time before the Lord. It is also a process that leads to *discernment* with respect to the healing ministry. Think of it as an occasion of co-working in harmony with the Holy Spirit in order to recognize God's calling. It is important to remember that in the discernment of ministry, it is not *whether* you have reached perfection that is at issue, rather that you are *on the road* that God has laid out for you.

Buy Yourself a Journal

The one condition is that you do your part. Spiritual work such as this can be difficult. I invite you to a time of more intense prayer and study. Throughout this chapter and in the other chapters of this book, there will be questions and reflections that I invite you to take to prayer. For this reason I suggest that without delay you purchase a journal or notebook in which to write down your reflections and prayers. I myself am not an everyday-journal-writer. However, in tasks of discernment, journaling has helped me immensely to be honest with myself and God, to commit things to writing and to see more clearly the hand of God.

A Disciple Named Flora

As if out of nowhere, Flora found herself in a small town in the middle of the Salinas Valley of California. Raised in Mexico, she and her husband Freddy migrated to the U.S. to be with Freddy's parents. Flora had spent long years away from the Lord until someone invited her to the parish prayer community. There she started her way back to God. A few weeks later, God began moving greatly in her life.

Her conversion took place when she got the courage to receive the Sacrament of Reconciliation. It was during a charismatic renewal marriage retreat that Flora received baptism in the Holy Spirit. She had been for a long time struggling with interior and exterior trials in marriage and family life. She had formed strongholds of shame and unforgiveness from which she had to be delivered. One day, while Flora was helping in a church service, the power of the leader's prayer pierced her soul. Through the ministry of brothers and sisters who cared, she was set free from these strongholds and diabolic influences.

Flora's freedom was the entrance into a new dimension in her relationship with God. Over time, this deliverance enabled her to venture into the healing ministry. The gifts of the Holy Spirit began to be manifested through her, and in the process God set her on the adventure of discipleship.

I remember when she first started to manifest in the prophetic gifts. She could not help but burst into tears while delivering prophetic messages. This and many other manifestations of her flesh were being purified. She soon began to be recognized for her gifts of healing and razor-sharp discernment. In this journey she came to realize that the damage in her family from so many years away from the Lord had caused great suffering and serious obstacles in her path. In addition, Flora had to endure humiliating and deep trials from within and without—at the hands of misguided Church leaders, even priests.

Through her commitment to deeply knowing and studying God's word, Flora brings the "sword of the Spirit" (Eph. 6:14) to bear in her extensive healing ministry. She has come into a maturity that stands out in her use of the gifts. One day she was reflecting with me on the phenomenon of "resting in the Spirit" that is common-place in charismatic renewal circles. She said, "Father, when one starts the life in the Spirit one often *falls backward* in order to receive from the Lord. But there comes a time in which one needs to *fall forward in prayer*—on one's face—in order to *give* to the Lord and his people."

This is the characteristic of Flora's prayer—"falling forward"—as she comes into greater growth in Christ. The same principle applies for anyone serving the Lord in the healing ministry. As we will see, it is a process of increasing spiritual maturity and intercession. A holy priest once told me that one should talk more to God about those who come for ministry than talk to them about God. This was Flora's attitude as she sought the Lord for his Body the Church. He saw to it that her family would be taken care of, in spite of tough trials. Today her husband Freddy has manifested gifts of administration and is looked up to as a man of God.

Flora has remained persistent in her discipleship. Because of that perseverance people come from all around the state to be ministered to by her. Priests and other leaders frequently consult and take her to healing ministry situations. On January 1, 2000, Flora was the first to publicly lead 2000 prayer warriors in spiritual warfare on behalf of northern California from the altar of St. Mary's Cathedral in San Francisco. Who would have believed that God would call this humble woman from Greenfield, California? But then, didn't he call a lowly virgin from insignificant Nazareth to be the mother of the Messiah? We can receive the call too!

The Bottom Line

God is not demanding that you be holy, healed and complete when you enter the ministry of healing prayer; the Church is a body of "wounded healers." But he does need our will. The most fundamental issues to discern the call to the healing ministry are as follows:

1. Are you genuinely and humbly seeking God's will for your life?
2. Are you on the road of discipleship?
3. Are you growing in the Lord with respect to your relationships?

THREE LIFE-PRINCIPLES FOR DISCERNING THE CALL TO MINISTRY

In this chapter and in that which follows, several principles need to be considered as you seek God's will for your life and ministry.

1. Conform Your Lifestyle to Christ

One purpose of this work is to help discern whether you are called to the healing ministry and, if so, to what extent. The Church and its members in any time of history must deal with the error of "legalism"—that is, following a system of rigid rules and regulations in order to be made worthy to participate in the Church's work. One must seriously take to heart the teaching of Christ and his Church when it comes to faith and moral behavior. Being a priest, I make it a point to respect the Canon Law of the Catholic Church, as well as its liturgical norms governing the correct order of the administration of the sacraments. This is important in order that others won't be imposed upon by leaders' particular tastes or agendas.

Still, life in Christ cannot be reduced to following laws and rules. Rather, it is a walking in the Spirit. St. Paul says, "if you are led by the Spirit, you are not under law" (Gal 5:18, NIV). For a Christian, the law of God is written on the hearts of those who believe by the presence of the Holy Spirit. This means that moral laws are useful to people in the Spirit in order to measure the degree they are following his *interior* guidance. For instance, someone who habitually lies manifests a serious deficit in letting the Holy Spirit guide his or her life. I would never knowingly seek out such a person for prayer

65

ministry to me for fear of being contaminated spiritually by untruth. It is the same for those who habitually use foul language and curse. How can a broken person expect to be blessed through one who uses the same tongue to curse? The apostle James puts it this way:

> With the tongue we praise our Lord and Father, and with it we curse men, who have been made in God's likeness. Out of the same mouth come praise and cursing. My brothers, this should not be. (Jas. 3:9–10, NIV)

Likewise, I have known people who do healing prayer who are in overtly sinful situations. Lorenzo was a man in the eastern part of El Salvador who lived in adultery, graft, and church politics for many years. Yet he was in the top leadership of the charismatic renewal. Because of him, the renewal in that area was given a bad reputation and fell into disfavor with Church leadership. In his perverted way of thinking, Lorenzo believed he was under "special circumstances" and the moral law didn't apply to him. In this case, even though he supposedly "flowed" in the gifts, the enemy used his personal life and lifestyle to impede the Kingdom of God.

Until those sinful situations are dealt with in God's way, a person should *not* enter or continue in the healing ministry. Like Lorenzo, some think that the basic moral guidelines of the Word of God do not apply to them. This is self-deception. No one, including leaders and ministers, is excused from the precepts of the Christian faith. These precepts are a measuring rod of whether the person is walking in grace and is in a position to assume a ministry. Again, God is not demanding perfection, but there are a few basic things which indicate that a brother or sister is moving in the Spirit of God sufficiently to take on ministry. St. James

God is not demanding perfection, but there are a few basic things which indicate that a brother or sister is moving in the Spirit of God sufficiently to take on ministry.

affirms, "confess your sins to each other and pray for each other so that you may be healed. The prayer of a righteous man is powerful and effective" (Jas. 5:16, NIV).

What does it mean to be "righteous," or "just," as the scriptures put it? It means that there is belief in and a commitment to the Lord Jesus such that the person is trusting in the power of Christ's redemptive sacrifice for the forgiveness of sins. It also means that his almighty power has begun to take root in such a way as to begin to bring all aspects of life and relationships under the dominion of Christ.

"But I Feel Unworthy!"

If you are like me, you may see some areas in your life and relationships that are continually in danger of being compromised by the power of sin. As we saw before, this we call "iniquity."[1] It habitually inclines us to act in sinful ways. Does the persistence of sin in your life mean that you "don't qualify" to be a minister of healing prayer? The answer to this depends upon two things:

a. Are you resolved to seriously deal with this sinful pattern through prayer and counsel?

b. Is there a danger that the Body of Christ would be in some way harmed by this brokenness—even as you struggle with it—if you were to exercise a spiritual influence such as healing prayer?

Concerning sin that remains in a Christian's life, Ramiro Cantalamessa draws an illuminating analogy to a dried up, dying olive tree:

What takes place in nature takes place in our lives. You can at times see some very old olive trees with chopped and withered trunks but which nevertheless still have a few green branches on their tops which, in the olive season, are full of lovely olives. If you look closely at them you will discover the reason for this. It's because somewhere there is still a "vein" of live wood rooted in the soil which gives life to the tree. That's what happens sometimes to the evil tree of sin in our lives. It should be completely dead and unproductive from the moment we no longer want sin which we have often confessed and rejected. Yet it continues to produce its fruits and the reason is that there are still some "green branches" rooted in the living soil of our freedom . . .

To discover our "green branch" we must look for the thing we fear will be taken from us and which, without admitting it, we defend and keep on an unconscious level. We keep it hidden for fear that our conscience will oblige us to renounce it. More often than a single sin, it is a question of a sinful habit or of an omission which must be overcome . . .

But what must we do exactly? In a moment of recollection, during a retreat or, even this very day, let us kneel down in God's presence and say to him: "Lord you know my weakness and I know it too. Trusting therefore only in your grace and faithfulness I declare that from now on I no longer want that particular satisfaction, that particular freedom, friendship, resentment, that particular sin . . . I want to accept the idea of having to live without it from now on. I have finished with sin and with that particular sin . . . After this, sin no longer "reigns" simply because you no longer *want* it to reign; it was, in fact, in your will that it reigned. If sin repeats itself in your life—and it will almost certainly do so—you will no longer be "conniving" with sin but simply "living" with it; that is you will have to live reluctantly with it, accepting it as part of your purification and struggle against it. But this is very different to the previous state when you were conniving with it, when you were its accomplice. There may be no apparent change, those around us may still notice the same faults in us but where God is concerned something has changed because our freedom is now on God's side.[2]

Journal Questions for Christ's Lordship Over Me

1. What areas of my life and relationships are still to be brought under the dominion of Christ? What sin have I been "conniving" with? What areas of my life are not conformed to Christ's image?
2. Go through the steps outlined by Fr. Cantalamessa.

2. Respect Family and Work

One of the friends and co-workers that God has placed in my life is Ernie VonEmster, a man dedicated to his family and also to his leadership role in the Archdiocese of San Francisco. At one of the gatherings of our ministry group called *Fire of Pentecost*, he was torn between our prayer ministry on one hand and some family tasks on the other. All seven members of the *Fire of Pentecost* took Ernie's situation to prayer. It was discerned that Ernie could, with confidence, lay down any activity with *Fire of Pentecost* for the sake of what God wanted him to do with his family. We released him to not participate with us the next day and we prayed for the family situation. To our surprise the following morning there was Ernie, cheerful and happy, witnessing to the quick work that had been done and how his wife had encouraged him to come to the gathering. The point is that he had put his priorities in order, and because of this was enabled for his ministry.

Family Life and Ministry

The balance among family, work, and ministry is a constant challenge. Further on in this book we will go into this issue in

69

more detail as it relates to ongoing ministry. The point here is the matter of discernment about *coming into* a ministry. I believe that even though members of your family might not understand the various issues of ministry, they do need to concur with your participating in ministry. Otherwise, you will not be able to "hear" the Lord correctly. This doesn't mean that all your family problems need to be resolved. That will never happen until we get to heaven! If going into a ministry would *unduly* compromise family or work, and the people involved are not in agreement, then that needs to be respected as the will of the Lord.

There is more to this: If you are married there needs to be a "baseline" of living in harmony with your spouse and children. Consider this text from the Apostle Peter:

> In the same way, husbands must always treat their wives with consideration in their life together, respecting a woman as one who, though she [physically] may be the weaker partner, is equally an heir to the generous gift of life. This will prevent anything from coming in the way of your prayers. (1 Pt. 3:7, NJB)

This instruction about a fundamental equality and partnership is a principle of discernment. Family life is a manifestation of God's covenant. If that covenant is intact and fundamentally in harmony with God's word, then the Spirit of God will be able to flow powerfully through ministry. People with healthy and supportive relationships in their marriages will be powerful ministers.

There are a number of sisters in the Lord with whom I have opportunities to minister in prayer. It is a great privilege to be in the presence of these women when they are in prayer ministry. They all have one thing in common: those who are married have the consent of their husbands that they do this ministry. On top of that, I make it a point to submit my relationship in all aspects with these women to their respective husbands and to my own spiritual family, the Oratorian Community. When there have been misunderstandings or problems, the principle of obedience to a "spiritual head" has guided me and brought about total clarity. If this were not a fundamental attitude, then neither I nor they could hope to hear the Lord correctly.

Work and Ministry

With respect to work, there are three considerations before entering ministry:

a. That your ministry will not jeopardize the well being of family, causing grave financial problems;

b. That your employment is morally correct; that is, that it doesn't lead you or others into sin;

c. That your work is done to please God and in its own way build his Kingdom.

Journal Questions for Priorities

1. Is your spouse generally in agreement with your ministry in the church? (That does not mean that he or she has to fully understand it!)
2. What importance do you give to quality time with your family?
3. How do you prioritize your schedule? Resolve schedule conflicts?
4. Are you fulfilling your work responsibilities in a godly way?

3. Come Under Spiritual Authority

The author of the Letter to the Hebrews lays down this principle for spiritual authority:

> Obey your leaders and defer to them, for they keep watch over you and will have to give an account, that they may fulfill their task with joy and not with sorrow, for that would be of no advantage to you. (Heb. 13:17, NAB)

Many years ago, when I was a seminarian in the community to which I belong, the army asked the two senior fathers who then presided over the community to be civilian chaplains at Ft. Ord Army Hospital. The fathers had discerned that this ministry was a leading of the Holy Spirit. I, however, wasn't impressed and was not interested in this particular ministry. At the time, I was seeing a new counselor for some personal enrichment and therapeutic growth—a nun who was on her way out of her community.

At a critical point the fathers drafted a letter to the army officials, accepting the ministry position. They wanted and needed the solidarity of the rest of the community, so they asked for the seminarians to sign the letter with them. I rebelled and refused to sign. Not only that, I enlisted the support of the therapist and felt myself fully justified in not signing a letter with which I wasn't in agreement. My counselor assured me that the "healthy" thing to do would be to not sign something with which I wasn't in agreement. The stubbornness of my character had shown through. The fathers, my spiritual heads, were requesting spiritual solidarity but I had every "reason" in the book to deny them. In my self-righteousness I even wrote the community a memorandum about it. Now I was conniving to rebel. The community's letter finally got sent off to the army, but without my signature. I was wrong.

Later in the week I asked the community to review this procedure. A few days after that the provost (superior) gave out a letter that began, "United we stand; divided we fall." He went on to expose my stubborn refusal to express solidarity with the spiritual family which I was joining.

I felt stung, angry, and disappointed. In the process of my "self-assertion" I had called into question the authority of my spiritual heads, injected spiritual poison into the atmosphere of the community and given reason for scandal by manifesting division and dissension with respect to the community's ministry. And I had made their accountability for me a sorrow instead of a joy.

Every Christian needs to deal with issues of the mind and heart when it comes to spiritual authority. Anyone coming into *any* kind of ministry, including the healing ministry, must have—in some way—a spiritual authority to which she or he is accountable. That means that we put our inspirations, gifts, and Christian walk under discernment and accountability.

When I was younger, every time the word "obedience" was mentioned, I would feel an instantaneous negative reaction in my spirit. I was bound by a spiritual stronghold of super independence that affected my thoughts, attitudes, and feeling-life. I can still see rebellious parts of myself, but thank God, he is in the process of dealing with them. Obedience is a big issue, especially when it refers to spiritual authority with the people God has placed in our lives.

The members of the community to which I belong are my "first line of discernment" when it comes to life and ministry. Even though at this time I happen to be their superior, I must submit to their discernment. If I would be negligent in this area I know my own "wisdom" would be like a shotgun without direction and God's plans would be frustrated. Fire of Pentecost, the covenant group with whom I pray regularly, is another line of discernment. These brothers and sisters deal with me in things that are often painful to handle because of my own sinfulness, but they love me and are like watchman not only for me, but for my relationship to the Body of Christ which I serve in ministry.

Marty, the Self-Styled Prophet

Marty was a self-styled "prophet" who participated in the Institute for the Healing Ministry I led from 1998 to 2000. At one point he came to me and said that he held the "office of prophet" in the church. No one in leadership had ever told him this. He had "discerned" it on his own. In the gatherings he attended, he often would give three or four "prophecies" and "visions" in a row. Sometimes he would even sing them. This man's actions had the effect of not only cutting off but also quenching others in the group. Invariably he would come late to meetings and begin to "prophesy." The prophecies would sometimes fit but most of the time they were off. Several years earlier his wife had left him and he was alienated from his children.

When Marty came to see me for inner healing ministry, I asked him if he was willing to submit to some kind of guidance and leadership in his ministry. He said he wasn't sure he needed that. I told him he should seriously think about whether he should speak so many prophecies in a row and that he should look at the effect they were having on the gathering—they were stifling the manifestation of the Spirit in other people. In spite of this, at the Healing Institute, he continued with the same routine.

Because he always arrived late I could not speak to him directly, since I was leading the meetings. Finally, I had someone give him a note on my behalf indicating that he was no longer authorized to speak or exercise any spiritual gift as long as he was not submitted under a spiritual authority. He became silent, but it was obvious that this was a terrible blow to his ego. Marty finally had to undergo serious psychiatric treatment.

I often think about that brother in the Lord. What if he had had an attitude of discipleship instead of an attitude of "needing to be needed," or of craving people's admiration of his "spiritual gift"? It was significant that in his life's circumstances he had two broken marriages, his children had rejected him, he had gone through two other churches, and now he was in the Catholic Church thinking he could carry on in the same way. He was an unsubmitted Christian and his attitude was, "I am a prophet." That's a dangerous combination!

Even though they may not go to Marty's extreme, there are many who "minister" out of the "need to be needed," rather than an authentic gift of the Spirit. Ministering because you "need to be needed" is a sure way to short-circuit discernment and to miss what God wants. If you suffer from this, begin to let the Lord take dominion over it. Our best assurance to avoid this dead end is to seek out and take seriously the legitimate spiritual authority under which God wishes to place us.

Journal Questions for Spiritual Accountability

1. What is your attitude toward making yourself and your ministry accountable to others in the Body of Christ?
2. Who are you currently accountable to? Have they accepted that role in your life?

---

[1] "Iniquity" is the scriptural term for the power of sin living in us. It is produced by the damage due to sin. The Catholic tradition has called it "concupiscence," again meaning that even though the guilt of sin has been taken away there remains an *inclination* to follow the same pattern of sinful behavior.

[2] Cantalamessa, Raniero, *Life in the Lordship of Christ*, Kansas City, MO, Sheed and Ward, 1990, pp. 125–126.

Chapter 6

READINESS FOR MINISTRY II: AN INVENTORY FOR PRAYER LIFE

In Chapter 5 we explored the dimensions of a Christian's readiness for ministry from the point of view of the way we live. In this chapter I invite you to let the Holy Spirit shine light on your present prayer life and spirituality as you discern this dimension of your preparedness for the healing ministry.

1. KNOW GOD'S WORD

The Word of God is a revelation of God's character and how he works with his people. If we know and use the scriptures correctly our spiritual compass will remain true. The psalmist said, "Your word is a lamp to my feet, and a light for my path" (Ps. 119:105, NIV). This applies first and foremost to our living out the life in Christ. But it equally applies to how we minister healing prayer. In the Bible we can see not only moral principles, but patterns of how God reached out his healing hand and lifted people into wholeness. Believers who are in healing ministry will reflect God's character, which is revealed in the Scriptures, and reach out in the same way with the love he has poured into our hearts through the

Holy Spirit. St. Jerome said, "To be ignorant of the scriptures is to be ignorant of Christ."

One day in 1959 some bishops asked Pope John XXIII how the proposed Second Vatican Council would renew the Catholic Church. He replied simply, "Read the book of Acts of the Apostles—that is our blueprint." Upon opening the Council he solemnly prayed for the Father to send a "New Pentecost" upon the Church. That would never have been possible without "opening the riches of the Bible." This is for the whole Church, and it is for each and every believer.

That doesn't mean we all need to be scripture scholars and theologians! Knowledge of the Word of God enables us to perceive what is in accord with his plans. It is a baseline of discernment for life and for ministry. We need to have not only knowledge of the Word of God but a commitment to it as it is reflected in the essential teachings of our Church.

I often ask people for healing prayer when I am in need of it (which is quite often). However, I would be very reluctant to ask a sister or brother to pray for me who doesn't have some understanding of the Bible. I would be afraid that the prayer could easily become misdirected, even harmful.

What does this mean in the practical order for those discerning a call to healing ministry?

- Every day, spend some time with the scriptures. I suggest that this time be a planned reading in succession. There are a number of guides through the Bible. This should take precedent over any devotional book or literature. That is not to say that these books are not of great value—they are. But first things first. If you are Catholic, you might want to start following the two-year cycle of daily mass readings (this is helpful, even if you don't go to daily mass) and the three-year cycle of Sunday readings.
- Learn how to use the Bible; that is, learn to look up texts by chapter and verse, find where the major sections of the Bible are, and what kind of material is found there.

- Get to know at least generally about some of the major figures in the Bible; how God called them, what struggles they went through, how God used them and saw them through their trials.
- Most importantly, through the gospels, have an overview of the life, teaching, and ministry of Jesus Christ. Especially learn about his death, resurrection, and sending the Holy Spirit, and what these mean for people of all times and places.

You may ask, Why is this important? For two reasons:

a. *Jesus ministered in this way*, based on his knowledge of the Word of God. He used it as a "sword" in his ministry. If we minister in his Body, we can confidently follow his way. St. Paul says that the Word of God is the "sword of the Spirit" (Eph 6:17) and the book of Hebrews says that the Word of God cuts like a two-edged sword into the deepest places of a person's being (Heb 4:12–13). That means that the Word of God is entirely suitable and necessary for work in the healing ministry.

b. *The Word is a standard for the discernment of our ministry*, giving us images and indications of how God works, which we can always use as the measuring rod of our own ministry. What is contrary to God's word we reject.

Journal Questions for the Word of God

1. How can you make the study of God's word a more important part of your life?
2. What are some Bible passages that have influenced your life in a meaningful way?
3. What do you know about Jesus' life? How does that affect your life?

2. LIVE IN HOLY COMMUNION

St. Paul wrote the following to the Christians of Philippi:

> If you have any encouragement from being united with Christ,
> if any comfort from his love, if any fellowship with the Spirit, if
> any tenderness and compassion, then make my joy complete by
> being like-minded, having the same love, being one in spirit
> and purpose. (Phil. 2:1–2, NIV)

Let's take a good look at the word "fellowship." It is one of the most important faith-words for any believer. The Greek is *koinonia*, meaning an attitude, a disposition, that is produced by the Anointing of the Holy Spirit, enabling people to be "of one mind and heart." You ask, How can I be of one mind with everyone in the Church? I can't even do that with my family members! Being of "one mind and heart" is not some lofty goal that we will achieve in heaven; it is a reality that is possible in the here and now. It doesn't mean that we are in agreement with respect to opinions or that we have the same sentiments.

The best translation of *koinonia* I know of is "communion," which gives a sense of spirituality to our sharing in common. To have *communion* with someone means a bond is established. We share or participate in something together. Christians are led to have a *holy communion* with each other; that is, by virtue of the Holy Spirit a bond is established in Christ. It is through him that we become bonded in a holy way to each other. Without a holy bonding, any ministry is impossible, because there is no connection with the Body of Christ on earth. All legitimate ministry is carried on from a standpoint of *koinonia*. Attempts at ministry apart from communion with a recognized Church body are disordered. They create more wounds in the Body of Christ. Even if your ministry is to the "broader" body of believers, cross-denominational, or even to non-believers, being in communion with a recognized community is essential, if a ministry would be rooted.

Communion as Sacrament

When most Christians think of "holy communion," they are referring to participating in the Eucharist. Paul declared, "The blessing cup which we bless, is it not a sharing [*koinonia*] in the blood of Christ; and the loaf of bread we break, is it not a sharing [*koinonia*] in the body of Christ?" (1 Cor. 10:16, NJB). The Eucharist is the highest and most magnificent bond of communion we share. It enables us to be bonded to Christ as he himself is to the Father and the Holy Spirit. It draws us into the very life of the Holy Trinity and creates many holy bonds between us.

Jesus himself declared in his sermon on the Eucharist,

> Whoever eats my flesh and drinks my blood remains in me, and I in him. Just as the living Father sent me and I live because of the Father, so the one who feeds on me will live because of me. (Jn. 6:56–57, NIV)

As a Catholic, I belong to a "sacramental" Church. This means that I recognize that the life-giving grace of God is normally poured into the Church through the seven sacraments of faith: principally the Eucharist and the Covenant of Baptism, but also through the sacraments of Confirmation, Reconciliation, Anointing of the Sick, Marriage and Ordination (Holy Orders). These are more than ceremonies and rituals:

> Sacraments are "powers that come forth" from the Body of Christ, which is ever-living and life-giving. They are actions of the Holy Spirit at work in his Body, the Church. They are "the masterworks of God" in the new and everlasting covenant.[1]

81

Some of the most profound healing I have seen has taken place at the celebration of the sacraments. In my own walk, daily devotion to the Holy Eucharist has kept me centered and connected with Christ and the Church.

In February of 1998 I attended a "pastors' summit" in which twenty-five local ministers (mostly evangelical) participated. At the conclusion of each of the three nights there was a celebration of Holy Communion among these pastors. They wanted me to partake of the elements. Although I couldn't, I united myself to them in prayer and ministry during those ceremonies. Making a profound impression, those moments have stuck with me because they showed me with what faith, devotion, and dedication those ministers approached Holy Communion as they conceived of it. These were worship moments of a deep outpouring of grace, bonding, and healing for all of us, whether they called it "sacrament," "ordinance," or another term. I realized that God is extravagantly generous with his grace.

Holy Covenant Bonds

Just as unholy and ungodly bonds such as hate, immorality, or occult practices destroy people, making them broken, sinful, and sick, living in holy and godly bonds produces inner and outer harmony, health, and joy. These covenant bonds are a baseline indicator that a Christian is ready for ministry. It is impossible to serve the Lord without participating in the normal life of the Body of Christ.

Despite our inevitable disagreements, feelings of unworthiness, and sometimes ill feelings toward others, the scriptures provide for us the example of the first Christian

> Living in holy and godly bonds produces inner and outer harmony, health, and joy. These covenant bonds are a baseline indicator that a Christian is ready for ministry.

community: "They devoted themselves to the teaching of the apostles [the Word of God] and to the communal life [*koinonia*], to the breaking of the bread [the Eucharist] and to the prayers [assemblies]" (Acts 2:42, NAB). The author of the letter to the Hebrews exhorts us, "Let us be concerned for each other, to stir a response in love and good works. Do not absent yourself from your own assemblies, as some do, but encourage each other; the more so as you see the Day drawing near" (Heb 10: 24–25, NJB).

What, then, is holy communion? What are these holy bonds? There are five types or expressions of holy communion:

a. *Communion of faith* - the teaching that has been handed on to us from the Apostles. This includes sharing in the Word, and rooting our life in it.

b. *Communion of the sacraments* - most excellently the Eucharist, those special moments of covenant that mark our lives and through which God pours his abundant grace.

c. *Communion of charisms* - the manifestations of the Spirit of God given for the upbuilding of the Body of Christ.

d. *Communion of goods* - the disposition that our property is the Lord's and we are his stewards to administer it according to the purposes of his Kingdom.

e. *Communion of charity* - a free giving of ourselves, time, material goods, and energy so that all may benefit.[2]

Journal Questions for a Life of Communion

1. Consider prayerfully the above aspects of communion.
2. Where are your strongest bonds?
3. Where are your weakest bonds?
4. Compose a prayer asking for a deepening of a life in communion.

3. EXERCISE THE GIFTS OF THE SPIRIT

The story of two teenagers

The Nuñez family lives about forty minutes from Monterey in a beautiful valley near Watsonville, California. Berenice, one of two children, began to receive prophetic words when she was fourteen, calling people to conversion and prayer. Her father was the first to give his life to the Lord. Subsequently, Berenice organized prayer and Word of God gatherings in the extensive backyard of their house. Hundreds of people from that valley joined them and gave their lives to Christ. I was impressed by the humility this young lady showed as she submitted all her words and the whole work to the discernment of her parents and to the priests.

Since then the whole family has conducted evangelistic and healing missions in Mexico and have a perpetual open house for prayer. Everyone is welcomed. In 2000, while on a mission to Mexico, Berenice, by then eighteen and trained in the healing ministry, led many people to Christ and led hundreds at a time in public prayer for healing. She is a young woman who has been through the discernment and the purification of her gifts. At the tender age of fourteen, she was willing to "step out in faith" even if it meant discipline. Now a co-worker in Christ, she is in love with God and his people.

The apostle Paul in Romans 12:3–8 encourages us to recognize and affirm the gifts that God has given us, to stay in our gifting and exercise them according to faith. I believe that God creates each person with exactly the right spiritual dimensions to be able to contain the gifts—natural and supernatural—that he has destined for that person to walk in. When we open ourselves to his purposes, he deposits the gifts to "fill out" those dimensions with spiritual power. If you are discerning healing ministry, now is the time to receive and begin to exercise those gifts. You might say you don't know what your gifts are. The first step is to say to God, "I'm ready to receive any gift you have purposed for my life." For sure, you at least are called to pray and ask for other people to be healed. It is a fundamental part of the Christian walk.

In the introduction I referred to a teaching that Joyce Meyer once gave in San Jose, in which she emphasized the need for people to flow more in the gifts. As a child, when I got sick my parents took care of me physically and emotionally by encouraging me. They were great from that standpoint. However, I never remember anyone in my family actually praying for me for healing. Why shouldn't parents or siblings pray for healing? Today, I think it is absurd that parents should not pray for their children's healing. How could God not hear and answer such prayer?

However, just because you exercise a *gift* of healing doesn't mean that you are called to the *ministry* of healing. Likewise, most Christians in some way can and should prophesy, even though that doesn't automatically indicate that they are called to full prophetic ministry. My purpose is to encourage you to start to use and move in the gifts so that it can be later discerned if you have a ministry of healing.

To be active in ministry we must get beyond ourselves and our "hang-ups" and get busy for the Kingdom of God. For the ministry of healing to be discerned and activated, the charisms need to be put into operation and to be tested. That is what has made Berenice such a powerful young believer. What we are talking about here are the charismata, or

Natural talents and abilities are very useful for the "packaging" of these gifts, but we must not confuse them or substitute them for the charisms associated with the healing ministry.

"spiritual gifts," which are needed for the healing ministry. Natural talents and abilities are very useful for the "packaging" of these gifts, but we must not confuse them or substitute them for the charisms associated with the healing ministry. The natural and the supernatural must be harmonized in just the right balance. Achieving that balance is a life-long, challenging and altogether fulfilling adventure.

There will be a great deal to say about the use of the gifts in the healing ministry toward the end of this book. We will explore how the different charisms are used. For now, the point is to begin to exercise the gifts, if only in intercessory prayer.

A year ago I dealt with a demanding father who wanted me to talk with his fourteen-year-old son, Danny, who was acting up. I know that this boy is a child of great promise for the Body of Christ. It is evident to me that God has given him prophetic gifts. One day I took him aside and, knowing that he prays, asked if he would pray for me. I was trying to get him to walk (just a bit) in God's purpose. Without being totally aware of what was happening to him, Danny began to "see" in prayer a danger that would come upon me as I drove that day to an important ministry commitment. He prayed that I would know what to do and that God, through his angels, would protect me. I wasn't aware of the prophetic nature of this prayer until an hour later when I almost got in a crash at high speed. Danny exercised in prayer a charism of the Holy Spirit. When he gets older, I have no doubt that if he continues to exercise those gifts, God will place him in a wonderful ministry in the Body of Christ.

On the other hand, there are those who began to exercise gifts and because of discouragement, misdirection, doubt, fear, or laziness, have left the gifts aside, even if they are in active church "ministry." I want to exhort you that if you are one of these brothers or sisters, for the sake of Jesus and his Body the Church, please return to the exercise of those gifts, so that he can put you into a ministry that will be his work and totally for his glory. I'm asking for a basic openness to receive, use, and grow in these charisms. In a later chapter we will focus specifically on the biblical "service gifts" of the Holy Spirit from 1 Cor. 12: 4–11.

Early on in the Institute for the Healing Ministry there were some brothers and sisters who, when we broke into groups to practice healing prayer, would start to wave their hands over supplicants, trying to "focus" or "channel" their energies. This became so distracting that people thought that they were practicing New Age techniques. Indeed, there was confusion between this and true healing prayer. Healing prayer relies on the manifestation of the Holy Spirit, not the individual's "powers." One sister, enthusiastic at first about developing her "healing powers," could not comprehend the role of the Holy Spirit and the charisms. She soon stopped coming.

Let's be clear that a call to the healing ministry is a call from a Sovereign God, not from me, you, or any human agency, even though it is discerned through human beings. We hold the treasure of God's gift in earthenware jars, not glorious gold vessels, "that the surpassing power may be of God and not from us" (2 Cor. 4:7, NAB). Today, let the glory of his power flow through you!

4. DEVELOP YOUR PRAYER LIFE

If we are docile, our prayer life is a work of art fashioned by the Holy Spirit throughout a believer's life.[3] Prayer exists so that we can become temples of the Holy Spirit, where God is glorified and his Kingdom is established by our obedience. It is a question of our destiny in God. God has a very special work of art he wants to make of your prayer life, and it corresponds to the calling he has purposed for your life and the unique way in which you will need to hear his voice.

St. Francis de Sales, an eighteenth-century master of the spiritual life, puts it this way:

[God] commands Christians, the living plants of his Church, to bring forth the fruits of devotion, each according to his position and vocation. Devotion must be exercised in different ways by the gentleman, the worker, the servant, the prince, the widow, the young girl and the married woman.[4]

Hearing God's Voice

Our Father wants to be able to speak to us at any time, day or night. This becomes particularly crucial as a person moves into the ministry of intercession, which includes the healing ministry. Many people go to prayer hoping that God will immediately speak or give them insight then and there. While he often does give guidance as we settle ourselves down and start to listen, I think that the expectation that he will clearly speak every time can be somewhat limiting. We affirm that God speaks mysteriously and wonderfully at his discretion. *Prayer sets up the conditions and ongoing connection with him so that we can be available to his voice—however it comes—in the midst of any activity.*

I know very few people who are genuinely satisfied with their prayer life, myself included. And that's the way it should be, since we all fall short of the glory of God as the flesh, the devil, and the world ever seek to encroach upon us or block God out. We can use the virtue of hope in our prayer to ask the Holy Spirit to take us into greater depths of the power of his Anointing. The power grows in proportion to being able to hear his voice. As Benny Hinn puts it,

You must learn how to hear His voice. Without knowing His voice, you will not know His power. As I said, the apostles, in Acts 1:2, 8, did not receive the power until they head heard the voice of their master . . . We are to follow Him daily. Hear His voice daily, Psalm 95:7 challenges us that each day, today, we must listen to God's voice, The question isn't whether God is speaking to you today; it is, are you listening to Him speak to you today?[5]

Everyone has a baseline of prayer to which God has called them. If we are not on that baseline, we cannot hear him. It will vary according to the calling of each individual. An attitude of flexibility about prayer life will enable it to grow and develop. The important thing is to start somewhere. For this, I recommend Linda Schubert's *Miracle Hour*, a practical booklet that contains the material that the Holy Spirit can mold, shape, and fashion. She writes,

> The prayers and reflections in this booklet are offered as suggestions to help you get started. The more you can personalize them and allow the Holy Spirit to lead you spontaneously in your own words, the more meaningful it will be. You can expect a tremendous awakening and continual deepening of your spiritual life through this daily "Miracle Hour."[6]

A disciple has to be in a position to hear the voice of the Good Shepherd. If not, then we are just hearing our own voice and doing our own thing. When we have set up the conditions to hear God, our ministry takes place in response to a purer perception the Lord's call. It will be a ministry of obedience to the Lord himself. It will be a manifestation of his power. That is what the prayer life of a minister is all about.

Journal Questions for a Spiritual Baseline

1. Do you have a prayer life that serves as a sufficient baseline for you to hear God and obey him?
2. Describe your prayer life.
3. What does your prayer life need in order to hear God more clearly?

Seeking God's Will about the Ministry of Healing

I would like to invite you to focus your discernment by a spiritual *seeking* of God's will. Let's do it through the eleventh chapter of Luke, where Jesus teaches about prayer.

> So I say to you: Ask and it will be given to you; seek and you will find; knock and the door will be opened to you. For everyone who asks receives; he who seeks finds; and to him who knocks, the door will be opened. (Lk. 11: 9–13, NIV)

Jesus' teaching on prayer presents the three dimensions of prayer. Let's put these three dimensions of prayer in the context of discerning your call to the healing ministry. I used to mistakenly think that these were three ways our Lord had of saying the same thing. Now I realize that asking, seeking, and knocking are three distinct dimensions of prayer.

Ask in prayer. We often go before the Lord and ask him in a petition, stating the desires of our heart. May I suggest that we take that prayer, turn it around, and ask the Holy Spirit what we should ask of God. He will begin to work in our hearts to indicate to us what we should ask of him. If someone you love is ill, start asking, "Lord, how would you have me pray for him or her?" Begin to intercede according to what you sense in your spirit. For beginners this is awkward and foreign, but as you become accustomed to this way of praying, it will feel natural and easy.

Seek in prayer. There is a dimension of seeking in prayer where we strive not to seek our own self-interests. We seek God's face in the interest of the Body of Christ. There is more. It is not necessarily a seeking of an answer to this or that question. It is a seeking the will of God in a profound way. We come before the Lord and we say with expectant faith, "Lord, reveal your will to me." "Are you calling me to this?" "Would you have me enter into a greater dimension of this ministry or are you calling me to something else?"

We seek God's will because we seek his face. This takes us into the realm of the prophetic.

Let this be our prayer:

> Hear my voice when I call, O Lord; be merciful to me and answer me. My heart says of you, "Seek his face!" Your face, Lord, I will seek. Do not hide your face from me, do not turn your servant away in anger; you have been my helper. Do not reject me or forsake me, O God my Savior. (Ps. 27:7–9, NIV)

Knock and enter in prayer. "Knock and the door will be opened"— so that we would stand outside? No, if we "knock" it is because God's door will be open and we enter in. May I suggest that this is the third dimension of prayer, an entering into his presence. Beyond asking and seeking his will there is a deliberate, purposeful "stepping inside" his presence and being in that spiritual place where he is able to guide us intimately in ministry. He will speak and deal with us in his own way, in his own time. He will open the door. Let's not stand outside, let's step into his healing presence!

Pray with me:

> *Heavenly Father, in obedience to your Son, we want to pray in your Holy Spirit.*
>
> *Your word says that when we know not how to pray, the Spirit enters in and intercedes through us with groaning too deep for words. Grant us the Holy Spirit so that we should know how to ask, intercede, and petition according to your will.*
>
> *We seek you, Lord; we seek not what you will do for us, we seek not our own will, we seek your will. What would you have us do?*

Father, we knock at the door, we knock at the door of your heart and we ask that you would open that door so that we can step in. We commit ourselves to stepping in when you open it. We will step in to a new intimacy. We will step into a deeper dimension of our ministry. We will step into that spiritual place where we will obey you and minister to you and do what you want.

In Jesus' name, Amen

TIME FOR AN HONEST CONVERSATION WITH GOD:

Three Basic Questions for the Healing Ministry

1. Is the healing ministry really what God wants for me?

   Or

2. Do I need to mature more and give myself—and the Holy Spirit—time for my spiritual growth before I enter into or continue this ministry?

   Or

3. Is God at this time calling me to give myself with greater generosity to the healing ministry?

---

[1] *Catechism of the Catholic Church,* #1116.

[2] *Catechism,* #949–953.

[3] *Catechism,* #2672.

[4] de Sales, St. Francis, *Introduction to the Devout Life,* New York, Image Books, 1989, p. 43.

[5] Hinn, Benny, *The Anointing,* Nashville, Thomas Nelson, 1992, p. 152.

[6] Schubert, Linda, *The Miracle Hour,* p. 3.

Part III

The Spirituality of the Healing Ministry

Chapter 7

A Baseline for Ministry

A Balancing Act

Our God is a covenant God, who provides just the right framework and conditions so that we can be both the recipients and conduits of his own life—the power of his grace—working in and through us. In every divinely appointed covenant there are conditions that keep the flow of grace intact. The energy of his life is meant to flow through four aspects of life:

1. prayer life
2. family life
3. work life
4. ministry life.

Maintaining a spirituality that provides a flow through all these areas of our life is *the* most difficult issue for a minister of healing prayer. It is a delicate balancing act that has to be revisited often.

God has graced me with ministry partners who walk in this covenant relationship in remarkable ways. One of these is Chip

Sundstrom, whom I've had the privilege to know over many years. He is a family man with a scientific profession in agriculture of working to provide the best quality seeds used worldwide. He is a husband of a loving wife and three wonderful (currently teenaged) children. Chip, like you and me, has struggled in some hard battles to keep those above-mentioned four aspects in balance.

Often, people sacrifice their families to do what they think really gives meaning to their lives, that is prayer and ministry. This is erroneous. Watching and working with Chip has taught me a lot about spirituality and how *nothing* in our lives lies outside of the Lord's covenant. Chip has experienced how, as a husband and father, he is God's instrument of life and blessing for his family. As a corporation executive, he is also responsible, through prayer and obedience, to see that God's principles govern the conduct of business. When things get out of balance, time, energy, and resources are dramatically wasted. Life bears no good fruit and blessing is blocked. All areas lose their focus.

Chip has a ministry of leadership, healing, and intercession. He is like a spiritual "radar" when it comes to discernment and the use of spiritual gifts. I've been in gatherings where he starts to pray in the Anointing that God has bestowed on him and I literally feel interiorly shaken from the power of that prayer. Because Chip has put the aspects of prayer, family, and work under God's covenant, he has been given a beautiful and powerful ministry, recognized all over northern and central California.

One day, when interceding for Chip, who was going through a crisis situation, I received a very strong image of a large sailing vessel—like the ones used by the explorers of old. I thought, "How strange, Chip has nothing to do with sailing." (By the way I studied as a midshipman at the U. S. Merchant Marine Academy, so God sometimes speaks to me in nautical terms. Chip often has agricultural "images.")

As I prayed about this vision and shared it with Chip, I sensed that the vessel was a metaphor for Chip's life. The keel of the boat with the rudder is his prayer life. The hull is his family life. The deck, with all its gear is the work life, and the sails are his ministry. If there is no prayer, there is no balance, no direction. If the family is not attended to in God's way, the hull is damaged and will take on water and eventually sink. If the gear on the deck or in the cabin is not functioning, the ship will not go anywhere. If the sails are tattered or not unfolded, the vessel will not be carried by the wind, which is the Spirit of God.

This all means that there is a way God desires for us to *navigate* through these four aspects of life. There are conditions to be met for each part of the ship to function in the way God established. Each of these aspects needs to be:

- soaked in the exercise of *faith;*
- purified by a life of willingness to be shown where the weak spots are for *repentance, conversion, and growth;*
- carried in the direction of the *Father's will.*

Once, after a trip to China, Chip said to me, "It's all one—all the aspects of our family, prayer, work, and ministry are meant to flow in the same way." Realizing that God allows the trials that cause us so much pain to bring this truth about in our flesh, I thought immediately of the ship. It would be absurd to have the hull on one vessel, the deck gear on another and the sails on a third. It is just as absurd to think that we can conduct our lives as independent little boats, each going its own way. A hard battle often ensues when God's Spirit starts working to this end.

"Little Girl, Get Up"

It is vitally important that, to heal as Jesus healed—that is, to work under the same Holy Spirit Anointing—we take him as our primary example and examine how he conducted himself in the ministry into which the Father had led him. Let us look at Jesus' own spirituality as he ministers. In Mark 6:35–43 Jesus is called to the house of a synagogue official to heal his daughter. On the way, the news arrives that she has died. Jesus exhorts the man not to fear, but have faith. He takes Peter, James, and John into house and expels the people who had arrived to lament and bewail the little girl's death. With the parents, Jesus and his companions enter the room. Taking her by the hand, he orders the dead girl to get up. She is then restored to life and given to her parents.

In my ministry as a priest and in my healing ministry, I often run into situations where there is a lot of commotion like the incident in the Gospel of Mark. For instance, when people die, commotion and confusion are often present among family and friends. That is often the case with illness, when it hasn't been placed in the Lord's presence. There are always the questions, Why does God allow this to happen? If God is so good and merciful, why does he allow suffering, death and illness to happen? In the gospel passage, there was desperation from the fact that a child was ill and then died. Jesus exhorted the father, who was the president of the synagogue, to have faith. But it was a hopeless cause in a hopeless situation. The first thing Jesus did was to put the unbelievers and wailers out of the house.

He took five people with him into the room. The parents' grief and emotions were a barrier for God to work in the powerful way that was needed. They could not conceive of what Jesus was about to do. Why did he take Peter, James, and John with him? These were the same disciples who would also be present at the transfiguration and in the Garden of Gethsemane. Peter, James, and John were part of Jesus' inner circle. There was something about their presence that corresponded to their high calling of faith.

I am convinced that Jesus took them into the room with him to promote a spiritual atmosphere of faith in the face of so much negative emotion. Jesus himself needed that atmosphere in order that the Anointing would flow out and heal. It was also part of the disciples' faith training: they needed to experience working and praying in a spiritual climate to later become effective ministers of Jesus' healing.

The necessity of doing healing ministry in an *atmosphere of faith* is a primary concern for the spirituality of the healing ministry. It is essential that whenever we are in a situation where God would heal, there should be an environment of faith. In the preceding example, as in the story of the paralytic and so many others, Jesus needed a spiritual climate of faith so that the Anointing of God could flow.

> It is essential that whenever we are in a situation where God would heal, there should be an environment of faith.

SEEK HEALING THROUGH WORSHIP

The best way I know to get into that spiritual climate is through worship. A Greek New Testament word for the Saxon word "worship" is *leiturgia*,[1] from which we get the word "liturgy," a term most often used in the Catholic tradition. It refers to spiritual work Christians do corporately to give God what is his due. Taking a close look at the way we worship as a body enables us to understand some things about our private devotion and relationship with God. Looking at how God works in worship and how we respond to him will give important clues about prayer for healing. In fact, it can be a true model for healing prayer, as well as the whole of our relationship with the Holy Trinity.

The Word of God teaches that there is no relationship with God the Father except through the Holy Spirit. There is no relationship with Jesus except through the Holy Spirit. If you come to know Jesus, that in itself is a work of the Holy Spirit. Our prayer life is a work of art of the Holy Spirit for he is the "artisan" of our prayer life.[2]

Let's now take a closer look at worship, or liturgy, and consider it as a model for our own ministry of healing. Of the many powerful works that the Holy Spirit does when we gather for worship, one is the special initial work of *preparation*. This applies equally to healing ministry. Of course, we know that God often miraculously touches people and changes them dramatically into believers, as he did with the apostle Paul on the road to Damascus. But healing normally takes place as God leads people to open themselves to receive it. Remember that Paul went away for fourteen years of discipleship and training before returning as an apostle to Palestine (cf. Gal. 2:1).

To have a deeper and more healing encounter with the Lord Jesus, we need to allow the Spirit to draw us into that "spiritual space" of openness and the dimension of spiritual intimacy. This goes for those seeking healing, and it especially applies to those who are ministering. I liken this openness to being on a "spiritual baseline"—drawn apart from worldly and selfish ways and lifted up by the Spirit of God to that "spiritual space" where we can meet the Lord Jesus with a full heart. Those who minister and those who receive ministry often need to be helped onto this "baseline" to meet the Master. Let's look specifically at the steps onto this meeting place with Jesus.

The spiritual meeting place with the Lord could also be called a "spiritual baseline." In medical terms, a person is at his or her baseline when he is at the normal level of functioning. When you are at baseline, it means that your vital signs, body chemistry, temperature, and other functions are working at least with a minimal normality. The patient can then undergo an operation or other treatment in order to heal. That is also true in the spiritual realm.

Our spiritual "baseline" is our spirituality as a *disciple*. The baseline means that we are on a certain level of faith, conversion, and adherence to the Father's will. In ministry we are listening for that which would be our own mission. In addition, we listen with regard to those whom God has placed in our lives, for signs of their mission and God's purpose. As long as we are on that baseline, God can speak to us at any time, at any place. He can speak to you on the mountaintop or he can speak to you when you are going through a dark valley. All he wants from us are the basic conditions of being his disciples.

> Our spiritual "baseline" is our spirituality as a *disciple*.

A HEALING ENCOUNTER WITH THE LORD

Preparation—Your "Spiritual Baseline"

There are three steps leading to that baseline of the meeting place with Christ. They turn out to be three "preconditions" to deeply meeting Jesus in prayer and worship. In the healing ministry these are the same three preconditions that lead to a healing encounter with the Lord Jesus Christ. Please look with me at key passage from the *Catechism of the Catholic Church* as it relates to the ministry of worship:

> The assembly should *prepare* itself to encounter its Lord and to become "a people well disposed." The preparation of hearts is the joint work of the Holy Spirit and the assembly, especially of its ministers. The grace of the Holy Spirit seeks to awaken faith, conversion of heart, and adherence to the Father's will. These dispositions are the precondition both for the reception of other graces conferred in the celebration itself and the fruits of new life which the celebration is intended to produce afterward.[3]

It is most beneficial to look at this paragraph line by line.

The assembly should prepare itself to encounter its Lord and to become "a people well disposed"

Creating a "people well disposed" was the mission of John the Baptist (Lk. 1:17). His work concerned the preparation of the nation of Israel for its encounter in history with the Anointed One (and his Anointing). It took place when the arrival of the Messiah was imminent. Since John was filled with the Holy Spirit from his mother's womb, his life was soaked in this calling. Can you imagine if there had not been this preparation? The Anointed One and his Anointing could have never been received! Jesus could have come, but the response would have been minimal.

The world changed as a result of the Jews' encounter with the Anointed One. It was truly an encounter, a meeting appointed by God so that the Anointing power of the Holy Spirit could be sent into the world. God has designed encounters for us, as well—life and ministry-changing encounters with the Anointed One to heal, restore, free, and save. If you and I are to be persons of encounter with God, ministers of intercession, we must be willing to prepare by stepping up to that baseline where Jesus will meet us and work through us.

The Oxford Dictionary says that to *dispose* is to "arrange in a particular position / incline (someone) toward a particular activity or frame of mind." In the case of worship, and in the particular case of healing prayer, a position before God of the heart, mind, attitudes, and soul becomes crucial to allowing the Anointed One and his Anointing have full sway.

The preparation of hearts is the joint work of the Holy Spirit and the assembly . . .

There is a common work that is being done when we gather together. Think of a tandem bicycle, but with the Holy Spirit doing most of the pedaling. If we do our part, he will move us along. If we are lazy, or even "back-pedal," he will respect our free will but we cannot expect to move ahead. The grace of God surrounds us, yet there is an active human consent to receive it and do something about it. Healing prayer is best when there is a group of people who are "called together" by the Spirit of God to pray for a healing: it is an *assembly*. On our part there is work to do, and the Holy Spirit can be trusted do his part. This is done so that we can get onto the "baseline" where God works most powerfully. The Holy Spirit will provide the steps, but we are the ones who have to step up!

. . . especially of the assembly's ministers

If you are ministering healing prayer at an event, the joint work of preparation especially applies to you. It is you, together with your fellow ministers who will, through the Holy Spirit's power, lead those who are broken and ill to their spiritual baseline so that they can meet in intercession with Christ the Healer. It is our job to make sure we are on the baseline of meeting so that God can use us as instruments. We will also model for our supplicants that prayer and that disposition or readiness that lets the healing power of God flow freely. In later chapters I will outline a model of this preparation, step by step. For the moment, we are concerned about the issues of spirituality.

The grace of the Holy Spirit seeks . . .

The Holy Spirit *seeks*; there is a passion on the part of God to make a connection with us and with those for whom we are praying. It was the same Spirit that made Jesus thirst and seek the faith of the woman at the well (cf. Jn. 4:7–10) and, from the cross, seek the salvation of anyone who would accept the Son of God (Jn. 19:28).

Journal Questions for Ministry Baseline

1. Where do you sense God wants you with respect to your:
   personal life, including spirituality?
   family?
   work?
   ministry?

2. Reflect on and describe your own preparation for prayer or ministry with others.

---

[1] See, for example, the gathering at Antioch in Acts 13:1, or the places in the book of Revelation that refer to the worship (liturgy) in heaven.
[2] *Catechism of the Catholic Church*, #1091, 2672.
[3] Ibid., #1098.

Chapter 8

THREE HEALING WORKS OF THE HOLY SPIRIT

In Chapter 7 we began to study the work of preparation that forms the "spiritual baseline" from which people minister in healing prayer. It is a "baseline" of spirituality, or relationship with God, that enables his power to flow unrestricted through us. We can go deeper. Ministers of healing prayer are the indicated ones to prepare in every way for healing events. Below are presented three distinct dimensions that can and need to be stirred up in us: to awaken faith, to move in repentance and deeper conversion, to have an attitude of adherence to the Father's will. These movements are for everyone, including the recipients of healing prayer. But the ministers are the key people to lead others in need of healing in their relationship with God.

1. The Grace of the Holy Spirit Seeks to Awaken Faith

Our connection with God depends on faith, so the Spirit seeks *to awaken our faith.* That is why Jesus always wanted people of faith to be with him when he ministered. Healing flows in the presence of faith. Notice the term "awaken." It is significant because it implies that faith can be dormant, or asleep. When prayer, assemblies, and the celebration of sacraments put you to sleep, the Spirit needs to wake you up, especially to awake those ministering. Worship should never be boring! Cooperation, which literally means a *co-working,* is needed on our part. In worship, in healing prayer, and in all of spiritual life, the first step is to press through our laziness. Laziness prevents a person from moving ahead in relationship with God and others.

Let's go further. What is it about faith that enables the encounter with Christ? Faith has two aspects: it is first of all a *personal* adherence to God. This implies that sooner or later, there has to be a decision that you will connect and stay attached to God, to the *Persons* of the Holy Trinity. The four men who brought the paralytic to Jesus adhered to God. So did Peter, James, and John. Even if they were yet immature in their walk of discipleship, they had a personal faith. Take a look at the word "adhere." Scotch® Tape is the brand name of an *adhesive* tape because it *adheres,* it sticks. The dictionary's definition of "adhere" is "to stick fast, to stay attached." Faith is first of all, an adherence to God. The person of faith stays attached to God as Scotch® Tape sticks to paper! The more we are devotedly attached to God, the more his power fills us and flows through us for healing.

Along with the personal adherence to God, faith is at the same time an "assent" to the whole truth that God has revealed. Assent is a "concurrence," a putting oneself into agreement with what is revealed by God. The biblical revelation is that faith confesses that Jesus has almighty power to heal and that he wants to heal. People often feel helpless about the suffering that is in their lives and in the world. This is a faith problem. The remedy is to be steeped in the Word of God, thus producing the knowledge of God and personal adherence to him.

Francis MacNutt describes an interesting awakening he had with regard to faith when he discovered that the Yiddish slang word "chutzpah" best describes the way Jesus would have approached healing prayer. Chutzpah means "nerve" or "brass," "extreme confidence in action." "In today's terms a person with chutzpah is someone who 'goes for it'."[1] Along with this, he maintains, "Our faith lies in the obedience of praying for the sick, despite our weakness, doing the best we can to show forth the mercy of Christ."[2]

Faith is not something that is passively received. Faith that results in healing is active: it involves *stretching out* a withered hand (Mk. 3:5); it means *getting up, picking up the stretcher and going* (Lk. 5:24); it demands *coming out* of the tomb (Jn. 11:43); it challenges *to go to your brother to be reconciled* (Mt. 5:24). There is a song that often rings through great healing services:

> Rise and be healed in the name of Jesus,
> Let faith arise in your soul;
> Rise and be healed in the name of Jesus,
> He will touch you and make you whole!

Jesus Is the Master of Healing

Some truths of faith are of crucial importance when we come to adhere to the living God. One is that we must know that we are not God, *he* is: we cannot impose our will on him. It also means that we can stand firm on his promises. There are some things that we have to believe about God, about who he is, about his character, that will enable us to get on the baseline for an encounter with the living Master.

Barbara Shlemon puts it this way, "To 'have faith in God' means to trust that the Father's will for us is much more wonderful than we can possibly imagine. Our attitude as we approach him in prayer, needs to be childlike in simplicity."[3] Father John Bertolucci adds that this faith needs to be persistent: "To persist in faith for healing simply means that we continue trusting in our Father's love. We trust that he knows our sickness and suffering, that he wants to set us free, that he will meet every one of our needs."[4]

When this trust is not present, people will become desperate. This drives them to seek other means of "healing," a relief that really isn't a healing at all, but a temporary remedy that puts them in greater spiritual jeopardy. To resort to psychics, witch doctors, esoteric healing, or the New Age is a breach of trust in God and his life-giving word. *Trust* and *surrender* are the key words in developing a mature faith. It was a lack of trust that led to the first sin. "All subsequent sin would be disobedience toward God and lack of trust in his goodness."[5]

Adhere to the God Who *Is* Healing!

God's character is revealed as the Scriptures speak to us about his attributes. One of the things that we believe about him is that he is a *healing* God. In Exodus 15:26 God declares, "I AM Yahweh-Rapha," literally, "I am the Lord-who-is-healing." If we are faithfully attached to God, we will adhere to his nature, which is healing. God identifies himself with healing so that when we stick to him we *believe* that he is a God who is in the act of healing us. That is *revelation*. If a person adheres to him personally, he or she will be healed. Just getting into the presence of God and surrendering ourselves to him will produce healing in a person's life.

> Just getting into the presence of God and surrendering ourselves to him will produce healing in a person's life.

There are some misguided expressions of spirituality that emphasize that brokenness and pain are always meant to be, without recourse to the God who heals. It is as if God were to say to us "just go ahead and suffer." This is a rather extreme and unscriptural point of view. I do believe in a sound "theology" of suffering, which will be discussed later in the chapter on the Catholic Church's teaching on healing. Yet suffering remains an issue that ministers of healing prayer must be able to handle without going from one extreme to the other. God's will is for wholeness. Francis MacNutt affirms,

> It is my belief that the ordinary will of God is that we should be whole. Usually, we glorify God more when we are healthy than when we are sick. Therefore we can and should pray to God with confidence for healing.[6]

The Word of God constantly reveals that it is his will for us to ask for healing. More often than not, when we ask in faith, suffering is diminished or eliminated, and there is *always* healing on some level. We do not believe in a God who says you must just suffer. We believe in a Jesus who said to the leper who asking for healing, "I do will it. Be made clean" (Mk. 1:41, NAB).

Faith is a personal adherence to God and a conforming of ourselves to his truth. This means not only *that* we believe, but also *what* we believe about God. Faith in Christ is different from our faith in any human person. People who run to this or that "faith healer" often believe in the *person* and that this person has special powers. Often people say to me, "Would you heal me?" I have never healed anybody in my life! The only thing that I can do is provide an atmosphere of faith and prayer so that person can be connected with the Lord, adhere to him and be healed. I believe that is *the* essential part of the ministry of healing.

The minister of healing must develop a unique spirituality. He or she needs to be a man or woman of faith, with regard to his or her own personal adherence to God. It is also vital to know about God—to know who he is, what he has revealed about himself, his character, and the way he works. Many people believe that Jesus was just a great human being. Some people even believe that he had supernatural or "psychic powers." This is foreign to the Christian belief. We believe that he is almighty God and therefore healing power flows from and through him. To adhere to Jesus is to get to know him personally in relationship. Faith is a condition for a firm and lasting healing. Our God *is* a God of healing.

Stand on Your Faith

Another definition of faith comes to us from Hebrews 11:1. This is the most talked about definition of faith in scripture. I would like to approach the text from a different angle. It says that "Faith is the realization of what is hoped for and evidence of things not seen" (Heb 11:1, NAB). The text goes on to talk about Old Testament heroes who had that kind of faith. In the scriptural view, faith is a substance of the things that we hope for. Substance is a translation of the Greek word *hypostasis*. *Hypostasis* is used two other times in the book of Hebrews (1:3 and 3:14), both referring to the substance of God himself. Paul exhorted the Colossians to "persevere and stand firm on the solid base of the faith" (Col. 1:23, NJB).

The faith on which I stand is a guarantee, a substance, and an assurance built on God himself. One does not adhere to a human being in the sense of absolute reliance. Nor does one adhere only to ideas about God. The believer adheres to a *Person*—to God himself. *We stand on the substance of God himself when we live in faith.* It is not some kind of idea, a system of belief or an "ism." Faith is the *hypostasis*, the *substance*, of the things that we hope for in God himself.

Now look at the phrase, "hope for." 1 Corinthians 13:13 says, "These remain: faith, hope and love" (NJB). There is a hope that takes its place in God. When we have a desire that someone would be healed, that desire is a holy desire. When that desire comes from God, that desire is a *potential* until it is achieved. This is more than "wishful thinking." In healing prayer, you are called to get into the desires of the Spirit for that person. Ministry in the Spirit means that things in the future of that person are revealed that couldn't be seen before. That is the virtue of hope. In the Scripture, it is the "evidence of things not seen" (Heb 11:1). God has wholeness in our future and this notion should always characterize our prayer. Because of the future orientation of healing prayer, there is a distinctly "prophetic" element to it.

As confirmed by the prophets, we believe in a future in which God himself will be our wholeness. When we step into that reality, when we adhere to it, then we walk into that wholeness. When we haven't achieved the substance part, we are in the realm of hope. Faith is a substance that produces a flow of grace that brings us directly into the wholeness of God himself: "I am Yahweh-Rapha." To know God as Healer is a defining characteristic of spirituality that every person ministering healing prayer needs to have. To know how to get to the desires of God's heart for someone is to have a spirituality of hope—to see where God wants that person, then we adhere to God so that he brings that future into the *now* reality of faith.

> To know God as Healer is a defining characteristic of spirituality that every person ministering healing prayer needs to have.

In Romans 4:17 Paul talks about faith, the faith of Abraham. He says, "Abraham is our father in the eyes of God in whom he put his faith" (NJB). Abraham not only adhered to God personally but he believed what God told him. He absolutely believed. Abraham didn't put his faith in a human; he adhered to and put his belief in the God "who brings the dead to life, and calls into existence what does not yet exist." Abraham had a living hope, based on the desires of the Spirit. That hope became faith, based on the substance of God himself.

Hope is a desire that is taken from the heart of God. Faith is what brings that which still does not exist into our realm. Taken from the heart of God, the desire for healing is brought into the realm of our human "here-and-now." That is healing! This is the spirituality, the "mind-set," and the heart of a person who is in the healing ministry. When someone has the charism, or gift, of healing, there is a faith that corresponds to that gift.

In one of the most beautiful and deep prophecies of Isaiah we find these words:

> Yet it was our infirmities that he bore,
>   our sufferings that he endured,
> While we thought of him as stricken,
>   as one smitten by God and afflicted.
> But he was pierced for our offenses,
>   crushed for our sins,
> Upon him was the chastisement that makes us whole,
>   by his stripes we were healed. (Is 53:4–5, NAB)

The last phrase, *by his stripes we were healed,* is very important. The Hebrew text uses the past tense to say that we *were healed* by his wounds. Healing is in our destiny, wholeness is our future, which already exists in God's realm. In the healing ministry God gives prophetic vision that enables us to see and walk into the future he has prepared.

Hebrews 11:1 says, in effect, that there will be a hope, an expectancy, that when a prayer connection is made in faith, a person walks into that which has already been accomplished for him or her by Jesus on the cross. We say this with regard to salvation and the forgiveness of sins. When we ask forgiveness, whether it be privately within ourselves or through the Sacrament of Reconciliation in the Catholic tradition, because of the cross, God's forgiveness is already there, just waiting to enter. We have simply to let it in, and the way we let it in is by faith. Forgiveness has been accomplished for us already. We are the ones who are so slow to believe. It's a belief issue, a faith issue. Healing works the same way as forgiveness. It is already accomplished for us. "He took away our infirmities / and bore our diseases" (Mt. 8:17, NAB). I suspect that we have missed out on many of the promises of God by simply neglecting to receive them.

F. F. Bosworth comments on this passage from Isaiah and also cites the example of obedient faith that brought down of the walls of Jericho. He puts it this way:

> Since it is "by His stripes we are healed," let us not forget what our healing cost, but with gratitude and love, and consecrated service to God, let us stand on His promise and "blow the ram's horn" of faith and thanksgiving until the walls of our affliction fall down flat.
>
> *Faith does not wait for the walls to fall down; faith shouts them down!*[7]

God, through his word, has made to us many promises based on our living out his covenant. Through his word we see clearly the promises he gives us prophetically for our personal, family, professional, and ministerial life. It is in the realm of faith that we receive these promises and they are brought into our existence as we live out our covenant relationship.

A couple of years ago, my friend Chip and his wife were put to the test with regard to their faith, their living out the covenant and entering into healing. Their son is a child of God's promises (as is each offspring in his or her own way). As alluded to earlier, he has been given gifts by the Holy Spirit—not just natural talents.

At one point, Chip's son was attacked by enemy forces that would have detoured him from God's promises and cut him off from the family. As Chip and I prayed this through, the Spirit of God quickened us to hold onto in faith the promises that related to the young man. The temptation for Chip and his wife was to give up on God's promises, give in to despair and take measures leading to defeat. There was a spiritual ground that had to be "staked out" and renewed. That intercession, based on the rock of faith in God's promises, enabled Chip to take the godly measures necessary and provide healing and freedom for this child of the promise. The prophetic word over him, together with God's word in scripture, used in intercession, provided guidance and wisdom that enabled victory.

An Invitation

If you are currently undergoing a trial that would detour your personal life, family, profession, or ministry, I would like to invite you onto a baseline of faith and there pray in an intercession of faith based on God's promises. You might not yet be aware of all the promises God has purposed for each of your issues. That is not important now. There are promises—even the most basic ones—that come from Scripture and can be applied to the situations. Here are just two of these promises that require a baseline of faith:

> We have this confidence in him, that if we ask anything according to his will, he hears us.
> And if we know that he hears us in regard to whatever we ask, we know that what we have asked him for is ours. (1 Jn. 5:15–16, NAB)

> [God] wills everyone to be saved and to come to knowledge of the truth. (1 Tim 2:4, NAB)

Let's lay claim to these promises and agree in faith for a loved one.

Lord Jesus, today we choose to put our confidence absolutely in you, we know you hear us, we affirm that what we ask for in faith is already ours.
We place in your hands this loved one,_____,
who is in need of a deeper relationship with you. Let your salvation and healing penetrate to his/her deepest need. We believe that as you long to be deeply known by him/her, you

will provide those circumstances, people and teaching that will form his/her ideas about you and guide his/her thoughts to you.

We ask this in your name Lord Jesus. Amen.

2. The Grace of the Holy Spirit Seeks to Awaken Conversion of Heart

The Gospel of Luke relates that John the Baptist "went through the whole Jordan area proclaiming a baptism of repentance for the forgiveness of sins" (Lk. 3:3, NJB). The second step of the spiritual baseline is *conversion of heart*. Conversion comes from the Latin *convertere*—to turn or change the direction. In Greek the word that is used in the New Testament is *metanoia*, meaning a "change of mind."

It is important that a person in the healing ministry be someone of true *conversion* or *metanoia*, so that he or she will be an instrument for others to encounter the risen Lord. If we are gentle instruments, God will insure that people will come into that change of mind for themselves. This means a change in the direction of our own minds, our own ways of thinking about things and people. Sin is an offense against reason, God's truth and a right conscience. This makes repentance and conversion something that takes place in the *mind*.

But it is also an issue of the *heart*. Sin is a failure in genuine love for God and neighbor. It is caused by a perverse (misdirected) attachment to things that may be otherwise good. But these are not in God's plan for us. A relationship calls for an adherence to God. A decision made to detach ourselves from God is obviously sin. The human heart is such that if we let go of God we will naturally turn and attach ourselves to something that is not God. Sin is a misdirected attachment to things, ideas, or persons that lead us away from God: we "miss the mark."

Look at the word "perverse." In Latin it is *pervertere* (*per* = a turn or alteration; *vertere* = in the course of). It is an alteration of course or misdirection, just as *con-vertere* means redirection or a turning back. We are meant to adhere to God with our whole being. In faith we are to absolutely adhere to what he has revealed. When we refuse to do so, we produce in ourselves a wound and this leads to sin. We have become misdirected. To be misdirected means that we "miss the mark" and that is sin. We are adhering to something which takes us away, which *perverts* us and leads us away from God. Since we were created for him, violating that for which we were created wounds our nature.

Sin also injures human solidarity. It causes brokenness in relationships with other human beings. We are created to live and be in communion with others. Sin breaks that communion. In order to function in the image of God, in the purpose for which we were created, there has to be a free giving of ourselves and an entering into communion with God and others.

A wound is caused in our own nature when we dis-adhere from God and cling to sin. When we unstick ourselves from him we become misdirected or perverted in what we believe about God's character. Conversion, or *metanoia*, means that we allow God to change our minds about the distorted way we think of him and the whole created order with its purpose. When we change our minds about what we are adhering to, we also change our hearts about what we have been directing our attention to and so return to cling to God. This kind of conversion is characteristic of the spirituality that defines a person in the healing ministry.

Let's look at a simple example. A sign of brokenness in the area of sexuality is when a person thinks and acts in a way that looks on others as if they were objects of self-pleasure. The mass media often portrays sexuality in this light. This way thinking and acting out is to pervert or misdirect sexuality. In contrast, a person who has allowed *metanoia,* or conversion, in this area of life looks upon sex and sexuality as a way of entering into communion with the other.

3. THE GRACE OF THE HOLY SPIRIT SEEKS TO AWAKEN ADHERENCE TO THE FATHER'S WILL

In Luke 3:10–14, people asked John the Baptist, "What must we do?" John's mission in preparing a people "well disposed" was to give them concrete guidance concerning God's will and plan for their lives.

We now come to the third aspect that defines a spirituality essential for people to encounter a living Jesus in the healing ministry. We have seen that the Holy Spirit awakens faith and conversion of heart. It is not enough to adhere to God himself or to believe what is right about God; Christians are called to grow in adhering to what he wills for our lives.

Who doesn't pray out of the desires of his or her own heart? The problem is when we seek to impose our human desires upon God's heart. Our task as healing ministers is to know what is on the heart of God, to listen to what God wants for the people we are ministering to and to know God's purpose for them. Once we hear and know the heart of God, we step out in faith. This spirituality of listening and obeying is of critical importance for a person in healing ministry. Attuning our hearts to the heart of God is arguably the major issue in intercession and healing prayer

> Attuning our hearts to the heart of God is arguably the major issue in intercession and healing prayer ministry and it separates those who authentically minister in the name of the Lord from those who seek their own agendas.

ministry and it separates those who authentically minister in the name of the Lord from those who seek their own agendas. Yet knowing God's will is often difficult and requires a growth toward maturity in mind and spirit.

"Adherence to the Father's will" is a discipleship issue. It means that the follower of Jesus seeks what God wants in all things. Otherwise we are in danger of manipulative prayer—and that gets very close to what some even call "witchcraft prayer." Despite any eloquence we may have in prayer, a secret desire may be to make oneself look good, spiritual, or holy in front of others. We might compensate for low self-esteem or we might put on a "spiritual" facade just because of pride and vanity. This kind of prayer is egocentric.

God's Heart: Love

A spirituality of adherence to the will of God means that the healer prays in the pure realm of God's own heart. This is absolutely necessary if we are to be instruments of God's healing and if we are to bring people into the healing he has prepared for them. This puts us squarely in the realm of true love for God. Every important spiritual writer, when dealing with God's will, reflects at the same time on what it means to love God, which includes the love of neighbor. It is a heart issue.

St. Francis de Sales was an eighteenth-century French bishop who sounded the depths of the love of God. He explores how the will of God is revealed to the believer who is attentive and striving to put his or her heart into that of God. He says,

> Conformity of our heart with God's signified will consists in the fact that we will all that God's goodness signifies to us as his intention, so that we believe according to his teaching, hope according to his promises, fear according to his warnings, and love and live according to his ordinances and admonitions.[8]

Later, St. Francis adds,

This same eternal God breathes and infuses into our souls the inspirations of supernatural life to the end, as says the great Apostle, that they may become "a life-giving spirit," that is, a spirit that makes us live, move, feel, and work the works of grace.[9]

The Inner Anointing

The best way we can become docile to obeying revelation when it comes is a constant exercise of the gifts of the Holy Spirit mentioned in Isaiah 11:2—wisdom, understanding, counsel, fortitude, knowledge, piety, and fear of the Lord.[10] Catholic believers who received the Sacrament of Confirmation had these gifts directly invoked upon them, normally by the bishop. They are what I like to call the *inner anointing* that draws a person through the Holy Spirit into a life of holiness. The spirituality of the healing ministry consists in a constant pursuit of the inner anointing of holiness. This produces in the heart and mind the docility to do God's will in the healing ministry.

Isaiah prophesied that these gifts would define the character of the coming Messiah. They are the hallmarks of those who share his Anointing. This focuses us on the Person of Christ who is our "holiness" (1 Cor. 1:29). He says, "My food is to do the will of the one who sent me and to complete his work" (Jn. 4:34, NJB). If we sincerely and constantly have this same mind-set, we will be on the spiritual baseline for healing ministry among God's people. We will enable others to receive his immense mercy and healing love.

Journal Questions for a Ministry Baseline

1. Have you ever "stepped out in faith" in healing prayer? Describe how you did it.
2. What kinds of things do you "have faith" to pray for?
3. What attitudes, ideas, actions, or concepts do you have about God that might be in conflict with a God who is healing?
4. Where might you need a change of mind or change of direction with regard to your personal conversion? Is there something you could do to practice this change on a daily basis?
5. What are some ways you can discern the difference between God's will and yours? Where can you go to receive help with this?

[1] MacNutt, Francis, Ph.D., *Healing: Revised and Expanded*, Notre Dame, IN, Ave Maria Press, 1999, p. 103.

[2] Ibid., p. 105.

[3] Shlemon, Barbara Leahy, *Healing Prayer*, Notre Dame, IN, Ave Maria Press, 1976, p. 45.

[4] Bertolucci, Fr. John, *Healing: God's Work Among Us*, Ann Arbor, MI, Servant Books, 1987, p. 43.

[5] *Catechism of the Catholic Church*, #397.

[6] MacNutt, *op. cit.*, p. 92.

[7] Bosworth, Fred Francis, *Christ, the Healer*, Fleming H. Revell Co., 1973, p. 104.

[8] de Sales, St. Francis, *Treatise on the Love of God*, Rockford, IL, Tan Books, 1975, p. 63.

[9] Ibid., p. 81.

[10] *Catechism, op. cit.* #1831.

Chapter 9

The Spirituality of Jesus' Healing Ministry

In 1993 I brought my mother to live in Monterey, California. God had put a desire in my heart concerning her: that I be the best possible son to her for the rest of her life. Taking care of an elderly parent is a difficult road many people can identify with. This was a road I had to walk very much alone since my sisters had moved to different places in the country, even though they offered me much-needed moral support.

I had prayed for many years for my mother. I prayed that she would be fulfilled in God in the best possible way. I also had a profound respect for my mother's Lutheran faith, which after all, was the one in which I had been raised.

In the fall of 1998 while in Stockton, in a center giving a healing retreat, word came on Sunday morning that Mother had suffered a fall and was taken to the hospital. The sixty people on the retreat asked if they could pray. There was such power in that prayer for Mom—more than in all the years that I had prayed for her. It was truly an encounter of intercession! During their prayer there was in my spirit a sense of something wonderful being deposited in Mom. This was new. This prayer was followed by an immense confidence that everything would be okay. Her favorite health caregiver was with her. There was peace that I could finish the retreat before going back home.

Weeks passed while Mom received rehabilitative care, but she was now at a level where she didn't get better and she didn't get worse. She had had previous episodes in which she had been brought low, but she always made her way back. This time there was something different; I felt a suspense that was in the spiritual realm.

One day after praying before the Blessed Sacrament, an interior word came to me: "You have been the best son that you could ever be for your mother over the past five years. Now you must be her priest." Upon hearing those words, my "flesh" resisted. I could not accept this. God was doing a work in Mother in the spiritual realm that was dealing with a negative spiritual barrier of mine—that of the need for greater obedience to the Lord. This boundary needed to be broken so I could come into a new dimension of ministry and a greater anointing. Mom was suspended between life and death while I struggled with God, who needed my consent at that meeting place with him. These were days of wrestling and protest in which I told the Lord, "I respect my mother's faith. I do not want to violate it. I would even call a Lutheran pastor for her, but I cannot be her priest because that would be forcing my Catholic beliefs on her!" Back and forth I went for four days in these "negotiations" with God while my Mom was suspended between heaven and earth.

It was around Thanksgiving Day when God spoke to my heart again and said, "She *gave you permission* for you to be her priest." "When, God?" He quickened to my mind a conversation we had one day in which she said, "Sometimes the son has to be the father, and the mother has to be the daughter." Now I realized that Mom was giving me permission to be her "father" and to lead her into deeper faith. He was forging a unity of faith between us. I *could* be her priest! Finally breaking down, I consented to be her priest:

"Okay God, I will be her priest, but *she has to accept this.*" He assured me that she already had.

I went to the convalescent home, prayer book under my arm, and strangely enough, there was a doctor waiting for me. He said, "Fr. Peter, your mother is moribund. She is going to die." This was the first time I ever heard those words, and they stung. Thanking him for his help, I rushed in to see Mom. She was fully conscious, but she couldn't move.

I nervously but solemnly uttered the words, "Mom, do you want me to be your priest?"

She looked up at me from her bed and said with all grace and dignity, "Sure."

I continued, "Do you want the fullness of what the Catholic Church has for you?"

Again, she said, "Sure!"

I led her in the profession of faith, followed by an examination of conscience in which she declared forgiveness for everyone who had ever hurt her in any way. I gave Mom absolution as a priest. Then she received the Sacrament of Anointing of the Sick. This was a moment that will forever be impressed upon my memory.

Two days later, Mom died, united with me in my faith. It was like what St. Paul declares: "Glory be to him whose power, working in us, can do infinitely more than we can ask or imagine" (Eph 3:20, NJB). It was sovereign favor from the Lord. Her passing to eternal life marked the point at which I really sensed that God called me to be his apostle. This turning point was built upon my putting aside preconceived ideas about the way I think or expect that God should act, about who I think I am, and on giving him my consent that his power should be released through me.

The emphasis for my life before Mom's death was that I was a disciple, and I still am. That is my spirituality. But there was a "before and after" her passing. Between them was a meeting place where a spiritual battle had to be waged. Negotiation and intercession went on in that meeting place. I have learned over the years that about ninety percent of prayer consists in our spiritual struggle to give true and committed consent to God for him to work in our lives.

Perhaps you are presently at a "meeting place"—in a spiritual struggle over what you think is "appropriate" for God to do for and through you. It is possible that the Body of Christ (or a part of it) is in suspension—in a spiritual waiting—for your consent to God. There are four steps to enter into the new anointing he has purposed for this hour:

1. Put aside all your built-up fantasies and ideas about how God should work
2. In prayer, give explicit, deep, and total consent that he should take over
3. Let him carry you along and open your mind and heart to new vistas
4. Obey him

Discipleship and Apostleship: The Spirituality of Jesus

As we have seen, the spirituality of a person in the healing ministry is based on a baseline of discipleship. A disciple is one who follows the discipline of the Lord. It is essential that there be an ongoing discipleship in which the Lord teaches and guides, and we obey. Settling into discipleship takes place *before* we can enter into ministry. As we have seen, an apostle is "one who is sent." There is a mission. We cannot be apostles before we are disciples. Many leaders in the Church have been trained to be apostles in all kinds of ministerial situations. Even in our seminaries, candidates for the ordained ministry have been put into pastoral positions, but without the adequate baseline training of disciples. Discipleship is not only for priests and ministers, but also for lay leaders and all Christians. This is what the lack of discipleship yields:

- Ministry burnout
- Moral failures and ruined ministries
- Lack of direction for individuals and entire communities
- A free-for-all atmosphere in which "anything goes" in the Body of Christ.

In charismatic circles, prayer meetings, and intercessory groups, there is sometimes a "charismatic free-for-all." I believe this occurs in part because people are trying to "minister"—that is, consider themselves apostles—before they have been true disciples. In the church as a whole, lay leaders, priests, pastors, and even bishops can create chaotic situations in their parishes and in their dioceses because they are not standing on the spiritual ground of basic discipleship that they are called to by the Lord. I propose that for healing ministry, the basic spirituality required is that of discipleship.

Many years ago there was a "discipleship" movement that abused the Christian notion of obedience. As a consequence of this extreme, many were hurt and the movement discredited. What I propose is *not* a return to that movement. To clarify what I mean by discipleship, I will focus on Jesus' own spirituality.

Archbishop Emile Guerry, Archbishop of Paris in the middle part of the twentieth century, wrote a book called *God the Father* in which he explores the relationship a disciple should have with God the Father. The first two lines of the book are these:

Jesus' devotion was to the Father.
How should His devotion not be ours?[1]

I remember meditating on this for many weeks. I realized that it was Jesus' own devotion to the Father that enabled him to teach on spirituality. As Jesus was, so we must be. Jesus' spirituality is "the drama of prayer" that is "fully revealed."[2] It is a *drama*. That is to say, there are high points, low points, victories, and defeats.

Most important, prayer is a drama because it is a dynamic story being written by the Spirit of God himself in the lives of each of us. Jesus' own spirituality reflects this dynamic: it is based upon "a humble and trusting surrender of his *human will* to the loving will of the Father."[3]

Jesus' primary devotion was to his Abba. The Old Testament word "devoted" has its roots in relation to the animal sacrifices made to God. Sacrificial animals are termed "devoted ones," or literally, those whose purpose is "for destruction." In discipleship, our will is devoted to the Father; that is, something has to die so that our dedication can be complete. "Not my will, but yours be done," Jesus said in the garden of Gethsemane. The author of the letter to the Hebrews asserts that Christ's "*will* was for us to be made holy by the *offering of the body* of Jesus Christ made once and for all" (Heb 10:10, NJB).

We all have a "drama" to be worked out in prayer life and ministry. It is not only the drama of learning to hear the Lord, but often the drama of a vigorous struggle of wills. The struggle culminates in putting our own reason, body, and will at the disposition of his. St. Philip Neri used to say that all holiness consisted in the space of three fingers. He would put three fingers to his forehead to indicate that the "mortification [putting to death] of the reason" and will is what matters in our relationship with God.[4]

Perhaps you are struggling to discover and follow the Father's will in your life and ministry. May I suggest that you make an explicit and honest commitment to let him have his way, even if it means that there would be no healing ministry, if that be his will.

Decisive Moments in Jesus' Personal Calling

Luke's gospel gives us insight on the role of the Holy Spirit and prayer in Jesus' ministry. Before his critical *personal* moments and decisions, his prayer became intense—he made sure his spiritual feet were on a firm ground, or baseline, of prayer. We can identify these times, as they are presented in the Bible: "before his Father's witness to him during his Baptism and Transfiguration and before his own fulfillment of the Father's plan of love by his Passion."[5] The gospels relate Jesus' personal, intimate relationship that he had with his Father.

Here is where we can see his spirituality. Jesus is fully centered on the Father and prays before the decisive moments that relate to his personal mission.

> The spirituality of the healing minister is built upon a solid spiritual ground, a meeting of the Father in prayer and intercession so that God's mission can come about through him or her.

As with Jesus, God calls us to intensive encounters in prayer as we come into a fuller realization of the Father's purpose for our lives. This imitation of Christ's devotion is essential in a healing minister's road of discipleship.

Decisive Moments in Jesus' Mission to the World

The scriptures give us example of Jesus' prayer before the decisive moments of his ministry:

- involving the mission of his apostles and his election of the twelve (Lk. 6: 12–13);
- before Peter's confession of him as the Christ (Lk. 9:18);
- at the prayer that the chief of the apostles may not fail when tempted. (Lk. 22:31–32)

Jesus' prayer before the events of salvation that the Father asked him to fulfill is a humble and trusting commitment of his human will to the loving will of the Father: "Not my will, but yours be done" (Lk. 22:42, NIV). Here again, we can appreciate Jesus' own spiritual baseline of adherence to the Father's will.

127

A Firm Spiritual Base

Following Jesus, therefore there are two aspects of prayer for anybody who is in a leadership position or in a healing ministry:

1. prayer that concerns a person's own mission in life
2. prayer of intercession concerning the people whom the person works with, ministers to, supervises or over whom there is any kind of spiritual authority

The spirituality of the healing minister is built upon a solid spiritual ground, a meeting of the Father in prayer and intercession so that God's mission can come about through him or her. This is what I sensed was taking place before and after my mother's passage to eternal life. I was at a meeting place with God. The spiritual baseline of prayer represents an ever-deepening of the perfection of personal life and public ministry to which God calls us. Past prayer, piety, and old patterns of holiness are not sufficient for the present hour in the Body of Christ.

Pray with me:

Father, I surrender all to you; through the Holy Spirit, make me like your Son.

Journal Questions for Surrendering

1. Reflect on a decisive and life-changing transition you have made in your life. What was you prayer like during that time? How do you think prayer helped you through it?
2. What parts of you are completely surrendered to the Lord?
3. What parts of you do you suspect are not totally surrendered?
4. What stops you from complete surrender?

---

[1] Emile Guerry, *God the Father,* London, Sheed and Ward, 1947, p. xi.
[2] *Catechism of the Catholic Church*, #2598.
[3] *Catechism*, #2600.
[4] Ponnell, L. and Bordet, L., *St. Philip Neri and the Roman Society of His Times,* London, Sheed and Ward 1979, p. 584.
[5] *Catechism*, #2600.

Chapter 10

FIVE EFFECTIVE ELEMENTS OF MINISTRY

1. ". . . BE PERFECT, JUST AS YOUR HEAVENLY FATHER IS PERFECT." (MT. 5:48, NAB)

The first letter of John says, "Whoever keeps his word, the love of God is truly perfected in him" (1 Jn. 2:5, NAB). This is an echo of the perfection that is talked about in the book of Hebrews, which says that Jesus had to learn obedience: "Son though he was, through his sufferings; when he had been perfected, he became for all who obey him the source of eternal salvation" (Heb 5:8–9, NJB).

Does this mean that Jesus wasn't perfect before? No. It affirms that every stage of life in his humanity had it's own fulfillment to reach. With us this occurs so we can show with greater transparency the glory on the face of Christ. St. Paul says, "And we, who with unveiled faces all reflect the Lord's glory, are being transformed into his likeness with ever-increasing glory, which comes from the Lord, who is the Spirit" (2 Cor. 3:18, NIV). With God we progress from "glory to glory"!

We are called to spiritual growth, but the only way to have that progress is to be on the spiritual ground he has shown us. This is what comprises the spirituality of the healing ministry. St. John adds, "whoever claims to remain in [Christ], must act as he acted" (1 Jn. 2:6, NJB). This is the basis of our spiritual path; it is patterned after Jesus' own spirituality. We are destined to reflect the image and likeness of the Son of God, who is the Word Incarnate, so that anyone acting *in the Spirit* needs to act like Jesus acted: Jesus' own spirituality has to be reflected in our spirituality. The "perfection" that Jesus calls us to is his own image and likeness, which reflected that of the Father.

That is our goal and purpose. A person in the healing ministry will heal in the way Jesus healed because he or she is growing into the likeness of the Lord, reflecting his character.

2. DEVELOP A SPIRITUALITY OF THE WORD

Earlier, explaining the process of discernment of the call to the healing ministry, I explained the importance of getting acquainted with God's Word. On the road from discipleship to apostleship is a spirituality of intense listening in prayer. We need to have the attitude of Jesus when he entered into prayer with the Father. It was not only a recitation of the prayers he had learned in his Jewish tradition, although certainly that was important. Jesus was first and foremost a *disciple* of the Father. Strange as it may seem, Jesus is the *first* disciple: he is the example of what it means to be a true disciple. He identified with what Isaiah had prophesied concerning the Messiah:

> Lord Yahweh has given me a disciple's tongue,
> for me to know how to give a word of comfort to the weary;
> Morning by morning he makes my ear alert to listen like a disciple.

Lord Yahweh has opened my ear and I have not resisted, I have not turned away. (Is 50:4, NJB)

Isaiah then goes into an amazing prophecy about what the Messiah would undergo during his passion, which was a confrontation with the forces of evil. Yet on the other side of the battle of the passion and cross—done through his alert ear and well-trained tongue, the victory of resurrection is achieved. He got to that place by opening his ear in prayer every morning as a disciple, listening for what the Father would tell him. The spirituality of anyone in the healing ministry is built on *hearing*. We pray that God will open our ears on a daily basis to hear what he will say.

In the previous chapter I reflected on the day and time when God spoke to my heart concerning my mother. It didn't matter that I happened to be shaving at the time! As long as we are on our baseline, we will be prepared to hear his voice at key moments in our life.

Through the Bible

The most important aspect of a spirituality of the Word of God is that we get to know the Bible. St. Jerome would say, "Ignorance of the Scriptures is ignorance of Christ." As we steep ourselves in its passages and they become part of us, the Holy Spirit then has an instrument, the "sword" of Ephesians 6:17, that can be used to change us—our thoughts, attitudes, broken places, anything that would receive the Word of God. A daily prayerful diet of scripture brings us into contact with the living Christ. It sows the word in our hearts.

Dutch Sheets, in the eighth chapter of his book *Watchman Prayer,* wrote an eloquent chapter on "Keeping Watch Over Your Heart." It is about the radical transformation of those who let the Word of God be sown in them. He relates a vital insight that the Lord gave him while reflecting on John 8:32, "Then you will know the truth, and the truth will set you free" (NIV). Pastor Sheets questioned why our lives don't always line up with the scriptures, if we know the truth:

> *Why doesn't the Word work for me?* I thought while meditating about this verse in John.
>
> Because all truth comes in seed form, He so clearly spoke to my heart. What you do with the seed after it is planted will determine whether or not it bears fruit in you.
>
> Suddenly, many other passages of Scripture made sense: the parables of the sower (see Mt. 13; Mk. 4; Lk. 8); the renewing of the mind (see Rom. 12:1, 2); abiding in the Vine by abiding in His Word (see John 15) and others. All of these involve planting seeds and working the process.
>
> I discovered . . . that this process of applying God's Word is both constructive and destructive. It is a healing scalpel and a destroying sword. It is a watering nutrient and a pruning knife. Through it God gives life to those who believe and releases judgment to those who don't. And most importantly, I realized its work in me was a process.[1]

3. "PRAY AT EVERY OPPORTUNITY" (EPH 6:18, NAB)

God asks from us an honest and constant regimen of prayer and submission to his will in obedience. This is the journey of all the saints, a thrilling journey of listening and obeying. A true disciple's prayer and obedience are fundamental conditions for the Anointing to be sustained in ministry. We don't presume to obey what we have not heard. That would be absurd! Yet people are going out in ministry without praying. It is a discipleship issue. If you are not on a base of listening and obeying, start now to take discipleship seriously. If we are ministering to people in prayer when we don't have a solid prayer base and sincere attitude of obedience, we are kidding ourselves. That is not ministry. It is doing our own thing! It cannot produce lasting fruit for the Lord.

Prayer Is Communion

The all-important challenge of living in God's covenant is that our devotion be soaked in the presence of the Holy Trinity.

> In the New Covenant, prayer is the living relationship of the children of God with their Father who is good beyond measure, with his Son Jesus Christ and with the Holy Spirit. The grace of the Kingdom is "the union of the entire holy and royal Trinity . . . with the whole human spirit." Thus, the life of prayer is the habit of being in the presence of the thrice-holy God and in communion with him. This communion of life is always possible because, through Baptism we have already been united with Christ. Prayer is Christian insofar as it is communion with Christ and extends throughout the Church, which is his Body. Its dimensions are those of Christ's love.[2]

4. DEDICATE YOURSELF TO BE MADE WHOLE!

It is vital for those in healing ministry to make a prayer-based dedication to be made whole. This includes purification of anything that has been allowed to poison us morally, spiritually, or even physically (referring to healthy nutrition and substances). One of the best definitions of healing that I know is that degree of wellness that enables us to best serve the greatest glory of God. We avoid two extremes:

1. That we neglect entering into a ministry because we are not perfectly well. We will always be to some degree "wounded healers."

2. That we deny that we need healing and don't seek it while attempting to be in healing ministry.

I know a number of people who do prayer ministry while they have not attended to their own brokenness or even admitted they have problems. These individuals pray and minister from their own needs. It is easy to see that their intercession is not coming from a legitimate spiritual baseline but is based upon their own brokenness.

A well-rounded spirituality includes an increasing awareness of that which is dysfunctional, or out of order, in ourselves. It means actively reaching out to the Lord for healing. St. Francis de Sales states,

> Since prayer places our intellect in the brilliance of God's light and exposes our will to the warmth of his heavenly love, nothing else so effectively purifies [heals] our intellect of ignorance and our will of depraved affections. It is a stream of holy water that flows forth and makes the plants of our good desires grow green and flourish and quenches the passions within our hearts.[3]

A person who is in healing ministry needs a certain baseline of spiritual, psychological, and even physical health. That person must be committed to wholeness every day of his or her life. In the natural realm one will discipline oneself to a healthy life-style and seek good advice and treatment from competent and proven healthcare givers. For some this may include Christian-based psychological therapy or even a twelve-step program for addictions.

A number of years ago I developed a painful rheumatoid condition in my right knee. From the pain, I could even predict with accuracy when a storm front would move in—I would sometimes markedly limp. While I had the pain I "offered it up" (like a good Catholic), but it was increasingly impeding my ministry. In the parishes where I worked, they would ask, "Father, what's wrong with your leg?" I used to answer facetiously, "Nothing, I'm just

Sometimes a commitment to wholeness means that we have to get "comfortable" with being uncomfortable because the process of healing is often painful.

trying to get sympathy." After many months, in prayer I was led to pray for my own physical healing. Sensing that God really did want to heal this affliction, I started "soaking prayer"—a certain amount of time dedicated each day, laying my hands on my knee and asking God to heal whatever was out of order. Within a few days I already felt relief and over several weeks of faithfully obeying him the condition was completely healed!

At other times I have availed myself of healthcare professionals. At the end of the day, not even the best doctor can heal. Many years ago I had a scratched cornea in my eye. The cornea had to be scraped away (that was major pain) and I was left seeing double out of the right eye for many months. I was struck on one of my frustrating visits to a Jewish ophthalmologist when he said, "Father, you know well that all I can do is provide in your eye the conditions that promote healing. God has to do the rest. You should be the first to recognize that." He was right; then I started to pray. It also taught me a lesson about the healing ministry: both for ourselves and when we intercede for others, what we are doing is providing the conditions in which God should work, so that our body, mind, and spirit can function the way they were created to function. God works for healing in tandem with the nature he created; as his ministers, so should we.

Sometimes a commitment to wholeness means that we have to get "comfortable" with being uncomfortable because the process of healing is often painful. This pain—physical/mental/spiritual—is often God's way of doing in us what he needs so we can be more powerful instruments of his healing, so that the Anointing on our lives can increase. It is also the reason that many do not face their personal inner healing task. Our healing is part of God's way of bringing us into discipleship. We should not be asking why we are in this pain; we should be asking rather, What is God doing in us through this pain? Let us be committed on all levels of our being to physical, emotional, spiritual, and even generational healing.

Some of the most powerful moments of healing in my life have occurred before generational healing retreats. In fact, I invariably have to face my own generational brokenness each time I prepare for these retreats. The Father is about building a spiritual foundation upon which I minister. He has brought to light specific brokenness that is in my past generations. I cannot presume to do generational healing or any other healing without first submitting my own brokenness to Jesus Christ. Again, it is not about relieving discomfort; rather it is about going to the root of dysfunction and illness, just as Jesus went to the root.

Seeking healing in your own life requires courage and faith on your part. This enables you to use the same courage and faith when you are called to intercession. Every work of intercession—whether personal or on behalf of others—is based on our willingness to wrestle with deep issues that enable us to be his transparent instruments. A spirituality that incorporates that kind of courage and faith will transform your ministry, and even your personal presence, into an instrument of God's healing and deliverance.

5. GROW INTO A SPIRITUALITY OF THE SACRAMENTS

Earlier I relayed that in 1998 I attended the Monterey Pastors' Prayer Summit. I was there at the request of the priest in charge of ecumenical relations of the Monterey Bay. This was a three-day retreat of mainly evangelical pastors who offer prayer support to each other. Among the many experiences that impressed me was the celebration of Holy Communion with these pastors.

Although I couldn't participate in the elements, I did accompany them in prayer throughout the services. I was truly built up by how seriously these men of God partook of Holy Communion, each from his respective tradition. It was edifying to experience not only the message and prayer that was shared, but the reverence that accompanied the partaking of the bread and grape juice, and the mutual ministry that took place in the process. Much healing took place as a result. Even though they may not be fully aware of it, these ministers have a spirituality that is "sacramental," according to the discipline of their respective traditions.

In the evangelical Protestant tradition, baptism and the Lord's Supper are usually observed as "ordinances" of the Lord Jesus, and are taken very seriously as moments of grace, ordained by Christ himself.

If you are an evangelical Christian interested in the healing ministry, may I say that it is vitally important that these ordinances be observed and deepened. They are moments of deep grace as the heart of the believer is opened to a remembrance of Christ's death and resurrection. Paul says, "Whenever you eat this bread, then, and drink this cup, you are proclaiming the Lord's death until he comes" (1 Cor. 11:26, NJB). When the "death of the Lord" is proclaimed, the effect of it is deepened in us, and that means atonement for sins, forgiveness, deliverance, and healing. Because it is an ordinance of the Lord, it must be a part of a Christian's spirituality—proclaiming at the Lord's table his death and letting its effects take greater hold on our lives.

The Catholic Sacramental Devotion

The word "sacrament" is used in the Catholic, Orthodox, Anglican, and many Protestant traditions to refer to those focal points of Christian worship. The Latin term *sacramentum* was used in the Roman army to signify the oath of loyalty to the emperor that soldiers took to solemnly express their allegiance and commitment to their state in life. Very early in Christian history the term was borrowed to signify particular forms of worship as allegiance and commitment to Christ and his church. These were principally Baptism and the Eucharist as well as other important moments where human commitment meets divine grace.

An important part of a healing spirituality is longing for the celebration of the sacraments. For Catholics, Orthodox, and many Protestant bodies this "sacramental spirituality" is essential to be a minister of healing prayer. Particularly for Roman Catholics and Orthodox Christians, this encompasses particularly the Sacraments of Reconciliation and Eucharist. We should know how to take our brokenness, wounds, sin, and iniquity to these sacraments. Jesus said, "Whoever eats my flesh and drinks my blood remains in me, and I in him" (Jn. 6:56, NIV). Our way of *remaining* in Jesus is the Eucharist. It becomes the all-important point of contact—the meeting place, where we remain in Jesus and he remains in us. It also expresses and deepens our communion with one another and all Christians in all places and of all times.

Every morning, as part of my personal devotions, I renew my Baptism. It is a covenant through which a rich flow of grace is bestowed and has the power to let us continue to stand and grow in grace. That is the reason that Catholics "bless themselves" with holy water—as a renewal of the baptismal commitment.

The Eucharist especially is a meeting place with God. There is a wonderful privilege in taking our intercessory life to the Eucharist. As healing ministers we can take the people for whom we pray to the Eucharist. There we intercede and meet with God on their behalf. His grace with its effect of healing can be poured forth even as we pray for those people that he has placed on our heart.

ACTIVE FAITH AND PRAYER

"Stretch Out Your Hand"

> Going on from that place, [Jesus] went into their synagogue, and
> a man with a shriveled hand was there . . . he said to the man,
> "Stretch out your hand." So he stretched it out and it was com-
> pletely restored, just as sound as the other. (Mt. 12:9, 13–14, NIV)

When we meet God in intercession, we have to do *our part*.
Jesus says to us, "Stretch out your hand." The man with the withered hand, just like the man with the paralyzed body, could have
complained, "I can't. It doesn't work." It is not enough to just hear
the words "Stretch out your hand" or "Get up!" He will not magi-
cally stretch our hands *for us* or set us on our feet without our
cooperation. To receive healing, growth, and work in ministry, we
must obey him and do our part in active faith.

Our past would tell us, "You are not able." People around us
would say, "you do not dare." The enemy would accuse us saying,
"Look at your sins—you can't!" But we must have the courage and
faith to be on a solid ground of spirituality no matter what opposi-
tion we face. With respect to our relationship with the Lord, spirituality is a discipline in which there is no room for laziness.

We saw that the spirituality of ministry in healing insists that
there be a common work between the Holy Spirit and the assembly, especially of its ministers.[4] There is a common work between
God and us and that common work takes place at the meeting
place of prayer. We work in prayer concerning ourselves and what
God has purposed for our individual lives and ministries. It is also
a common work of intercession with respect to those whom God
has placed in our lives for healing. Because we have "arisen" from
whatever paralysis—physical, emotional, or spiritual
woundedness—and walked, because we know to "stretch forth our

hands" from disability, we in turn can then say through the power of his grace, "Rise up and walk" and "Stretch out your hand" to the broken. The spirituality of a minister of healing is that of prayer, obedience and wholeness.

Pause for a moment of prayer.

Father, I desire to meet you and seek your face, listen to your voice and work out the issues of the discipleship you have called me to. Take my life and ministry: shape and form it according to your beautiful design. Form me into the image of your Son. Let your Spirit move in me bringing forth your character. In Jesus name. Amen.

Journal Questions for Living on Your Spiritual Baseline

1. Describe a time, after your conversion, when you felt God calling you to serve him in ministry.
2. What are the conditions under which you sense you can hear the Lord most clearly?
3. In what ways have you sought healing—spiritually, emotionally, and physically? Identify some ongoing areas of healing that you need.
4. Evaluate your appreciation of and your life in the sacraments. How important a role have they played in your life of discipleship?

[1] Sheets, Dutch, *Watchman Prayer*, Ventura, CA, Regal Books, 2000, p. 137.
[2] *Catechism of the Catholic Church*, #2565.
[3] de Sales, St. Francis, *Introduction to the Devout Life,* New York, Image Books, 1989, p. 81.
[4] *Catechism*, #1098.

Chapter 11

THE MEETING PLACE: BECOMING AN EFFECTIVE INTERCESSOR

Mark's Intercessors

Mark had been wounded from childhood as he was the son of a young teenage mother, and an absent father. As a child, Mark had been sexually abused. He grew up in Catholic Church culture without a personal relationship with Christ. When he reached adolescence, he detoured into drugs and the party life, finding nothing but emptiness and inner pain. This was a wounded soul looking constantly for relationships that would make up for the loss of his parents. Going into a religious sect (a "Jesus-only" denomination), he "accepted" Christ as his Savior and became defensively self-righteous about anything to do with more "orthodox" Christian teachings. He often looked for arguments and the opportunity to persuade others about how wrong they were. Mark was slipping into a deep legalism with regard to his— or anyone's—relationship with God.

The odd, and at the same time wonderful, thing about Mark is the high calling God placed on his life and the striking spiritual gifts with which he endowed Mark. He was to be a minister of the gospel. After an enormous struggle, he found himself back in the Catholic faith through the good influences of a well-known priest. Only this time he had carried his legalism with him. Mark stood up to several priests for their "heterodoxy" and was often at odds with his Catholic brothers and sisters (although many admired him, his testimony, and his gifts). The problem was that because of the wounds of his childhood, which he unconsciously felt he had to cover with his legalism, he could not hear the call of God, and was alienating himself into his own little world.

Two people, a brother and sister in Christ trained in healing ministry, prophetically sensed the high calling on Mark's life. At the same time they saw through to his wounds. As they interceded, God provided the opportunities for them to minister healing prayer to Mark, going to some of the deepest wounds. Mark was empowered to begin to recognize the work God was doing in him, pulling down the strongholds of legalism and self-righteousness and instilling a sweet and gentle spirit. God arranged strong circumstances and permitted trials to enable him to seek and receive deeply this healing intercession.

As great as Mark's story is, it is really a testimony to the power and healing grace that was poured through that brother and sister's prayer and healing ministry. Many times, as they prayed and battled for Mark, they were led to hold on to the prophetic element in Mark's life—God's call. They went to the sacraments for him and with him. It is an intercessors' story of persisting each day for the sake of what God would do in the short and long run in his Son's Body, the Church, through Mark. This story is an example of what can happen in healing prayer when ministers stand their ground and model the character of God: lives get changed through healing, enemy strongholds come down, the voice of God is heard more clearly in his Church and people give their consent to his plan.

The Ministry of Intercession

Jesus Christ our Savior is the source of all intercession. He is the only High Priest worthy to present petitions on our behalf before the throne of God. When we approach the throne, it is only because we belong to him that our prayer reaches God. Consider these important verses on the ministry of intercession:

> The fervent prayer of a righteous person is very powerful. (Jas. 5:16, NAB).

> It is due to him that you are in Christ Jesus, who became for us wisdom from God, as well as righteousness, sanctification, and redemption. (1 Cor. 1:30, NIV).

> For there is only one God, and there is only one Mediator between God and humanity, the man, Jesus Christ (1 Tim. 2:5, NJB).

> Therefore, [Christ] is always able to save those who approach God through him, since he lives forever to make intercession for them (Heb. 7:25, NIV).

Yet we are members of his Body, filled with the Holy Spirit who prays through us. Therefore we share in the mission of intercession he makes before the Father in heaven.

The word "intercession" comes from the Latin *inter* (between) and *cedere* (to go or pass). It is the act of reconciling the differences between two parties. It assumes that the party standing in between has the right and the call to do so.[1]

One who is involved in the healing ministry must be a person of intercession because this ministry, properly understood, is essentially intercession. For a more complete treatment of this aspect I recommend Dutch Sheets' book, *Intercessory Prayer*.[2] It has been a wonderful contribution to my ministry. Many people have called intercession "standing in the breach" or "standing in the gap." Indeed it is that, and much more. The word that is used most often for "intercession" in the Old Testament is the word *paga*, literally, "a meeting place." Just as Jesus "met with" the Father in the crucial moments of his life, he also met with the enemy in spiritual battle. In heaven, his humanity as our High Priest is eternally meeting with the Father in union with the Holy Spirit.

Intercession: Meeting God

Apart from Jesus, the figure of Moses is "the most striking example of intercessory prayer" among the distinct types of prayer that God has revealed.[3] Through Moses, God produced a spirituality that corresponded to the call he had for him. Therefore, Moses had some difficult tasks to work out with the Lord in order to be formed into his call. Consider with me this passage on intercession from the *Catechism of the Catholic Church*:

> God reveals himself in order to save them [his people], though he does not do this alone or despite them: he calls Moses to be his messenger, an associate in his compassion, his work of salvation. There is something of a divine plea in this mission, and only after long debate does Moses attune his own will to that of the Savior God. But in the dialogue in which God confides in him, Moses also learns how to pray: he balks, makes excuses, above all questions: and it is in response to his question that the Lord confides his ineffable name, which will be revealed through his mighty works.[4]

It is no accident that intercession has to be *learned*. The drama and battle that Moses sustained in learning how to intercede yielded powerful fruit—first revelation and then Moses' becoming the conduit through which God poured forth his mighty redemption for the Israelites. For Moses, intercession was the way that led him into the prophetic realm that enabled him to be the outstanding leader he was. This course of action is our school as well, learned through the same, often dramatic, process of spiritual battle against the flesh and against the enemy. Persist like Moses, and God will give you revelation; you will walk into the mission he has marked out for you!

God had to meet with Moses on the mountain of Sinai. The people were in rebellion against him and God was poised to wipe them out.

- There was a *meeting*: Moses had to go up the mountain to meet God in a *paga*, an intercession.
- The third and fourth chapters of Exodus reveal a *spiritual struggle or confrontation* within Moses that enabled him to change the way he was thinking about the issues involved. Later he would spiritually do the battle of intercession and prevail over the Pharaoh of Egypt and, still later in the desert, against the Amalekites as exterior enemies. First the inner struggle has to be waged and won. Only then, can we release God's mighty power in our exterior battles.
- There was a *boundary*, a *breach*, between heaven and earth that had to be crossed for the people to be saved from the consequences of their idolatry.
- There was a *negotiation* that had to take place with God so that the people of Israel could be spared and forgiven.

All of this is paga, intercession.

People in the healing ministry are always meeting God on behalf of others, most often in situations where they cannot see the real needs. Therefore, the call to this ministry invariably means that one is appointed to learn the dynamics of Spirit—led intercession. It will mean meeting with like-minded people who are acquainted with this type of prayer, for when two or three are gathered he is in their midst. There is also the dimension of meeting God sacramentally in Eucharist as well as meeting him in private prayer and in intercession gatherings.

A Eucharistic Paga

Many Catholics will remember the Church calling them to spend time before the Blessed Sacrament and to develop a devotion to the sacred heart of Jesus to do a collective "reparation" for sin. This "reparation" was a *paga* before the Eucharistic Presence of Jesus, an intercession on behalf of those who are alienated from the life of God, blinded by sin and iniquity. This was, at its roots, an intercession for healing. Remember that "salvation" and "healing" in Greek are parts of the same reality.

This tradition of the Church is being revisited. Many, including me, are called to intercession before the Blessed Sacrament; we have had the benefit of teaching concerning how to do this type of prayer. This prayer-meeting with God in Eucharist—often flows into prayer for every dimension of healing—physical, emotional and spiritual. Indeed, the phenomenon of "healing masses" is a beautiful expression of this Eucharistic *paga*, where we can open the floodgates of Calvary and let its healing flow into brokenness of our own selves or of others before the eternal sacrifice of Jesus.

Whenever any Eucharistic celebration takes place there is a *paga*, a meeting of intercession. The Catholic practice of having "mass intentions" represents the Church's intercession on behalf of the person for whom the mass is being offered. This is united with the "General Intercessions" of the Church before the Liturgy of the Eucharist. In the Eucharistic Prayer, after the consecration of the bread and wine into the body and blood of Christ, who is the Lamb of God and at the same time our great High Priest, intercession is done in this most intimate of sacramental moments.

The ancient Orthodox writer Nicholas Cabasilas reflects the teaching of the Church, East and West, as he describes this holy moment of the liturgy:

> When this sacrifice has been thus completed, the priest, seeing before him the pledge of God's love of mankind, the Lamb of God, uses him as his intercessor and with him as advocate, makes his petitions known to God, and pours forth his prayers in sure and certain hope; he asks that the intention which he commemorated when the bread was brought, those for which he prays at the preparation for the celebration of the mysteries, and those for which he pleaded when offering up the gifts and asking that they might be found acceptable may now have their effect, since God has been pleased to accept our offerings.[5]

Intercession: Confronting the Enemy

In prayer, we all must meet with the Father; but we will also meet the enemy as we walk with the Lord. This meeting place, or *paga,* is of crucial importance in the healing ministry. The word *paga* also means a border, a boundary, literally a place of meeting for spiritual battle. Jericho, with its walls, was a meeting place of the people of God and their spiritual enemies. Doesn't it seem strange to "intercede" by walking around the walls seven times in seven days? The seventh day there was a shout and that shout itself was an intercession. The walls came down and the enemies were despoiled. Why? Because God had marked out Jericho's walls as a divine meeting place that was key to entering into and taking possession of the promised land. This place of *paga* was a divine appointment on behalf of the people of God.

In the letter to the Ephesians, there is a very strong example of *paga*—a familiar passage, yet one worth reading again, this time, from another point of view:

Finally, be strong in the Lord and in his mighty power. Put on the full armor of God so that you can take your stand against the devil's schemes. For our struggle is not against flesh and blood, but against the rulers, against the authorities, against the powers of this dark world and against the spiritual forces of evil in the heavenly realms. Therefore put on the full armor of God, so that when the day of evil comes, you may be able to stand your ground, and after you have done everything, to stand. Stand firm then, with the belt of truth buckled around your waist, with the breastplate of righteousness in place, and with your feet fitted with the readiness that comes from the gospel of peace. In addition to all this, take up the shield of faith, with which you can extinguish all the flaming arrows of the evil one. Take the helmet of salvation and the sword of the Spirit, which is the Word of God. And pray in the Spirit on all occasions with all kinds of prayers and requests. With this in mind, be alert and always keep on praying for all the saints.

Pray also for me, that whenever I open my mouth, words may be given me so that I will fearlessly make known the mystery of the gospel, for which I am an ambassador in chains. Pray that I may declare it fearlessly, as I should. (Eph 6:10–20, NIV)

Normally, when there is a teaching on this passage, it stops with verse 17, "Take . . . the sword of the Spirit, which is the Word of God." The next phrase (often edited to be a new paragraph) is meant to be associated with it, "And pray in the Spirit on all occasions." In other words, Paul is exhorting us that to enter into effective intercession, we first must "stake out" and stand on some spiritual ground and we need to avail ourselves of the full armor of God.

There is a spiritual reality I would like to propose for healing ministers—that of becoming in yourself a "meeting place" for God. It is often a place for battle in prayer.[6] It is both a battle with ourselves, which is against the flesh, and a battle against our spiritual enemy, Satan. For ministers of healing prayer, *paga* takes place each day of our lives if we are in ministry; it is an essential part of our spirituality.

Such a person of *paga* was Saint Padre Pio. For a time, when God had him in training for an international intercessory ministry, he would go into his hermitage for prayer. People often heard loud noises and the crash of pots, pans, and furniture as he would be assaulted by demonic spirits. Later, he received the *stigmata*, or wounds of Christ, so that he could be more conformed to our Savior in his redemptive sacrifice (Gal 6:17). God was shaping his prayer life and character. When the stakes got higher, he would, like Moses, be ready to stand his ground, firm on his spiritual foundation with the full armor of God. From there he interceded for God's people with great power and wonder-working. (Not that I am suggesting that you will have the same manifestations as Padre Pio!)

Look with me at the pattern found in the Ephesians passage above. It is really a strategy for intercession given successively in four steps:

1. Stand your ground.
2. Take up the full armor of God.
3. Pray in the Spirit.
4. Pray for all . . . and pray for me.

1. STAND YOUR GROUND

First, Paul exhorts us, "stand your ground." We stand our ground in prayer so that there can be a meeting place. When one army goes against another it is always on the basis of the territory that is claimed. The battle is then engaged on that boundary. Often, Christians in prayer do not know what ground they are standing on. The boundaries have become so fuzzy that it is easy to give ground to the enemy. For example, when we are called to fight battles involving moral issues, the blurry boundaries produced by ignorance or indifference can affect whether people are brought into the life in Christ or remain in bankrupt pagan values.

Recently I was talking with a sister in the Lord about how to bring a mutual friend out of depression. Amy lives in a "free union" with a man who is married to another woman. This sister kept referring to the man as Amy's "husband." When I objected, she said glibly, "For all intents and purposes, he *is* her husband and she presents him to others as her husband. You know how people think these days." I realized this was a spiritual battle for Amy. In this day, Christians need to be *standing their ground.*

Only a life of greater virtue that corresponds to the likeness of God himself will enable you to do effective spiritual battle.

In spiritual battle one always asks, What is at stake? Whether the issue is cheating, abortion, teaching moral rectitude in schools, countenancing homosexual "marriages" or whatever, it's not only the "moral fiber" of the country that is at stake. Even more important is the damage and wounding—spiritual, mental, and physical—done by the enemy as a result of Christians not standing their ground. It is the damage and iniquity that must be healed. Moral exhortations, however eloquent, do not make sin go away.

This "standing" is a defining of spiritual boundaries at which *paga* takes place, at which the work of intercession comes forth in a Christian's prayer. If you are in healing ministry, every day you will deal with the wounding described above. In addition, you will be dealing with the level of direct evil influence that is allowed in your own and in others' lives. That is your spiritual terrain.

2. Take Up the Full Armor of God

The Ephesians passage describes the spiritual armament of a soldier in battle who is *standing his ground* and *meeting* an enemy that moves against him. The spirituality of those who are in healing ministry begins by "clearing the decks" with spiritual warfare. The minister of healing has to conduct daily spiritual warfare.

The section in Ephesians[6] is often used in daily prayer as images. The Christian *imagines* oneself literally putting on a belt, breastplate, taking up a shield, etc. I want to challenge you to go far beyond the "imaging" of this prayer.

The armaments of spiritual warfare are only analogies of the deeper reality. In the book of Isaiah and the book of Wisdom, it is God himself who is presented as being clothed as a warrior.[7] The Ephesians text is an exhortation to take on the attributes of God himself and reflect those: truth, righteousness, justice, zeal to propagate the good news, etc. Mere mental images of the belt, breastplate, shield, etc. will not protect you from the evil one. Only a life of greater virtue that corresponds to the likeness of God himself will enable you to do effective spiritual battle. Prayer each day of putting on the armor of God is prayer to be clothed with the virtues of God himself. Being Christ-like is the first and principal armor in spiritual warfare.

Pray with me:

Father, in Jesus' name I ask for the spiritual armor to stand my ground. Make me more like you in my desires, attitudes, and actions. Today I choose to clothe myself with the power of your Son as I stand the ground you have given me. Lead me to be an intercessor docile to your Spirit. Let him take hold of my prayer and lead me to where I will be victorious with the victory of Christ your Son.

3. PRAY IN THE SPIRIT ON EVERY OCCASION

There can be no effective intercession without a spiritual battle. However, it cannot stop with the spiritual battle. Those who do spiritual battle and stop there are not fulfilling the deeper call to intercession. The Word of God says that we should be in prayer and entreaty, and pray in the Spirit on every possible occasion. Though I am not saying that "prayer in the Spirit" is always the gift of tongues, in the charismatic renewal it has been associated with prayer using the gift of tongues. That seems altogether reasonable and has been proven to work, for a numbers of reasons.

In 1 Corinthians 14 Paul describes the conduct of the Corinthian Christian assembly. In verse 15 he affirms alternately praying and singing "with the mind," or understanding, on one hand and "with the Spirit," clearly referring to the gift of tongues, on the other. His point is that we need both. The spirituality of intercession needs to be as full as possible, "taking up *all* God's armor."

When people pray in the Spirit, there is an intimate connection between their human spirit and the Spirit of God. I maintain that this connection is necessary in order to know the desires of God's Spirit. Prayer in the Spirit brings them to an explicit expression as the intercessor proceeds in *paga*. Part of the ministry of intercession is to prophetically call God's plan into existence. Prayer becomes prophetic intercession as the intercessor works increasingly in harmony with the Spirit of God.

Intercession is both a confrontation and a prayer, an entreaty, a prayer in the Spirit on every possible occasion. Not only does a spiritual battle take place in this *paga* but there is also a meeting with God, a positive thrust. In healing ministry, this intercession is purposed toward the wholeness of the person in God. There is a spiritual battle and there is a spiritual "working things through" with God himself on our spiritual baseline when it is concerning those people that he brings to us for healing ministry.

4. PRAY FOR ALL . . . AND PRAY FOR ME

Evidently for Paul there is a progression as we enter more deeply into prayer. The Anointing is increasingly manifested and takes hold of our prayer. Only after the first stages do we begin to hear the Spirit of God and know what is on the Father's heart. We come to the specific issues that God is concerned about. I have found that going through the stages of intercession makes an enormous difference in what I pray for. If the first steps are skipped, prayer comes from human criteria. It is prayer in the flesh. God wants something better from us! Our following the pattern of God's word enables him to inspire through the Holy Spirit those things that he needs us to pray for, as members of the Body of his Son. "Needs" is a strong word, as if God "needed" anything from me.

But this discloses something critical in the ministry of intercession: it is a mystery of God's will and human consent. He has set the world up such that, in our stewardship, he "needs" our consent to bring about a greater realization of his Kingdom. We see him do this in sending the angel Gabriel to the virgin of Nazareth. In that prophetic encounter, without her consent, "May it be done to me according to your word" (Lk. 1:38, NAB), the incarnation of the Word of God could not have taken place. Intercessory prayer—and specifically prayer for healing—works in much the same way. It is a dual process of the revelation of God's plan and of human consent for the release of his almighty power. The greater the plan, the more there is "at stake."

Prophetic Intercession

Whenever we ask ourselves before God, "What's at stake?" we are likely to border on the prophetic because we are going to the "borders" of the person's or group's life. It is here that spiritual battle is most often engaged, and certainly that which is blocking fuller growth in God. This is the *paga*, the leading edge of healing prayer. Let's be clear that we are not talking about "fortune telling" or the "psychic line." We are engaged seriously with two aspects of a person's life that denote Christian prophecy:

- that which is more immediate and seasonal—what is called *God's purpose*
- that which is eternal—called a *person's destiny*

If either of these two are in consideration—and I maintain they *should* be to some extent when we are doing healing prayer—then there is the potential of the prophetic realm in prayer. All intercession, including prayer for healing, takes on the character of the person's future *in God*. That is where the Anointing is most manifest.

Cindy Jacobs defines prophetic intercession as "the ability to receive an immediate prayer request from God and pray about it in a divinely anointed utterance."[8] This simply means that when we are in the Anointing of prayer, God himself puts in our hearts those things that are on his heart for the person(s) for whom we are praying. To some this may sound presumptuous. Safeguards, discernment, and experience all come into play. But the scriptures, lives of the saints, and Christian teaching reveal that, when God ordains it and our motives are right, we *can* know the heart of God and therefore know how to pray in more than simply general ways. After all, "he who searches our hearts knows the mind of the Spirit, because the Spirit intercedes for the saints in accordance with God's will" (Rom. 8:27, NIV). And, "we have the mind of Christ" (1 Cor. 2:16, NIV).

When you are in intercessory prayer for healing, it is always appropriate to have a spiritual "ear" or "eye" directed in God toward the person's or group's future and formulate your prayer by that. Again, we are not looking to some "mystical" clairvoyance. Rather we simply pray that God should bring forth his purpose and destiny in the lives of those for whom we pray. Healing cannot be truly understood without this.

Still, how do we know we are praying in his will, or with the mind of Christ? Joy Dawson gives some short and clear guidelines:

Prayers directed by the Holy Spirit:
- will be according to God's will (1 Jn. 5:14–15)
- will glorify the Father through the Son (Jn. 14:13)
- are based upon God's character, ways and Word (Jn. 15:7)
- come from a clean heart (Jas. 1:6)
- are prayed in full assurance of faith (Jas. 1:6)
- are asked in Jesus' name (Jn. 14:14)
- They always get answered![9]

To this list I would add that prayer needs to be in harmony with the teaching of the Bible and the wisdom of the Church, through which the Holy Spirit corporately speaks to Christ's Body.

Ten Principles for Effective Intercession

All of us continually need help and growth in our ministry of intercession. This acknowledgment of need is a principle mark of the spirituality of persons in the healing ministry. Our healing prayer should be wonderfully different and more mature than it was even last year. With God's help it will be a continual "work in progress." To guide our growth and maintain us on a strong foundation, Joy Dawson has some godly principles for our intercessory prayer:

1. Praise God for who He is. God's power is especially released through worshipful song.
2. Make sure your heart is clean before God by giving the Holy Spirit time to bring any unconfessed sin to mind.
3. Acknowledge that you can't really pray effectively without the Holy Spirit's enabling.
4. Deal aggressively with the enemy. Come against him in the all-powerful name of the Lord Jesus Christ and with the sword of the Spirit—the Word of God.
5. Die to your own imaginations, desires and burdens for what you feel you should pray.
6. Praise God now in faith for the remarkable prayer time you're going to have.
7. Wait before God in silent expectancy, listening for His direction.
8. In obedience and faith, take action on what God brings to your mind, believing God will intervene redemptively.
9. If possible, have your Bible with you should God want to give you direction or confirmation though His Word.
10. When God ceases to bring things to your mind for which to pray, finish by praising and thanking Him for what He has done, reminding yourself that "from him and through him and to him are all things. To him be the glory forever! Amen" (Rom. 11:36).[10]

Pray several times today:

Lord, make me into your powerhouse of intercessory prayer.

Journal Questions for Intercession

1. In your prayer life, how important is intercession?
2. Which of the following dimensions best describes your intercession: a meeting, a spiritual struggle, a boundary, a negotiation? Given the "burdens" you feel in prayer, what dimension do you feel you could expand more?
3. What are some spiritual grounds that you need to hold in intercession?
4. Describe the way you use "spiritual armor" in prayer.

---

[1] Cf . P.J. Mahoney, "Intercession" in *New Catholic Encyclopedia*, Catholic University Press, 1967, p. 566.

[2] Sheets, Dutch, *Intercessory Prayer*, Ventura, CA, Regal Books, 1996.

[3] *Catechism of the Catholic Church*, #2574–2577.

[4] *Catechism*, #2575.

[5] Cabasilas, Nicholas, *A Commentary on the Divine Liturgy*, Crestwood, NY, St. Vladimir's Press, 1977, p. 83.

[6] The *Catechism* dedicates 21 paragraphs (#2725–2745) to the concept of "battle" in prayer.

[7] Isaiah 11:4–5; 59:16–18; Wisdom 5:17–23.

[8] Jacobs, Cindy, *The Voice of God*, Ventura, CA, Regal Books, 1995, p. 39.

[9] Dawson, Joy, *Intercession, Thrilling and Fulfilling*, Seattle, WA, YWAM Publishing, 1997, p. 158.

[10] Ibid., pp. 74–78.

Part IV

The Character of a Healing Minister

Chapter 12

HEALING MINISTRY WITH AN ATTITUDE

HEALING MINISTRY BEGINS WITH FAITH AND FRIENDSHIP

Ministering with an Attitude

The Oxford dictionary defines attitude as "a settled way of thinking or feeling." Alternatively, a person with an "attitude" is someone who persistently exhibits "self-confident or aggressively uncooperative behavior." Both these definitions are applicable to the minister of healing prayer. A man or woman with an attitude is someone who brings to the healing ministry habitual mind-sets, or ways of thinking and feeling, that can either enable the power of God to flow or can obstruct it. In my ministry, I can think of times when I "got it right" and other times when my attitudes made me an obstacle for God's healing grace to flow. In this chapter we will explore three "Be-attitudes," or positive mind-sets, for people who practice healing prayer.

In Matthew 5:3–12 and Luke 6:20–21, Jesus teaches us the Beatitudes that characterize those living in the Kingdom of God. There are other beatitudes throughout the Bible. These define the blessings that flow when we are living in God's covenant. I believe that healing is a dimension of covenant living that brings people into happiness and fulfillment in God and allows blessing to flow through us unobstructed. For those in the healing ministry, being conduits of God's covenant blessing requires the cultivation of certain fundamental attitudes or "settled ways of thinking or feeling." These attitudes define how we are "to be" with our supplicants (those we pray for).

"Please Sit Down, Father!"

There is nothing in the area of human relationships that makes a person feel better than being with another who cares enough to be totally compassionate and non-judgmental, even though one is full of faults and sin. That is what a true friend does, even when it is necessary to tell the other the truth. That is how the Samaritan woman must have felt as she conversed with Jesus. He made himself a true friend to her.

One Christmas Eve many years ago, after having celebrated an evening mass, I was invited to a house where a light meal was served. I entered a crowded room where all the people welcomed me and were flattered that a priest should come by. While they were preparing me a sandwich, I was invited to sit down. They indicated to me the only place available—a tiny space between a large man and a woman who was obviously a "lady of the night" (so to speak).

Sizing up the situation, I declared, "Oh, I'd prefer to stand," with embarrassment in my voice.

Several people insisted, "Please sit down, Father." They were squirming to make room for me. I hesitated, but thought they would truly be offended if I didn't sit. So I nervously squeezed into the space. When I am uncomfortable, I tend to put a blank stare on my face and go inward.

The woman on my right exclaimed to me, "Fa-a-ther! I know you!"

"Oh, yeah?" I muttered, starting to feel pressured as my legs were rubbing right next to this lady and the overweight man on my left.

"Yes, I know all about you," she continued, "I even have your picture on my dresser."

I must have broken out in a cold sweat, at a complete loss for words, wondering if I was having episodes of multiple personality, as I did not know her. Or maybe this was some kind of set-up—or a joke. I was becoming indignant. "How do you know me?" I whispered, trying to lower the pitch of the conversation so we couldn't be overheard.

She said frankly, "You see, Father, I am a ba-a-ad woman. I have regular clients and they tell me about you and one gave me your picture, which I put on my dresser, so now I get to meet you in person."

By this time I was saying self-righteously to myself, "What do I do to get out of this place?" And "How dare these people do this to me!" But it was clear that she wanted to talk. She went on to explain how, after the birth of her two children, her husband had abandoned all of them, and she, unskilled, felt forced by economic desperation into a life of prostitution. She believed in God, but had no idea how she would be able to come out of that life and get close to him.

It was a setup, alright—by God. Right then and there, I was convicted by the Holy Spirit. I sensed an inner voice saying, "You hypocrite! This is what Jesus was about and it is what you are about, too." I remembered the criticism of Jesus related in Luke 15:2: "This man welcomes sinners, and eats with them" (NAB).

Jesus was innocent, totally without sin, yet associated with and wanted to be seen associating with sinners. We, on the other hand, are filled with sin and need every day to receive, like the woman found in adultery, his gracious forgiveness, and yet we often minister with attitudes of superiority!

I needed to change the way I saw this broken woman. I needed to change how I thought of her and my reactions to her. In short, I needed an attitude change—and quick—if she was going to have a lifeline to Christ and his Church. She needed a true friend at that moment, and the Lord sent me to be—at least in that opportunity—the prostitute's friend. He gave me that grace! I have never seen her since, but it became a moment of healing and encouragement for her as we conversed.

That incident was turned into a key time when God instilled in me what had to be a fundamental attitude for the healing ministry. I know that I have failed on many occasions by sometimes retreating into the stronghold of being cold, aloof, or haughty, but at least God hasn't given up on me with respect to the bottom line of dealing with others with compassion and friendship.

MINISTRY BEATITUDE # 1: BLESSED ARE THEY WHO ARE FAITHFUL FRIENDS

While maintaining appropriate boundaries, we are called to be spiritual friends of those whom God places in our lives for healing. This sometimes means conveying a hard truth, but it always implies compassionate love and never judging. It is a call to create holy bonds through which flow God's healing grace. If we habitually are in attitudes of judgment and superiority, we need to repent of it, allow God to change us, or simply not do healing prayer ministry.

Four Friends of a Sinner

Let us approach this from a different angle by returning to the example from the Scriptures on the power of faith and friendship that we studied in Chapter 3. This time we will look at the story from a different angle. In Luke 5:18–20 we read that while Jesus was teaching, some men came with a paralyzed man on a cot. They wanted to get him to Jesus, but the crowds rebuffed them. They then went up on the roof, and lowered the paralyzed man through the tiles, placing him in front of Jesus. "When Jesus saw their faith, he said, 'Friend, your sins are forgiven'" (NIV).

This was an important moment in the ministry of Jesus. Remember that Luke says in verse 17 that the "power of the Lord was present for him to heal the sick" (NIV). While Jesus was teaching, there was a flow of the Anointing that enabled him to heal. Healings would follow Jesus because he was flowing in the Anointing. But there was something else flowing that day—the connection of faith that the paralyzed man's friends had with Jesus. This mirrors the role that people in the healing ministry need to take so that the flow of faith sets up the conditions for God's divine intervention.

In this Scripture account, men who were bringing the paralytic to Jesus were obviously dedicated people of great faith. They would not stop at the rebuff of the crowds. The afflicted one was paralyzed physically and he was also paralyzed spiritually. He needed to break through—not only through the roof but in the deepest part of his being. He seemingly did not have the faith that would connect him to the power of God. He did, however, have loyal friends who were willing to exert, even risk, themselves to bring him to Jesus. Faith will enable you to do on behalf of others things that you never thought of doing before.

Now, imagine yourself as the owner of that house and seeing your roof all of a sudden being dismantled. It is bizarre having a man lowered down on a cot through your roof! But these men were willing to go to those lengths to put their friend into contact with Jesus. Put yourself in that moment and feel the astonishment, the indignation of that crowd. You can hear someone in the crowd saying, "We came here to hear Jesus teach, not to have our meeting interrupted by an invalid." The Pharisees and Scribes came to hear Jesus the teacher. They were the "heady" people, interested in fancy rituals, deep meditations and brilliant insights. The needy man interfered with their session. But it was his friends who, through their faith in Jesus, were willing to take on any obstacle.

A Faithful and Faith-filled Friend Connects Broken People with Jesus

A spiritual connection took place, but it wasn't at first a connection between the paralytic and Jesus. Jesus saw and admired the faith of the paralytic's friends. He saw faith in their eyes and in the expression on their faces.

Imagine Jesus looking up at those four heads peering expectantly through the hole they had made. They are looking down to see if their connection will be contagious; they yearn for their friend to have a connection with Jesus in order to be made whole. Jesus looks up at the friends; he looks down at the paralytic. He looks up again. He sees the expectancy on the faces of those men. He senses a hope turned into an expectant faith. He feels the connection of faith they have made. He sees in their eyes that they know something is about to happen. Anybody who comes into contact with Jesus in faith knows that there will be a supernatural intervention.

Jesus looks at the paralytic and he goes to the heart of the real healing he needs and says, "Your sins are forgiven." Jesus looked beyond the symptom of physical paralysis. Because of the faith connection between the friends of the paralytic, Jesus went to the root of the problem.

Isn't this the perfect model for the kind of intercession we call healing prayer? True believers put their friends in the presence of the Lord, knowing he will touch them where the need is greatest. This is the goal of healing ministry. My purpose in healing ministry is simply to get people to the presence of the Lord. When people are willing to enter his presence there is always healing.

Let's "track" further the process of this event. Jesus needed an atmosphere of faith in order to speak to the real need of the paralytic and to cure him of this paralysis, spiritually, emotionally, and physically. These true friends provided that atmosphere. True and godly friends create around them that positive sense of faith that enables the power of God to flow.

Friendship Is a Divine Calling

If you are called to the healing ministry, you will be called to friendship; to be like the four friends of the paralyzed man, seeking the presence of the Anointing to put the people under that mighty power. Ben Sirach says,

A faithful friend is a sturdy shelter;
he who finds one finds a treasure.
A faithful friend is beyond price,
no sum can balance his worth.
A faithful friend is a life-saving remedy,
such as he who fears God finds;
For he who fears God behaves accordingly,
and his friend will be like himself. (Sirach 6:14–17, NAB)

Several years ago, I used to pray regularly in prayer teams with my friend Chip. One day we arranged to pray with two people who had distinct physical and emotional needs. We spent the better part of the morning praying for Michelle and her many difficult health afflictions. We asked the other lady, Toni, to intercede for

Michelle as we were working with her. Only in the afternoon were we able to enter into prayer for Toni. That night Toni called me, angry and frustrated. "How could you let that needy woman lead you and Chip around by the nose all day?" (So much for my great ideas of bringing needy people together to pray for each other!)

Several days later Michelle called to give a report on how well she was doing since the prayer. It was a wonderfully uplifting praise report. At the end, she said, "Thank you for laying your life down for me on Saturday, and thank Toni, when you talk with her, for laying her life down, too." I did talk to Toni, who was still clinging to her anger over all the attention Michelle had received, and conveyed Michelle's message. It was the "conviction of the Holy Spirit" that hit Toni as she suddenly realized not only that she had been selfish but that when you pray for healing you have to be a friend, not a judge.

It was a great lesson for me. You must lay down your own wants and needs, even suffering for a time, when under the Anointing. This laying down, or self-emptying puts to death the flesh, and there is nothing so important as that for the Anointing to flow. Prayer ministry seldom works when there are judgmental attitudes at work, because judgment shuts down faith. Rather, it is a time in which we lay down our lives for our friends. No matter what the venue—a service, healing mass, ministry session for a few, or one on one, the ministry of healing is one of love, sacrifice, and putting aside oneself.

The paralytic's friends risked being made laughingstocks and fools. They incurred material damage expenses in the man's house. They risked the disdain of the prevailing religious leadership. But they were faithful and faith-filled. That's the attitude we must have as ministers of God's healing grace.

Ministry Beatitude #2: Blessed Are They Who Seek the Mind of Christ

People seeking healing most often simply want relief from suffering. Supplicants' minds are not usually focused on what God is going to do in them as they go through a process that involves suffering and seeking God. Most people just want to get through it and over their illness.

We cannot allow ourselves to be egocentric in our ministry.

This makes the mind-set of the minister key if one is to work as Christ Jesus did, flowing in the Anointing of the Holy Spirit. The same Anointing that was on Jesus' life can be on our lives as ministers. Healing took place as Jesus allowed the flow of God's power to go out through him—through his prayer, his ministry, and his teaching. When people approached him in their needs, he took those needs and used them as occasions to bring them into a deeper relationship with God. The deepest healing that took place was their coming into a place—spiritually, emotionally, and physically—where they would be able to love and serve God.

Today I invite you to ask yourself, If I am (or were to be) in a healing ministry, what should my mind-set be as I seek to do God's will in this ministry? It needs to be the mind of Christ. St. Paul exhorts the Christian community at Philippi on how they were to act toward each other as ministers of God and in relationship with others in the community:

> Nothing is to be done out of jealousy or vanity; instead, out of humility of mind everyone should give preference to others, everyone pursuing not selfish interests but those of others. Make your own the mind of Christ Jesus. (Phil. 2:3–5, NJB)

171

Paul is speaking to us about the relationships we have in the Body of Christ. The people who would minister in conventions, masses, or any kind of healing event may have the tendency to think that through them God is going to make people feel better. This way of thinking, of course, can be very good for the ego of the person ministering. Indeed, it builds the ego to see the demonstration of power. But that is not where God wants our minds.

Laying Aside Self-Centered Ministry

We cannot allow ourselves to be egocentric in our ministry. As we have seen, people sometimes do ministry because of their own ego needs and they "minister out of those needs." I know of brothers and sisters who have told me, "People will learn how valuable I really am if only they see God's power working through me." Or, if they are in marital problems, "My spouse will see that others appreciate how God works through me." What they are doing is relieving their own psychological pain in some way by doing healing ministry. This is what it means to "minister out of your need." But it is not the "mind of Christ Jesus."

Having the "mind of Christ Jesus" means deliberately cultivating within ourselves attitudes that reflect the Lord's. Paul does not say, "Have the mind of Jesus Christ." Nor does he say simply "Have Jesus' mind." Rather, he affirms, "Have the mind of Christ Jesus" (Phil. 2:5). "Christ Jesus" is Paul's favorite way to refer to our Lord. Why is this? He refers to the Christ, who is Jesus. The Greek word for anointing or the Anointed One is *Christos*. Paul is saying, Have in you the same mind, the same attitudes, the same approach, the same desires for the person asking for healing prayer as the mind, thoughts and attitudes produced by the Holy Spirit who is in the Anointed One, Jesus.

Remember from Chapter 3 that the Anointing is the presence and power of the Spirit that lifts the burdens and breaks ungodly yokes. Jesus tells us to look for what is deeper. This must be the

172

attitude of anyone who would approach the healing ministry. What I often see at healing events is that prayer stops with the relief of symptoms. Praying so that someone can simply feel better is wrong-headed. Jesus did not have that mind-set. As the Anointed One, Jesus allowed his mind to be guided by the Holy Spirit. As ministers we need to have a mind that is likewise anointed by the Holy Spirit. When you are praying with someone, ask yourself, What is the Holy Spirit doing deeply in this person? The Holy Spirit is lifting burdens; he breaks the ungodly yokes in every level of our being—physical, emotional, spiritual—so that we can come into that wholeness that will enable us to serve God and live in covenant relationship with him.

The first letter of John tells us:

> But anyone who does keep his word, in such a one God's love truly reaches its perfection. This is the proof that we are in God. Whoever claims to remain in him must act as he acted. (1 Jn. 2:5, NJB)

Healing ministers are called to act as Jesus acted. In pursuing the mind of Christ, we must have the same actions of Jesus. Our healing ministry must reflect his healing ministry; we must heal like Jesus healed, carry on our ministry like Jesus did his.

Jesus tells us in John's gospel, "I tell you the truth, anyone who has faith in me will do what I have been doing. He will do even greater things than these, because I am going to the Father" (Jn. 14:12, NIV). Jesus went to the Father so that he could pour out the Holy Spirit upon us. There was no general outpouring of the Holy Spirit before he went to the Father. Now in his Body we continue his work on the earth, and multiply it far beyond the reaches of what the historical Jesus of Nazareth could do. We, as ministers of God's healing, are purposed to carry on the same work as Jesus did and to have the same Anointing. It is not a different Holy Spirit that is poured out upon us than was poured out on Jesus, the man. It is the same Holy Spirit! The same work! God forms in us the same mind that is in Christ Jesus. It gives us the same attitudes and the same "desires of the Holy Spirit."[1]

Shepherding Supplicants into a Relationship of Worship

Jesus said to the Samaritan woman, "A time is coming and has now come when the true worshipers will worship the Father in spirit and truth, for they are the kind of worshipers the Father seeks" (Jn. 4:23, NIV). The Father seeks a relationship with all who are healed by his Son. True healing ministry takes place when a supplicant—who had been focused on his or her pain—turns the focus around to seeking God in a deeper relationship of worship.

As ministers of his grace, let us have a mind to work to remove whatever obstacle there would be in their path toward God. If the real obstacle is pain or discomfort, then healing means the relief or removal of it. Sometimes healing takes place when pain, rather than being eliminated, is united with the Lord Jesus' suffering on the cross. This is a hard thing for many to accept—that pain could unite them with God. When any circumstance—including sickness—is placed in the presence of the Lord, things change.

Ministry Beatitude #3: Blessed Are the Sons and Daughters of Encouragement

. . . Joseph, a Levite from Cyprus, whom the Apostles called Barnabas (which means Son of Encouragement) (Acts 4:36, NIV).

Barnabas was considered an apostle by the early church because of his deep involvement in the ministry of establishing churches and his missionary journeys. In each of the incidents in which he appears in the Bible he is always engaged in a positive upbuilding of the church. Whether it be giving financial help, taking in Saul of Tarsus when everyone was afraid of him, or taking Mark his cousin (the probable gospel writer) under his wing. So much did he encourage that they nicknamed him Barnabas, literally the Son of Encouragement. As healing ministers, we need to follow in this great apostle's footsteps of edifying the Body of Christ.

Paul writes:

> Blessed be the God and Father of our Lord Jesus Christ, the Father of compassion and God of all encouragement, who encourages us in our every affliction, so that we may be able to encourage those who are in any affliction with the encouragement with which we ourselves are encouraged by God. For as Christ's sufferings overflow to us, so through Christ does our encouragement also overflow. If we are afflicted, it is for your encouragement and salvation; if we are encouraged, it is for your encouragement, which enables you to endure the same sufferings that we suffer. Our hope for you is firm, for we know that as you share in the sufferings, you also share in the encouragement. (2 Cor. 1:3–7, NAB)

It seems clear that "encouragement" was an important part of Paul's vision and vocabulary! The Oxford dictionary says that to encourage means, "give support, confidence, or hope to." In both of the passages cited above, the Greek word for encouragement is derived from *paraklesis*, literally to be "called to one's side" as a counselor or comforter. It is the same word used by Jesus when speaking of himself and the Holy Spirit in John 14:16: "I shall ask the Father, and he will give you another Paraclete [Jesus being the first] to be with you for ever, the Spirit of truth" (NJB). To be a Barnabas—a paraclete or encourager—means that we reflect this essential and powerful dimension of God's character in our life and ministry.

In English the word encouragement has a sense of instilling courage in someone by an act, word, or prayer. The word courage comes from the Latin root word *cor* which means heart. Encouraging is what we as intercessors are called to do, to come to the side of our brothers and sisters to give them heart. They can then expose their real wounds for God to heal. As we have seen, symptoms are most often not the real wound that God wants to heal. It goes much deeper, just like with the paralytic. He was paralyzed and his sins had paralyzed him. Through the encouragement and act of intercession by his friends, Jesus went to the root cause—his spiritual paralysis of sin.

From Magic to Relationship

In the case of the paralytic, Jesus performed an instantaneous healing miracle. It took place as a sign to shake up the prevailing religious authorities who were in the audience. Most "healings" (despite many dramatic experiences at services and masses) are more gradual. Why is this? One reason is that many people are not ready or willing to expose their *real* wounds. That is why healing is often a process, and usually not instantaneous or miraculous.[2] Healing is often prolonged because of our unwillingness to expose what is really hidden in our darkness. The process of exposing this darkness is often a process of gaining trust. As the light of God brings those areas to the Lord, deep and significant healing takes place. At that point one's real self is brought to the Lord.

In our flesh, all of us can have a false quality about our relationship with God. Even with him we can attempt psychological games in defending the hurting parts of ourselves. This is where ideas of magic come in. Many think of healing as a kind of magic, but it is not. Healing is a relationship in which we face ourselves and God honestly. The relief of symptoms in and of itself, by somehow twisting God's arm by our prayer, can be a deceptive game we

play with ourselves and others. In this game-playing we can ig-
nore the root causes of brokenness. Often we think that the more
fervent our prayer or the more religious practices we heap up, the
more we will somehow make God finally concede to us. If we
"tweak" our prayer just right, the "God-machine" will produce
healings. If we attend the right service, say the right deliverance
prayer, go to the right "healer," or go the right number of times,
we will get it tweaked so that our healing will come through. Healing is not about magical practices; it is about a love relationship in
a living faith.

Healing is a covenant relationship with God that frees a human being to love and serve God and his people in the most transparent of ways. It is a relationship with God in a spirit that is free
from darkness and it enables us to do, physically, emotionally, or
spiritually, those things that he has called us to do for him.

I believe the healing ministry needs a shift in thinking to prepare the church for the season that is upon us. The ministry is not
about "choosing" the service in the church where we will feel the
most fulfilled, but where we will be guided by the Spirit of God to
"lay down our lives" that others can be built up in healing love. It
means coming to that spiritual and mental "place" where we can
most readily perceive what is on God's mind and in his heart for
the people he brings to us. Yes, it means having a willingness to
shepherd people who experience brokenness, knowing that we are
many times just as wounded and fragile, and so impart the power
of God's love, not our own brokenness. With God's guidance, we
can become *paracletes*—called to the side of others who are
wounded, in order to counsel, comfort, give them courage, and
minister healing.

Let us pray together:

Lord Jesus, instill in me your mind and your heart. Free me to avoid the pitfall of self-centered ministry. I give my consent for you to change the way I think, act, and talk. Let this show forth in all I do for you. Amen

Journal Questions for Ministry Attitudes

1. Can you be a faithful, faith-filled friend?
2. Where in your attitudes do you need more of the "mind of Christ," i.e., Spirit-directed ways of thinking?
3. Where in your prayer and service do you sense you may need to lay aside "magical" ways of thinking about God and his healing?

---

[1] The *Catechism of the Catholic Church* uses the phrase "the desires of the Holy Spirit" in several places: see for instance, #1091 or #2737.

[2] Note the distinction in 1 Cor. 12 that Paul makes between the charisms of healing and the gift of miracles, or "wonder working," which is an immediate dramatic demonstration of the power of God, often through miraculous or instantaneous healings.

Chapter 13

ILLNESS AND HEALING: THE CATHOLIC VIEW

This chapter is written with two purposes in mind:

1. *For Catholics*, the purpose is to provide a center point and a rooting in our tradition. Some groups of Catholics are suspicious or fearful of the "healing ministry," especially as it has been expressed in the charismatic renewal. This chapter is an attempt to get beyond the pros and cons of this or that expression of healing prayer and find common ground. It will be apparent that essentially I am following the *Catechism of the Catholic Church*, so that there should be no doubt as to where the Church stands.
2. *For non-Catholics* this chapter is written to provide a solid base on what Catholics believe as a body, so as not to form preconceived notions from the private opinions and practices of Catholic brothers and sisters. I also hope this chapter will provide some background for Catholic practices and concepts that might have been hard for Protestants to understand.

"What Do You Expect? I'm Just Trash"

Many years ago, a fourteen-year-old boy made his way from Oaxaca, Mexico to Carmel Valley, California. He was seeking to provide for his grandmother, having been abandoned by his father and discarded by his mother at the age of four. Manuel had no one to provide and care for him, so he would take any job and accept any living situation. He came across an old man who sent him to live in a water-pump shed, sleeping on cartons and eating the few tortillas and beans the old man would give him. In exchange, Manuel worked his field by irrigating, fumigating, and weeding.

Manuel was introduced to me by a friend who was appalled by his living conditions. When I met him, Manuel was in rags, hungry, and in tears. Most of all, he was starving for someone to love and care for him emotionally and spiritually. Thank God I had several compadres upon whom I could call and trust to provide for Manuel's physical needs. I was able to become a "guardian *ad litem,*" meaning I would be personally responsible for him with regard to the court issues. I worked with the California Rural Legal Assistance (CRLA) board to remedy the situation of virtual child slavery that he had lived in for almost a year. When his story hit the local *Monterey Herald*, he was ensured the sympathy of anyone of goodwill. We finally reached a settlement that would provide disbursement of a compensation for many years.

Manual considered me a father figure. We lived through rebellion, the heartbreak of people trying to take advantage of him in every way possible, grueling legal hearings, adolescent crushes, alcohol, a suicide attempt—everything. Manuel was constantly defeating himself by wanting that which would do him harm (an exaggerated version of the typical American teenager). One day, after a session at CRLA, Manuel was being stubborn about his responsibilities. We argued for a long time, then he said, "Well if I can't do what I feel like doing, then once and for all let's just end our relationship." Then tears welled up in his eyes, and he brought back the refrain, "My parents abandoned me when I was four. What do you expect? I'm just trash."

From that point on I realized that people often do things that "put them in the trash" because they think that's where they belong. It becomes an attitude held very strongly—a "stronghold." Manuel's dramatic odyssey parallels that of the fallen human race.

Many of us have felt alienated and have insisted on being left to ourselves. The reality is that our woundedness has its source in being treated like slaves of the enemy. We thought we were much less than the worth that God gave us—being bought from slavery by the price of a spotless Lamb who was God himself, and being called to be his sons and daughters. The more we rebelled, the more we deprived ourselves of what he wanted to lavish on us. If we are to be in God's family, we need to know and respect the way he has arranged the household, and the working of his grace.

To remedy this, God has provided for us a household that we share with the saints. It is a holy house, called "church" and it is full of the opportunities we need to live as his sons and daughters. This household has been set up to provide for our ultimate happiness and healing. St. Paul writes to the Ephesians:

> So then you are no longer strangers and sojourners, but you are fellow citizens with the holy ones and members of the household of God, built upon the foundation of the apostles and prophets, with Christ Jesus himself as the capstone. (Eph. 2:19–20, NAB)

Manuel at root had a "household" problem. He had never heard the words, "You are my beloved son," either from an earthly father nor from his Heavenly Father. He had never known the order and ways of people in a true household. If he was to receive that which would have been provided, he had to unlearn the ways of dysfunctional and ungodly households and bring himself into line with the way normal ones function. In addition to meeting Manuel's natural needs, I knew it was my responsibility to guide him into God's household. One day he and another young man decided to accept God's offer and that of the Church, and received Jesus in the Eucharist.

What a heart-warming day it was to see him—indeed to see anyone—receive the Lord in that way! Jesus says,

> I tell you the truth, unless you eat the flesh of the Son of Man and drink his blood, you have no life in you. Whoever eats my flesh and drinks my blood has eternal life, and I will raise him up at the last day. For my flesh is real food and my blood is real drink. Whoever eats my flesh and drinks my blood remains in me, and I in him. Just as the living Father sent me and I live because of the Father, so the one who feeds on me will live because of me. (Jn. 6:53–57, NIV)

Living in the Father's household of faith means we have the privilege to remain in Jesus through his community and the provision of the sacraments—especially the Eucharist. We form the Body of Christ! We will be always in Jesus and he in us. There is no greater truth that I could have imparted to Manuel.

THE SACRAMENT OF THE SICK: A MODEL FOR THE HEALING MINISTRY

God's household provision of the sacraments can serve as a model for all of spiritual life. It is the same Holy Spirit who works through all. Let's look at the work of the Holy Spirit specifically in the Sacrament of the Sick. Through this sacrament we can learn what the Church teaches concerning illness and healing. What we are most concerned with is applying the spiritual principles found in the Sacrament of the Sick to our own ministry.

The roots of this sacrament are in the healing ministry of Jesus himself, when he ministered under the Anointing of the Holy Spirit. In the gospels Jesus indicated to the disciples that an important part of their ministry would be that of healing. We see this continued in the early Church in the letter of James:

> Is anyone among you sick? He should summon the presbyters of the church, and they should pray over him and anoint [him] with oil in the name of the Lord, and the prayer of faith will save the sick person, and the Lord will raise him up. If he has committed any sins, he will be forgiven. (Jas. 5:14–15, NAB)

The administration of the Sacrament of the Sick is reserved to the ministry of the ordained priesthood, yet we can draw on the patterns it presents for all healing ministry:

> This sacrament gives the grace of the Holy Spirit to those who are sick: by this grace the whole person is helped and saved, sustained by trust in God, and strengthened against the temptations of the Evil One and against anxiety over death. Thus the sick person is able not only to bear suffering bravely, but also to fight against it. A return to physical health may follow the reception of this sacrament if it will be beneficial to the sick person's salvation.[1]

Suffering and Illness in the Hands of the Divine Artist

It is important to establish what is taught concerning illness and suffering. "Illness can lead to anguish, self-absorption, sometimes even despair and revolt against God."[2] The healing mission of Jesus is to take those evils—self absorption, despair, and revolt against God—and remove them so they will not block our destiny.

If, through prayer and faith, we let the Spirit of God take hold, then even suffering becomes a tool with which the divine Artisan can work.

Sickness, suffering, and sin are all evils that we face, personally and collectively, as human beings. On September 11, 2001, with the terrorist campaign against the United States, we witnessed unspeakable suffering in a diabolical manifestation of evil. Believers and non-believers perished together in New York, Washington, and Pennsylvania. Subsequently, what Satan purposed for evil and suffering, we saw God transform into goodness, grace, and moments of glory. Individually, we all face evil every day.

What the Sacrament of the Sick teaches us is that whenever there is evil, sickness, and suffering, and our human will consents to what God desires, then suffering and evil are transformed. This consent of our human will to the purpose of God is what is meant to share in the sufferings of Christ. What Satan purposed for the destruction of the highest work of God in his Son, turned out to be Satan's own defeat. "You intended to harm me, but God intended it for good to accomplish what is now being done, the saving of many lives," said Joseph in Genesis 50:20 (NIV), prefiguring this deep Christian truth.

What Happens If After Prayer, Suffering Remains?

Sometimes, even after the most persistent prayers for healing by the most gifted people, illness and suffering remains. During this time the believer has to endure it and by doing so the trial can become "redemptive suffering"—in which the person suffering purposes that pain to "plant the seed" of suffering for God's Kingdom. It makes no difference whether the suffering comes from persecution, hardship, misunderstandings, bad will, inflicted harm, or sickness; the same opportunity is given to the believer to *unite* this to the all-sufficient sacrifice of Christ. Suffering in union with the cross of Christ, becomes like a seed that is planted. It is important to understand that the suffering is united to that of Christ and not added to it. The human will has to die to itself so that God can apply the unction of his grace. I think this is the deep meaning Paul expresses to the Christians at Corinth:

> For we who live are constantly being given up to death for the sake of Jesus, so that the life of Jesus may be manifested in our mortal flesh. So death is at work in us, but life in you. (2 Cor. 4:11–12, NAB)

Illness "can also make a person more mature, helping him or her discern in life what is not essential so that he can turn toward that which is. Very often illness provokes a search for God and a return to him."[3] Has God directly caused illness so that people can suffer? Our Christian faith says emphatically, No! But we do know that according to the promises of God, every trial and every temptation can be a way that the Holy Spirit can turn what blocks our destiny into a work of art for God. "And we know that in all things God works for the good of those who love him, who have been called according to his purpose" (Rom. 8:28, NIV). This includes the trial of sickness.

> In the healing ministry we place illness and suffering into the hands of Jesus. When we do, this has a transforming effect. It becomes a sowing in God's Kingdom.

Christians are not exempt from evil and the effects of evil any more than Jesus was. The Christian message is that we can become victors over evil—including the suffering of illness—by uniting ourselves to Christ and his cross. In the healing ministry we place illness and suffering into the hands of Jesus. When we do, this has a transforming effect. It becomes a sowing in God's Kingdom.

Discerning Trials and Temptations

There is a difference between a trial and a temptation. In healing ministry a specific discernment is necessary when confronted with trial and temptation. We seek the wisdom of the Holy Spirit who allows us discern among trials, which are necessary for the growth of the inner man, and temptation, which leads to sin and death. We also discern between the act of being tempted and consenting to temptation.

This discernment "unmasks the lie of temptation whose object appears to be good, a 'delight to the eyes' and desirable when in reality its fruit is death."[4]

When we apply this teaching to the mystery of illness and suffering dealt with in the healing ministry, we can see that our task of discernment requires some degree of knowledge and maturity. We need to discern whether this illness is bringing genuine inner growth or is leading to a spiritual death that is not of God. It also requires that a minister of healing prayer encourage Catholic supplicants to seek spiritual orientation and help in the Sacrament of Reconciliation regarding that which is sinful, and when the line between temptation and sin has been crossed.

Carlos was a young man in his early twenties when he sank into a major depression and developed significant physical problems. Burdened with guilt feelings and hopelessness, he begged for prayer. Several weeks went by and he felt he was losing control. He would often call me to explain how bad he was feeling, on the verge of desperation. "What will become of me?" he repeatedly asked.

One day I was invited to a birthday lunch to which Carlos had also been invited. He sat across from me. I sensed something was very wrong. As we began to talk, I saw a bulge under his tee-shirt.

"Carlos, what's that?" I asked.

"Nothing," he replied with embarrassment, starting to turn a noticeably darker shade of his already dark Mexican complexion.

"It *is* something. Show me," I insisted. At that point he uncovered an occult amulet.

"I already feel better since my dad took me to get this." He went on to explain how his father (at that time a non-believer) had taken him to the central valley of California to a well-known witch doctor, who performed occult rituals and gave him the amulet to wear as "remedy" for depression. After some conversation he gave it to me to destroy. Within a couple of days, Carlos had become so noticeably worse that he quit his job and went to live with his mother in Mexico. A month later the bishop of that Mexican area came to Carlos's town to administer the Sacrament of Confirmation. Carlos, still desperate, asked to see him for the Sacrament of Reconciliation and confessed his involvement in the occult. That night he became well, and within a few days returned to the U.S. Since then, he has never had a reoccurrence.

Like Carlos, many people, acting outside of the light of the gospel become superstitious in the face of despair when they are seriously ill. They may have added the idolatry of witchcraft or other occult practices, which compound the problem by poisoning the human spirit and jeopardizing a person's covenant relationship with God. These issues also need to be discerned.

God does not cause illness, but *allows* it in order that people can experience growth and maturity in the inner person. It is in this dimension that the healing ministry can make a difference in drawing a person into greater maturity.

Christ's compassion toward the sick and his many healings of every kind of infirmity are a resplendent sign that God has visited his people and that the Kingdom of God is close at hand. Jesus has the power not only to heal but also to forgive sins. He has come to heal the whole person, soul and body. He is the physician that the sick have need of. Healing is not only a spiritual sign, but there is also a physical aspect. Christ's healings are real and they manifest themselves physically. As we saw in the first section, healing is sign of the Anointing.

"It Was Our Infirmities that He Bore, Our Sufferings that He Endured," (Is. 53:4, NAB)

The evangelist Matthew declares that Jesus "took away our infirmities and bore our diseases" (Mt. 8:17, NAB). That phrase is quoted from Isaiah 53:4. But it is striking that the *Catechism* affirms, "but he did not heal all the sick." Why this apparent contradiction? We have to understand this as it is important for the healing ministry. It is a fact that Jesus did not restore to physical wholeness all the people he encountered.

Here is a case in point: Jesus went many times in and out of the temple to worship. We know from Acts 3:2 that there was a man crippled from birth who sat daily by the Beautiful Gate and begged. Jesus most certainly saw him. Yet he went in and went out without curing him. The man probably begged Jesus for alms because that is what he did every day for many years.

Peter and John were purposed to be the vessels of healing for that crippled man. So it is true that Jesus in his earthly ministry didn't restore everybody physically. If he had, all of Jerusalem would have been instantly converted, but he didn't and it wasn't. What is the meaning of this? Again, we have to get beyond seeing healing as the relief of symptoms. Going deeper, we see that healing is a restoration of the person so that one can choose freely to follow God and walk in one's destiny. As we have seen, that involves faith and it takes place on God's timing, not ours.

The signs of Jesus *announced* a more radical healing, the victory over sin and death through his passing from death to life through the cross. Christ took upon himself the whole weight of evil on the cross. He took away the sin of the world, of which illness is only a consequence. By his passion and death on the cross,

Christ has given new meaning to suffering. It can henceforth conform us to him and unite us with his redemptive passion.

What about those people who go to miracle services, healing masses, healing sessions for years and are not made well in their body but continue to suffer? A superficial way of looking at this is to say they weren't healed because of their lack of faith. Some people do say this and I believe it is cruel. Anyone who would be at a healing service or a healing mass knows that people reach out in faith to Jesus. Maturity in Christ means coming to the understanding that when we have to suffer, we become an icon of Jesus crucified, redeeming the world.

A few months ago I had the opportunity to be at a meeting of many local evangelical pastors. One of them shared with the group that after many attempts of praying in faith and many prayers from his congregation and other pastors, he still needed several leg operations and was in constant pain. He himself had prayed many times for others, who had been healed. He gave testimony that he had gained immense spiritual growth through this illness, making him a much better Christian and pastor. That was a healing!

One of the founders of my community in Monterey, Fr. Emeric Doman, never ceased saying for many years, "Love without the cross is unthinkable; the cross without love is unbearable." If a person through suffering is enabled to love, I suggest that the person has indeed received healing.

WHAT THE CHURCH BELIEVES ABOUT THE HEALING MINISTRY

The Catholic Church, echoing the words of Jesus to his disciples, exhorts us: "Heal the sick!" Following Jesus *is* a call to compassion and healing. In the *Catechism* we read,

Christ invites his disciples to follow him by taking up their cross in their turn. By following him [in discipleship], they acquire a new outlook on illness and the sick. Jesus associates them with his own life of poverty and service. *He makes them share in his ministry of compassion and healing.* (Italics added)[5]

If we are disciples of Jesus, we will always share in his compassion and healing, no matter what our ministry may turn out to be. We are called to do what Jesus asked his disciples to do: "They went out and preached that people should repent. They drove out many demons and anointed many sick people with oil and healed them" (Mk. 6:12–13, NIV). It is a mandate of the risen Lord. "In my name . . . they will lay hands on the sick, and they will recover" (Mk. 16:17–18, NAB).

Every Christian at some point will be called upon to do healing prayer in Jesus' name. However, there are individuals who are endowed with healing charisms, which point the way to a ministry of healing. In the Body of Christ "the Holy Spirit gives to some a special charism of healing so as to make manifest the power of the grace of the risen Lord."[6] The Roman Catholic Church accepts the charism of healing as a manifestation of the Spirit today. A document from the Vatican of September, 2000 affirms not only the healing ministry but also declares that we cannot limit the Holy Spirit in what he would do in manifesting charisms of healing.[7]

The Sacrament of the Sick and the Charisms of Healing

The same instruction referred to exhorts us to be aware of the important distinction between the Sacrament of Anointing of the Sick and the charism of healing.[8] There is healing that comes through the Sacrament of Anointing the Sick itself. It is a gift that is exercised, in this case, by virtue of the Sacrament of the Sick. There, healing flows by virtue of the ordained ministry of the presbyter (priest), i.e., through the laying on of hands and anointing with oil that has been blessed for this purpose and prayers in the liturgy for the sick. The instruction is careful to say that this is *not* the *charism* of healing, as such. The sacrament is a "hierarchical gift," given by virtue of the power that was handed down through the apostles at ordination.

There are also *charismatic gifts* (manifestations) of healing. The Holy Spirit, irrespective of person, class, or category, is sovereignly manifested in charismatic gifts of healing. God bestows the gift of healing to male and female, young and old, and even sick and well. I know many people who have a powerful charism of healing who are not well themselves. Those of us in the healing ministry are *all* wounded healers. Some have a special connection to the suffering Christ that has allowed tremendous power to flow through their ministry. One of the most heartwarming things I have seen is children inspired by the Holy Spirit laying hands on people. Powerful gifts of healing have been manifested through the prayers of children. We should be respectful—and thankful—for what the Lord has done in his household: he has provided for an abundance of healing, both in the hierarchy and in the general Body of Christ through the charisms. "He has done everything well, . . . He even makes the deaf hear and the mute speak" (Mk. 7:37, NIV).

Ministry to the Sick

The Catholic Church views and recommends ministry to the sick in three dimensions:

> *Caring for the Sick:* The word "care" is derived from the word cure and means to attend to the sick by whatever means. It means to do something for them, whether taking care physically, encouraging, or praying with them.
>
> *Exercise the Prayer of Intercession:* We are encouraged to exercise the prayer of intercession. Ministers of healing

prayer are exercising a form of intercession for the sick. This is where the charisms of healing can be used.

Presence of Jesus and the Holy Spirit: The Anointing of God is particularly active through the sacraments and in a special way through the Eucharist. St. Paul suggests that the Eucharist is the bread that gives eternal life and is connected with bodily health (cf. 1 Cor. 11:27–30). We will know wholeness when we come to the Eucharist, which is the full expression of the Body of Christ and communion with him and one another. We not only hear about wholeness in the Word of God, but we will see wholeness in operation in the Body of Christ in the sacraments and we receive the Divine Physician himself in Eucharist. The Eucharist, as has often been said, is the Sacrament of Healing *par excellence* because it contains all the dimensions of God's healing.

FIVE THINGS YOU CAN EXPECT
IN FAITH FROM HEALING PRAYER

One important theme in this chapter is that it is helpful to use the Sacrament of the Anointing of the Sick as a paradigm, or model, for what happens in healing ministry. Paragraphs 1520–1523 in the *Catechism* set forth the effects that occur when the Sacrament of the Sick is administered. Analogously, we can expect these things when there are charisms of healing in operation:

1. Strengthening Takes Place

Against the temptation of the evil one (who would try to work through illness in order to detour a person's destiny) there is strength. In other words, through healing prayer there has been a spiritual battle against the temptation to discouragement and anguish in the face of death. Strength, peace, and courage are given together with healing of body and soul.

2. There Is Forgiveness

Just like the paralyzed man who was lowered through the roof in front of Jesus, people seeking healing need a word of forgiveness and a cleansing of their conscience. James 5 not only talks about the Anointing of the sick; James, like Jesus, connects healing and forgiveness. Many people are sick in body, mind, and soul because of sin, but that doesn't mean that everybody who is sick is in sin. However, some people have a pattern of sin in their life and it shows in their bodies and in psychological manifestations. There is a ministry of reconciliation in the Sacrament of the Anointing of the Sick and, in a parallel way, there is a ministry of reconciliation that takes place in the ministry of healing.

3. There Is Union with the Passion of Christ

A frequent effect of healing ministry is the restoration of bodily wellness. Another effect of healing prayer is union with the passion of Christ. In the Sacrament of the Anointing of the Sick, and whenever there is prayer ministry to the sick, there is a consecration that takes place. The word "consecrate" means to "separate out" for a specific purpose. A person so consecrated will be taken to a different dimension from those who suffer without God. They will be conformed, or united, with the passion of Christ. Only then does suffering become redemptive and meaningful. The healing ministry likewise has a consecratory effect. Holiness is bestowed, and the person enters into a new dimension: "Now I rejoice in what was suffered for you, and I fill up in my flesh what is still lacking in regard to Christ's afflictions, for the sake of his body, which is the church" (Col. 1:24, NIV). In this way, we become "God's co-workers" (1 Cor. 3:9, NAB).

4. There Is a Sharing of Spiritual Goods

A beautiful dimension of healing prayer is that through such intercession illness becomes an instrument for communion, *koinonia*. In other words, if we gently encourage our supplicants to unite their pain—while they have it—to Christ in love through prayer, then that illness can become a conduit through which Christ can pour more grace into his church. Again, St. Paul says, "So then, death is at work in us, but life is at work in you" (2 Cor. 4:12, NIV). *Koinonia* means that your grace is my grace and my gift is your gift, because we belong to the same Body. When we pray for healing, that which is alienated is through the blood of Christ brought near into one Body in Christ (Eph. 2:13). Sometimes physical relief doesn't happen, but union with Christ in his passion and resurrection puts one on course to God's purpose. This is healing.

5. There Is a Preparation for the "Final Journey"

I have prayed for healing with many people who soon afterwards died. Everybody who has been in the healing ministry has had this experience. Some people feel that they have failed in their prayer. This is not correct. If the supplicant is close to eternal life, healing prayer is vital.

A couple of years ago a friend who is a Church of the Nazarene pastor called with the news that his Catholic father was very ill and could possibly die. He had been "hanging on" for many days and it occurred to my friend and his mother that his father might need a priest. As we all gathered and, in faith, I administered the Sacrament of the Anointing of the Sick followed by the Last Rites, my orientation, as always, was toward healing, in any way God would want. A noticeable change of expression came over the man's face as I laid hands on him and anointed him. I left, with Pastor Brian and his mother walking me out to the driveway. As soon as I got home, Pastor Brian called and said his dad had gone to be with the Lord. When they walked back into the room, his dad had just died with total peace. Brian never ceases to gratefully recount the story of his dad's greatest healing!

The Ultimate Healing

When we pray for someone and the person dies, we must understand with our hearts that through death God healed that person with the ultimate healing of the resurrection. God has brought that one into the full union with him—and that is healing. We should not be afraid of death. Nor should we be afraid of praying for dying people and praying for their healing, however and whenever the Lord might want to do it.

I have also seen people come back from the verge of death through healing prayer. One time I was called to the hospital in Monterey to pray for a twenty-six-year-old woman named Martha, who was a teacher in Salinas. She was in the intensive care unit with tubes everywhere. Her doctor, a friend of mine, said, "It doesn't look like she is going to be around much longer, even for a few hours." She was dying. Nobody had prayed for her healing beyond general devotions. Her mother and siblings had obviously prayed for her, but no one had actually laid their hands on her and ministered in healing prayer.

Martha wasn't conscious when I prayed for her. I remember there was a tremendous sense that the Lord's power was very present in that room. Intellectually I agreed with the doctors who told me she was going to die. As we prayed and administered the Sacrament of the Anointing of the Sick, I sensed the power of God.

The next day they took one of the tubes out of Martha and she remained stable. She was getting better, so they took her off the respirator. As the tubes came out, it was apparent that the Lord had worked a total healing. Today she is teaching and knows she was brought back from the verge of death by the power of God.

This healing took place through the Sacrament of the Anointing of the Sick. I have also seen people brought back from the verge of death by praying for healing without the sacrament. And I have also seen many people in my priestly ministry die. They die after prayer because God has given them the ultimate healing—entrance into eternal life.

What can we expect when there is prayer for healing and openness on the part of the supplicant? We can expect physical, psychological, and spiritual strength. We can expect a mystical association in Jesus' redeeming work. We can expect that the household of God, which is the Body of Christ, will be built up and we can expect that there will be a preparation to meet God face to face when he chooses to call us to his side. One thing is for sure: when we lead people to the presence of God, nothing can stay the same!

Journal Questions

1. What stands out for you the most with respect to the Catholic Church's teaching on illness and ministry to the sick?
2. What could you do in your ministry that would bring it more into this model of the Holy Spirit's masterpieces of the sacraments?
3. Describe a time you have seen suffering and sickness transformed by God's healing grace. How did healing take place?

[1] *Pastoral Care of the Sick*, Introduction, No 6. New York: Catholic Book Publishing Co., 1983.
[2] *Catechism of the Catholic Church*, #1501.
[3] *Catechism*, #1501.
[4] *Catechism*, #2847.
[5] *Catechism*, #1506.
[6] *Catechism*, #1508.
[7] *Instruction* on Prayers for Healing, Vatican Congregation for the Doctrine of the Faith, September 14, 2000, #5.
[8] Ibid., #3.

Part V

Guidance in Healing Prayer

Chapter 14

HOW TO PREPARE FOR A HEALING EVENT

Several years ago I was called to a healing mass in the city of Hayward, California where five hundred people were expected. An experienced prayer team would be ministering with me and they could be relied upon for any spiritual need. Being in a joyful mood, my mind carried me to different songs that I like and, in particular, the type of songs that bring great delight—Argentine tangos. They are fascinating to listen to and sing. Sometimes I play them on my violin. It is an adventure to watch and listen to tangos. Someone had just given me a new tape of tangos. I thought, "What's the harm in waiting to get to the church to do my prayer preparation? The prayers of those powerful people ministering with me will be enough to prepare for the mass." Several tangos filled the air of my car.

Before long Hayward came into view and I had been listening to and singing tangos along most of the hour-and-a-half trip. But there was a problem: tangos are not the most spiritual of musical genres. They talk about lost loves, betrayals, poverty, and the low places in life. You might compare them with soap operas. I was on the verge of a healing mass—and had saturated my mind and soul with the stories and rhythms of tangos!

Upon exiting the freeway, I turned the stereo off, thinking, "Better do some praying!" Entering the church early, the ministry team and I went through the routine of spiritual preparation in prayer. Little did they know! I put on my most pious countenance and we prayed many beautiful prayers, but I was not on the "spiritual baseline" necessary for conducting a healing mass. Tangos were still rolling through my mind as I struggled to pray along with the healing prayer team. I was the principle one responsible for this mass and I was not spiritually prepared.

Deacon Joe Alvarez, a man of God, was celebrating mass with me that night, being his usual gracious self. After we began the mass, the readings followed and I began to preach. As I spoke, there was the sense of being "shut down." It was a feeling of being "shrunken" before the people. My movements were being restricted increasingly and the unsettling sensation of my voice going out to nowhere. Before long, I was at a loss for words, in confusion and literally groping to get out a message, which was blurry and unrefined. Then I started to actually feel sick in my body. Who knows what message finally got out?

Deacon Joe saw there was something wrong. After preaching, I went to sit down and confided desperately, "I need prayer and I need it now!" During the offering he and I joined hands and he began to pray. As he did, my strength came back and the mass continued. Later on, we found out that a witch had come deliberately to that mass to work against it and to work against me specifically! Being unprepared, I was vulnerable to that spiritual influence. The Body of Christ had suffered because I, as the one in charge of the event, had not done my work.

Spiritual Preparation for the Healing Event

If you are involved in any kind of conference, healing mass, or service, or if you know you are just going to pray for somebody for significant healing, there is a preparation that needs to take place. We will divide this preparation into two parts, "remote" and "immediate." Remote preparation takes place starting a few days before an event, while immediate preparation is what occurs immediately prior to the event, usually in the same location.

> The Anointing of the Holy Spirit is enabled to flow freely in a person who has prepared well for his or her ministry.

Six Elements of Remote Preparation

The Anointing of the Holy Spirit is enabled to flow freely in a person who has prepared well for his or her ministry. As the healing event approaches, I invite you to consider the steps that follow. Eventually, they become a habitual mind set as you deepen your ministry.

1. Before All Else, Get on Your Spiritual Baseline!

Previously, we discussed the preparation that has to take place by the assembly—and especially by its ministers—for there to be a full encounter with the Lord Jesus.[1] When we are ministers in a healing event, whether it is a mass, prayer meeting, or other type of service, there is a preparation that takes place by the people who are most responsible for it. It is crucial for us as ministers that we attend to our own "spiritual baseline" of expectant faith, repentance of sin, and adherence to God's will. These conditions need to be met *in us* before such a healing event or session.

2. Put Yourself in a Listening Mode

Along with establishing a spiritual baseline as a mode of preparation, there is the issue of discipleship. It is patterned after Jesus' own discipleship. What form discipleship takes often depends on the faith tradition the disciple comes from. We have many rich and diverse traditions and some can get somewhat complicated. I suggest that no matter what our tradition, we always look to the essentials of being a follower of Jesus. That is the center where the healing ministry must always return.

Discipleship consists of hearing God's directions and obeying them. This is the secret of the Anointing. It means attuning our ear to the voice of the Good Shepherd, who speaks to us. Jesus said that the sheep that belong to him listen to his voice (Jn. 10:4). The hearing is followed by obeying. Discipleship is a life of hearing the voice of God and obeying it. This is essential for any kind of ministry, and most especially for the healing ministry because so much is at stake. When preparing for a healing event, there is an attitude of listening that accompanies the planning for the event. A habitual attitude of listening will enable you to discern, days or even weeks in advance, what you are to prepare for and how you are to prepare for it.

I have found it of great help to ask the Lord open-ended questions about courses of action in ministry. It amounts to asking for a word of wisdom from the Lord, who so loves to bestow it. I wonder how many ministers of healing prayer stop and ask the Lord, How would you do this ministry, Lord? or, What is it that you wish me to say as your servant? The answers usually become clear as we wait patiently for his voice. We hear his voice in any number of ways and often how we least expect it! Yet it is the voice of the "Good Shepherd who never leaves his flock untended."[2]

3. For Catholics: Love the Lord in the Sacraments

Our remote preparation should include an intensive participation in the sacraments, for those who are in the sacramental tradition. If there is sin in our lives, let us approach the Sacrament of Reconciliation. In my own life I often am made aware of my utter unworthiness to carry on any ministry. Un-dealt-with sin impedes me from being God's instrument. I'm sure you have experienced this. Repentance and acceptance of his forgiveness places sin "under the Blood of Jesus." For Catholics, the Sacrament of Reconciliation powerfully allows us to soak all our personal sin and iniquity in the blood that flowed from the wounds that healed us.

When we know we will be ministering in a healing event, let us take that event to the Eucharist. The placing of that event, in anticipation, before the body and blood of Christ in a *eucharistic paga*—that sacred meeting between God and us in intercession—bonds the event itself to the redemptive sacrifice of the Lamb of God on Calvary. For those of us in the Catholic tradition, this is a natural way of preparing for a healing event. God speaks to us powerfully as we are before the Lord pouring ourselves out in intercession. The substantial presence of Christ in the Blessed Sacrament is an intense and privileged mode of his presence.[3]

"I Want You in the Discipleship of Peter, James, and John"

Several years ago I was in Chicago attending the international conference of the Association of Christian Therapists. During this conference there is always a special place reserved for prayer before the Blessed Sacrament (as Catholics like to call the reserved Eucharist). As I sat before the Lord, he spoke quietly and strongly to my heart: "I want you in the discipleship of Peter, James, and John."

This thoroughly puzzled me. Asking about this, I sensed him say, "I will be showing you, but for now, *I just need your consent* to lead you there."

Bewildered and half-incredulous, I managed to say, "Yes."

That consent in prayer before the Blessed Sacrament unleashed one of the most powerful—and painful—periods of my Christian walk. He showed me, step by step through the gospels, what he had to take out of and put into Peter, James, and John, the three disciples of his inner circle, as he trained them for the ministry.

My consent to face and let go of things in myself that I thought were part of me, and accepting things that I never imagined would be, has been the greatest asset to my ministry. Kathryn Kuhlman once said "the Lord doesn't need perfect vessels, just yielded ones." Yielding to the Lord's way of thinking, talking, and acting is the greatest of all challenges. Yet it draws down the Anointing powerfully on the ministry of those who accept it. I received strength, insight, and teaching as I went each day before the Holy Eucharist in prayer and intercession to yield my life and ministerial situations. This discipleship remains for me the essential fount from which I draw in order to accomplish his work.

4. Intercession and Fasting

The secret of all intercession is our consent to what God asks from us. We must be able to yield our wills in all aspects of life, especially in ministry. This act of the human spirit, by the grace he gives, releases his Kingdom on earth. When we go before him as we prepare for ministry events, he prepares in the spiritual realm what he intends to do later in the physical realm concerning his Kingdom. Dynamic and wonderful things take place as we come before him in this kind of anointed prayer. As a spiritual event approaches, it is vitally important that we come before God and "seek his face" as this is a time of personal revelation.

Fasting along with intercession during remote preparation makes prayer sharp and excellent. It is hard—almost impossible—to minister in the Spirit and hear his voice when the stomach is full. Fasting is a wonderful tool that enables us to focus on the Spirit of God. Jesus never said, "*If* you fast . . ." but rather "*When* you fast . . ." (Mt. 6:16), thus ordaining that his followers should fast.

I'm not saying that every minister of healing prayer will go for extraordinary times without food; this is a very individual thing. Yet discipline, exercised in the realm of bodily cravings, likes, and dislikes, is essential. Fasting must be accompanied by prayer or it just becomes "mortification" for its own sake. It is easy to become "legalistic" about fasting and this should be avoided. Some people maintain that this or that fast is the way God wants everyone to fast. That is not correct and subjects a person to making judgments about other ministers. It may be as simple as rescheduling a meal to avoid a full stomach during prayer and ministry. So how does one learn how to fast? I suggest that you might take this issue to prayer and ask the Lord how he would have you fast, then check out your leading with the person who holds spiritual authority and discernment in your life.

5. Pray in the Spirit on Every Possible Occasion

On January 1, 2000, about two thousand prayer warriors gathered at St. Mary's Cathedral in San Francisco. The purpose for the gathering was to do strong and serious worship, repentance, spiritual warfare, and intercession. We called it *Jubilee Prayer Explosion*. It was a unique event that I had sensed God moving me to organize since July of 1999. It was preceded by four worship gatherings of some sixty leaders of the charismatic renewal from all over northern California. To organize such an event was way out of the "game plan" for my ministry and beyond my abilities. Then there were the "naysayers" who said that a totally bilingual and multi-faceted event like this could not be done in five months. The spiritual stakes were high.

By a rich outpouring of God's grace, many vital spiritual developments took place beforehand and after as a consequence of that gathering. I want to state categorically that such a process would have been impossible unless there was a constant flow of the Holy Spirit in the leaders of the event. This flow took place by virtue of "prayer in the Spirit."

Early on, my friend and co-worker Nancy exhorted me, "This event will never come to pass unless you commit yourself to praying in tongues at least fifteen minutes a day." At first I thought, "This is an exaggeration, and really kind of strange." Soon, however, I came to accept that Nancy's word to me was a leading of the Spirit of God. The five months before the New Year were some of the most special of my ministry, in which I learned deeper dimensions of ministry in the Spirit. I sensed God taking a significant segment of the Body of Christ into a new time. It was truly a birthing process! And it truly could not have been done without obeying the word I heard through Nancy.

The Gift of Tongues

What was this praying in the Spirit that I was exhorted to do? Commonly called a "prayer language," it was a use of the gift of tongues as remote preparation for *Jubilee Prayer Explosion*. I call the gift of tongues a "threshold" charism. Indeed, this gift, which is officially recognized as a gift for our time by the Catholic Church,[4] can be called the least of the spiritual gifts. And being the least it gets us in the door in order to yield us to the higher gifts. In the New Testament, at least four uses of this charism can be discerned:

a. *A proclamation and a sign.* On the day of Pentecost in Acts 2, when the disciples were filled with the Spirit, they began to give utterance, using the gift of tongues. The people from many parts of the known world in Jerusalem each heard them speaking about the marvels of God in their own tongue, or language.

In 1 Corinthians chapters 12, 13 and 14, Paul elaborates on this gift with the following uses:

b. A *speaking forth* in the Christian assembly, followed by an interpretation that seems to mirror a prophetic word (1 Cor. 14:5).
c. A *praying with the (human) spirit* (1 Cor. 14:15) that has the external manifestation of utterances that are not understood, either by the one praying or anyone else. This is for the edification of the person praying, because the spirit is praying, or connected to God (1 Cor. 14:4).
d. A *singing with the (human) spirit* (1 Cor. 14:15) that is not understood by the mind.

Paul affirms, and at the same time differentiates, between the audible prayer of the human spirit and the prayer of the human mind, or understanding: "So what is to be done? I will pray with the spirit, but I will also pray with the mind. I will sing praise with the spirit, but I will also sing praise with the mind" (1 Cor. 14:15, NAB).

There is something about praying and singing in tongues that puts a believer into a spiritual connection with the Spirit of God. The reason is because of the affinity with which God has created us in the spiritual realm to be in communion with him. Paul says, "The [Holy] Spirit himself joins with our spirit to bear witness that we are children of God" (Rom 8:16, NJB).

> The gift of tongues correctly used can be (and I believe is meant by God to be) a basic and immediate school and tool for divine and human collaboration.

Later he adds, "The Spirit himself intercedes for us with groans that words cannot express. And he who searches our hearts knows the mind of the Spirit, because the Spirit intercedes for the saints in accordance with God's will" (Rom 8:26–27, NIV). It is in this context that we can better understand Paul's exhortation that "With all prayer and supplication, pray at every opportunity in the Spirit" (Eph 6:18, NAB).

Addressing this sometimes controversial matter, I think that Dutch Sheets puts it well:

> I don't believe the intercession of the Holy Spirit spoken of in [Rom 8: 26, 27] refers only to "tongues." However, most of us in Pentecostal and charismatic circles believe it has to include this gift, which we believe allows the Holy Spirit to literally pray through us. It is not my intention . . . to prove this, nor am I implying that those who do not practice it are second rate in their praying.[5]

To summarize, once released and matured in the believer, the gift of tongues can be used in a variety of contexts and occasions, according to what is discerned to be appropriate and in order. Enabled by the Spirit of God, it is an utterance giving audible expression of the spiritual dimension of us to God in prayer so that the believer and/or the community can be edified. Once the gift develops and matures, it is an elegant example of how the energies of the Holy Spirit and our human energies can harmonize and work in concert for our own building up and also that of the Body of Christ. In this way, it sets the stage for the other, more important, gifts to be manifest.

The gift of tongues correctly used can be (and I believe is meant by God to be) a basic and immediate school and tool for divine and human collaboration. Can the other charismatic gifts, such as healing or the word of knowledge, be manifest without the gift of tongues? Yes they can, but I believe in its absence the disposition to the Spirit of God will be handicapped and awkward. It is kind of like trying to paint a room from outside by reaching through the door or windows. Using—and using maturely—the gift of tongues will enable you to cross over the threshold into the house of spiritual gifts so you can have much freer access to that which is in the house.

Many people in ministry, having this gift, use it only when they are praying with others who have the gift and during certain designated times. That is the way I under-used this gift for many years. But God has given the gift of tongues for personal and corporate edification. When used personally, a spiritual intimacy with the Spirit of God is produced. Beyond that—and this is the point here— just having that kind of connection for a significant amount of time will *set up the conditions* in which you will be able to hear God more clearly and to respond to a greater degree to what he wants.

Any gift, however extraordinary, is always oriented toward sanctifying people in grace and is intended for the common good of the Church. Gifts are at the service of charity, which builds up the Church.[6] Whether you believe that the gift of tongues is or should be ordinary Christian practice, or whether it is an extraordinary gift, given for an extraordinarily wonderful ministry like healing, the goal is the same: not for selfish interests, but in love, healing and sanctifying the people of God.[7]

If you have been released in the gift of tongues, I would like to encourage you start the discipline of using it more often, even every day, and for longer periods each day. Dedicate even more effort as you approach ministry events. At first this might feel somewhat strange. Before long, however, you will experience five ways in which you will be edified:

- You will know greater intimacy with God.
- Your "prayer language" will increase, develop and mature.
- You will receive revelation about your personal walk with the Lord.
- You will be able to understand spiritual realities in deeper ways.

- You will receive revelation about ministry events in which you are to engage.

What should you do if you have not yet yielded to this charism? Ask the Lord for it—he delights in bestowing gifts on his Body so that it can be edified. If you haven't investigated and participated in a seminar for the baptism, or release, of the Holy Spirit, actively seek this gift and humbly ask others who have it to agree in prayer with you to receive it. I have yet to find anyone who has actively sought this gift and has been open to it who didn't receive. Here are four important dispositions:

1. An attitude of genuinely seeking the gift
2. Humility and repentance
3. Becoming accustomed to pronouncing sounds that you don't understand with your mind
4. Stepping out in faith, and allowing these sounds to flow and multiply, while you focus your spirit on God

6. Create a Spirit-Filled Atmosphere

In preparing for an important spiritual event, I strive to saturate the atmosphere around me in prayer and with the holiness of God. Praise and worship CDs and tapes are important tools for accomplishing this. They are readily available over the internet and in Christian bookstores.

Filling the atmosphere with music that God has purposed to help bring believers into his presence drives away the power of the enemy and prepares us to hear God. As believers become increasingly attuned to the Holy Spirit, there is manifest a discernment between anointed and un-anointed music (however well executed it my be). It is important that you seek out *anointed* praise music that directly and intentionally glorifies God. It is not just a matter of "lifting your spirit or mood," nor am I talking about "meditation" music or classical works (as great as they are). Anointed music purposefully directs and carries your spiritual faculties to glorify the Father, the Son, and Holy Spirit. It opens you to his presence and his working as you unite yourself to this anointed worship. God makes his home in the praises of his people (Ps. 22:3).

Because God has given psalmists, who are anointed music and worship leaders, a special gift, he pours out his Spirit through them so that the spiritual atmosphere literally changes when they start to sing and play. In Chapter 3 we discussed some of the qualities of the Anointing of the Holy Spirit so that we can recognize Jesus. The same applies to the preparation for healing events. Anointed music will lift burdens and destroy yokes. It will quickly get our focus where it belongs—on God's glory.

Let's pray together:

Father, I choose to hold nothing back in seeking your will for my service to you. Make me a "yielded vessel." Teach me to never presume, but always seek your Anointing before I enter ministry. I open myself to all that you would do in me and through me, so that I can be your minister. Release it in me! Let it happen! In Jesus' name. Amen

Journal Questions

1. How do you hear the voice of the Lord when you need wisdom? That is, how does he speak to you?
2. Describe your prayer and fasting with regard to ministry events. Prayerfully ask the Lord how he would have you improve or modify it.
3. What is your "prayer in the Spirit"? What is your attitude and practice with regard to praying in tongues?

---

[1] *Catechism of the Catholic Church*, #1098.

[2] *Roman Missal*, Preface II for the Apostles.

[3] Catholic teaching defines various "modes" of the presence of Christ, holding up in a special way the Eucharistic presence. See *Catechism*, op. cit. #1373–1374.

[4] *Catechism*, #2003.

[5] Sheets, Dutch, *Intercessory Prayer*, Ventura, CA, Regal Books, 1996. p. 96.

[6] *Catechism*, #2003.

[7] *Catechism*, #1999.

Chapter 15

MANIFESTING THE ANOINTING: THE IMMEDIATE PREPARATION

In this chapter, we shall reflect on the preparation that will enable us to accomplish our ministry as Jesus did. He is our model and we are invited to follow his example, for the Bible says that the one who remains in him must "act as he acted" (1 Jn. 2:6). When we enter into healing ministry, we can conduct ourselves along the lines revealed in the Word of God. In Jesus' life, his ministry didn't just happen. He prepared himself for ministry, not only during the first thirty years of his life, but in a habitual daily walk of discipleship. And he also prepared for specific ministerial situations. We can do likewise.

Earlier we discussed some of the dimensions of Jesus' own spiritual baseline and preparation for his ministry. Luke relates that the news of Jesus and his healing ministry "spread all the more, and great crowds assembled to listen to him and to be cured of their ailments, but he would withdraw to deserted places to pray" (Lk. 5:15–16, NAB). Later, the same evangelist states, "In those days he departed to the mountain to pray, and he spent the night in prayer to God" (Lk. 6:12, NAB). What was he doing? It is apparent that he was listening as a disciple to the voice of the Father. In this passage, one of the most momentous occasions in the history of the church was about to take place—the selection of the twelve—and Jesus knew that he had to seek the Father's will about this.

Before he could be the Father's apostle—one who was sent into the world—Jesus had to himself be a disciple in prayer and obedience. The text goes on: "When morning came, he called his disciples to him and chose twelve of them, whom he also designated apostles" (Lk. 6:13, NIV). Jesus was not only on his baseline; for such an important event he needed an immediate preparation time of prayer.

The steps in this chapter can be done alone but are much more effective when done with fellow ministers.

STEP 1: PRAISE AND THANKSGIVING

"Enter his gates with thanksgiving, and his courts with praise" (Ps. 100:4, NIV)

It is when you go into the presence of God that real prayer starts to happen. The Word of God gives us a strategy: it is called praise and thanksgiving. The book of Psalms was the official prayer manual of the Jewish people. A great many of the Psalms are praise and thanksgiving. Praise is a declaration of the greatness of God's being and his attributes, as in this psalm:

> The LORD is king: the peoples tremble; he is throned upon the cherubim; the earth quakes. The LORD is great in Zion, exulted above all the peoples. Let them praise your great and awesome name: holy is God! (Ps. 99:1–3, NAB)

By way of contrast, thanksgiving is a recognition and declaration of what God has done in his mercy:

> Give thanks to the LORD, invoke his name;
> make known among the nations his deeds.

214

Sing praise, play music,
    proclaim all his wondrous deeds!
Glory in his holy name;
    rejoice, O hearts that seek the LORD!
Rely on the mighty LORD;
    constantly seek his face.
Recall the wondrous deeds he has done,
    his signs, and his words of judgment. (Ps. 105:1–5, NAB)

Linda Schubert writes, "The very 'sacrifice' of praise—working at it when we don't feel like it—draws us into the presence of the Lord."[1] She understands the spiritual truth behind starting any prayer with praise. In the book *Miracle Hour*[2] you can find a Litany of Praise that can be followed and personalized as you learn greater depths of this worship form.

Often we are faced with any number of distractions—internal and external—that would prevent us from being fully present to the Lord. Praise and thanksgiving are the best strategies I know of to deal with these.

> I have found that to do ministry, I often have to push through in prayer and praise to the presence of God. It is a "sacrifice" because the egocentric focus within us has to die.

I have found that to do ministry, I often have to push through in prayer and praise to the presence of God. It is a "sacrifice" because the egocentric focus within us has to die. Declaring God's greatness, blessing him, and giving thanks takes the focus off ourselves and our concerns and places it on him. It sets up and models a right relationship between God and his creation. Praise and thanksgiving are an antidote to what is idolatrous in our lives. In praise, you march forward with firm purpose enter his Presence where your worship becomes serious.

STEP 2: THE BLOOD OF JESUS

Deal with Your Sin

Invite the Holy Spirit to Convict You of Sin

Jesus said that when the Spirit of truth comes, he will convict the world in regard to sin (Jn. 16:8). We have worldly parts in us that need this light. Often we are not even aware of these until we receive this precious light. We will never hear the Holy Spirit convict us unless we are willing to ask him where our need lies. Real courage is required to do this as we hand over control to the Holy Spirit. The guilt of sin is dealt with before the cross of Christ.

Repent and Ask for Forgiveness

John says in his first letter, "If anyone does sin, we have an advocate with the Father, Jesus Christ, the upright. He is the sacrifice to expiate our sins" (1 Jn. 2:1, NJB). Admitting to our failures and rebellions, rejecting sin, and asking for forgiveness places them in Jesus' atoning sacrifice. They can no longer be rightly used to detour us.

Forgive

Jesus emphasized that we receive God's forgiveness on the condition that we forgive others (Mt. 6:14). At a healing event this becomes critically important for two reasons: a) If we do not forgive, we are in sin and this is an obstacle for Spirit-led prayer; b) a lack of forgiveness contaminates our prayer to the extent that we minister through those old wounds. Ask the Holy Spirit regularly whom you need to forgive. Remember, forgiveness is not a feeling; it is a decision of the will.

Do Spiritual Warfare

Do Personal Spiritual Battle

Beyond the specific guilt of particular sins, there is in us the issue of "sinfulness," or the inclination to sin. Here we are often dealing in the area of "strongholds"[3]—sinful attitudes, thought patterns, and disordered passions. As we walk in the Spirit of God, he reveals these to each of us. I suggest that if you are dealing with attitudes, thought patterns, or disordered passions in yourself that would interfere with healing ministry, it would be in order to name them directly and renounce them in Jesus' name.

Some typical strongholds that impede healing prayer are lack of forgiveness, false guilt, manipulation, anger, vanity, lust, attitude of inferiority or superiority, judgmental spirit, and many more. If you recognize anything that you battle with on an ongoing basis, it has probably become what is known as a "stronghold." Each of us has his or her particular strongholds to contend with. The blood of Christ is the most powerful of tool we have in spiritual battle. St. Paul says, "The weapons we fight with are not the weapons of the world. On the contrary, they have divine power to demolish strongholds" (2 Cor. 10:4, NIV).

Do Corporate Spiritual Battle

"Be self-controlled and alert. Your enemy the devil prowls around like a roaring lion looking for someone to devour. Resist him, standing firm in the faith" (1 Pt. 5:8–9, NIV). Because Satan was defeated on the cross by the blood of the Lamb, this moment in prayer, while focused on Christ's blood, is an appropriate time to do spiritual battle both for the event itself that we are embarking upon and for our personal ministry in the event.

Each location and community where we minister has its own spiritual battles corresponding to the great work God has purposed for it. This is the spiritual battleground and it involves our spiritual work. Satan tries to impede this work. There is no way with our intelligence to "outwit" the schemes he has devised. Yet God has given us the means to thwart those plans through spiritual work: it is one of the effects of the blood of Christ.

Spiritual Warfare in the Institute for the Healing Ministry

Much of the material in this book is an elaboration on the Institute for the Healing Ministry I directed for three years. The format of each meeting naturally consisted in remote and immediate preparation. After initial praise and prayer, we gave free reign to the Holy Spirit for whatever he wanted to do. We worshiped for about an hour and a half before the formal teaching began. Invariably we did spiritual warfare prayer at the beginning, so that the members should be trained in it, by way of the preparation we have been talking about. But they also frequently needed spiritual warfare in their own lives and ministries. The most frequent comment I kept hearing about these sessions was that the discipline that was maintained in discernment and the use of the gifts, even with a large group, enabled the Holy Spirit to act freely with striking results in a variety of dimensions.

That was never more true than of sessions held in Oakland. They were some of the most powerful ministry sessions I had ever seen, and for many of the sisters and brothers it was a "laboratory experience" in the use of the gifts. One of the aspects that affected us the most was the fact that we were led to spend a significant amount of time doing the remedial work of repentance and spiritual warfare. I never ceased to be amazed at the oppression—even in those attempting to do healing prayer—of people who had diabolic influences, curses, witch-doctoring, and other occult practices in their background.

Week after week, as we dealt with these issues, it was exhilarating to see the growth and maturity in the ministries of a great number of these sisters and brothers as they learned and practiced the preparation. But it was often a hard struggle. When we reached the step of spiritual warfare in our preparation, we could not continue until these issues had been dealt with, sometimes at great length. Afterward, we were released into deeper ministry through a full manifestation of the gifts. We saw how both individuals and communities can become unblocked and unstuck through this type of preparation.

Lamentably, as time has passed, a few communities have left this work off of their preparation because it involves too much effort. Some leave it off through neglect or even the poisonous ideas of untrained naysayers. When this happens it is all too easy to see the results in loss of spiritual power, infighting, and drift in focus: they have neglected to put on the armor of God!

One word of advice: it is important that when doing preparation that includes strong spiritual work such as described above, brothers and sisters who have the spiritual authority and maturity need to lead it. If people who have recognized prophetic gifts or mature leaders are present, they are the appropriate ones (for many reasons) to lead this type of prayer and be obedient to whatever the Spirit indicates needs to be done.

Step 3: Praying in the Covenant

Accept Forgiveness

"God proves his love for us in that while we were still sinners Christ died for us. How much more then, since we are now justified by his blood, will we be saved through him from the wrath" (Rom 5:8–9, NAB). One of the worst fears of Christians is not measuring up to God's standards and not feeling worthy of living in him. I think this is one of the greatest tasks of Christians: to know and be confident that our sins are forgiven.

There are many who spend their whole lives in repentance, in sorrow for past sins. This is wrong. *Asking* for forgiveness is often easier than *accepting* the fact that we are reconciled with God through Christ. Covenant prayer means that, after the "dirty work" of repentance, of dealing with the ugly aspects of our condition as fallen and broken people, we now *receive* what was done on the cross. We give up dwelling on the past and press forward. You can have confidence in God's grace—enough confidence that you are considered clean and justified before God, ready to enter into more intimate aspects of his life. Yes, all of us are unworthy in ourselves, but Christ died for our unworthiness, and through his blood, he has made us worthy. "Let us then approach the throne of grace with confidence, so that we may receive mercy and find grace to help us in our time of need" (Heb. 4:16, NIV).

Live the Present Moment Fully in God's Covenant

Forgiveness, healing, deliverance, living the life of grace, and being ministers of God's grace are all part of covenant living. A covenant is a sacred agreement in which, according to the Bible, God makes us his people and we agree to receive this gift. The covenant sealed in Christ's blood is the spiritual structure, or conduit, through which this divine life flows. It is not a matter of being there one moment and not being there the next. Living in the covenant is a constant. Forgiveness, healing, deliverance from evil, and all grace are ours constantly. Christ died not only for your past sins, but those of your future as well. When we fall, our covenant right, bought and paid for on our behalf by Christ, allows us to repent, get back up to our spiritual baseline, dust ourselves off and go forward.

In the healing ministry, one of the important deceptions of the enemy is the false conviction that we are not worthy to do this ministry. That would be true if it weren't for the covenant sealed in the blood of Jesus. It is sealed and done as far as God is concerned. Our only task is to let the grace in. Covenant prayer means that I am constantly aware that I must be on the receiving end of grace, if

I am to let it flow through me. Walking in forgiveness, I must maintain myself open, ready and eager to receive the healing of my own brokenness. We must get beyond ourselves and our feelings regarding unworthiness so we can be used by God for our sisters and brothers.

Journal Questions for Covenant Prayer

1. What are the most persistent obstacles you face when you start to pray for ministry events? What do you need to do on your part to overcome them? How can praise help with this?
2. What effect of the blood of Christ do you most need in order to be free for ministry? What aspects of yourself need to be put to death?

Put on Your Armor: The Prayer of Protection

When there is much at stake spiritually in a ministerial event (and in healing prayer there usually is), you can be sure that the enemy is going to want to block it. That is why at every event where I minister in healing prayer there will be a Prayer of Protection. This prayer follows the same process of preparation that is outlined above.

Below you will find a model for such a prayer. I recommend that anyone who is involved in healing ministry pray this or something similar every day. When we are involved in anointed ministry, that is, lifting burdens and breaking yokes, the enemy will try to detour us at every opportunity. He will try to "take us out" where we are the weakest. We need protection in prayer. Individually, prayer like this can form an important part of our spiritual baseline. In addition, we can use this prayer in our immediate preparation before each spiritual event. Because healing events vary so widely, the prayer can be modified, as the Spirit leads, to fit the occasion.

Before you continue, I recommend that you carefully read this Prayer of Protection. Ask God if this is something that he would have you use in a personalized form for your spiritual baseline or a modified version for spiritual events. There may well be concepts and phrases in this prayer that you do not yet understand. They will become clearer to you as you study more about the ministry. In a later volume, we will study the prayer in more detail. When it is prayed in common, it can be adapted to the plural.

Introduction: Focus on and Praise God

Heavenly Father, I [we] praise you for all you are and thank you for all that you have given me. You are my Creator and have redeemed me through the blood of Jesus Christ your Son and you have sealed me with the Holy Spirit for the day of redemption.

Bind Yourself to Jesus

In Jesus' name, I bind my whole person—heart and desires, soul and spirit, body and emotions—to the precious blood of Jesus Christ; I bind my mind to the mind that is in Christ Jesus and I bind myself to your highest and best purpose for my life. Father, anoint me and anoint my prayer as I seek your guidance. [Pray in the Spirit]

Repent of Your Sins and Forgive

I acknowledge my sins before you, Father, repent and ask forgiveness for my sins and failings. I open my heart, Lord, and receive your forgiveness. I also choose this day to forgive all who have ever offended me and in the name of Jesus loose from me any strongholds of unforgiveness.

Bind and Cast Out Evil Spirits

In the name of Jesus Christ, I bind in his precious blood and break the power of all evil spirits of the air, earth, fire, water, and under the earth. I bind all satanic principalities, dominions, thrones, and powers in the blood of Christ. I bind all ministering, generational, and occult spirits and spirits of the capital sins in the blood of Jesus. I command these spirits and any spirits operating through my weaknesses in the name of the Father, the Son, and the Holy Spirit to leave peacefully and quietly and go immediately and directly to the presence of Jesus Christ to be disposed of by him and never again return to harm me.

Come Against and Reverse Curses

In the name of Jesus I come against, cancel, loose from me, and reverse all hexes, curses, spells, and incantations, programs, or assignments ever perpetrated against me, my family, loved ones, finances, property, or ministry.

Cut Unclean and Unholy Bonds

Father, heal my negative emotions and the wounds of my heart and spirit. In Jesus' name I destroy and loose from me every stronghold against the knowledge of God and obedience to Christ. I take the sword of your Spirit, the Word of God, and in Jesus name, cut and sever all unholy and unclean bonds between me and any other person, group or organization.

Ask for the Holy Spirit

Father, fill me completely with your Holy Spirit that I may overflow with your abundant love. Seal me with this same Spirit and anoint me so that guided with His power I may walk in that which you have purposed for me [ask for specific charisms]. All this I ask in the name of Jesus Christ who lives and reigns with you in the unity of the Holy Spirit, one God for ever and ever. Amen.

STEP 4: INVOKING THE HOLY SPIRIT CORPORATELY

The last part of this Prayer for Protection provides a model for praying for the gifts of the Holy Spirit, as they are needed for any particular event. No matter how you pray for protection, it is important to ask for an outpouring of the Holy Spirit. This kind of prayer is useful and excellent:

- God delights that we ask him for his gifts as a body of believers.
- Prayer for the Spirit makes the Church conscious that we need the Anointing so that the ministry of Jesus can be continued.
- It avoids the dangerous pitfall of thinking that just because I am there, God will move. God can always do things in a sovereign way, but he delights that we should pray in awareness of our need.
- In asking for the Spirit, we are surrendering our will to God's and giving consent to what he wills to do.

Experience will teach you about the combinations of spiritual gifts that are needed and therefore can be asked of God. You as a minister will often be able to sense in a general way what God is about to do. Then you can pray for the gifts that will shape that event. As with all preparation, you will need to come into agreement with all who are ministering and work in concert with the leader.

With prayer that the Father, in the name of his Son, pour out a manifestation of his Holy Spirit, your immediate preparation is complete. You can now enter with confidence into the temple of God's glory!

---

[1] Schubert, Linda, *Miracle Hour*, p. 5.

[2] Ibid.

[3] The issue of "strongholds" (2 Cor. 10:3–6), is of vital importance in the healing ministry and forms part of spiritual warfare prayer. They are treated in my third volume of this series. Interesting work on personal strongholds has been done by Dutch Sheets in *Watchman Prayer*, chapter 8 and Liberty Savaard in *Shattering Your Strongholds*, chapter 3. Also, Francis Frangipane presents a helpful perspective in the first part of his work, *The Three Battlegrounds*.

Chapter 16

THE HEALING EVENT

I n this chapter we will review the healing event step by step. Each aspect of the event applies, whether the venue is a healing mass, a large convention, or an individual healing session. The focus and goal of our study of the healing session is to be able to heal as Jesus healed, for we are members of his Body, filled with the Spirit of love and compassion.

STEP 1: FIRST THINGS FIRST—EXTEND HOSPITALITY!

The late Fr. Leo Thomas, a Dominican priest, and Jan Alkire wrote in their beautiful book, *Healing as a Parish Ministry,*

> The power of hospitality is the power of love. If prayer teams offer a supplicant nothing more than their hospitality, that act itself is healing. By welcoming a hurting person into their hearts, team members remove isolation, helplessness and hopelessness—three major blocks to healing. A supplicant who experiences the unconditional love of a prayer team is free to be herself, with no mask and no role to play.[1]

Hospitality is the very first thing individuals should sense when they come to us for healing. It is an atmosphere that is created and provided by you who are ministering. Hospitality is a way we show people respect and love. In a healing event, hospitality is not just a polite reception and making supplicants feel comfortable. It goes beyond that.

Being a minister of healing prayer is being a host. The word "host" comes from the Latin word *hostia,* which means "victim" of a sacrifice. At any healing event we know it is really Jesus who is the Host. Catholics call the bread that is used for Holy Communion the Host. We call Jesus in the Blessed Sacrament "the Host," because he was the victim of sacrifice, the Lamb slain for the forgiveness of sins. In the time of the healing event we, like Jesus, put aside ourselves and pour out our lives for the supplicant in prayer. In that way we are "hosts."

People who are broken need restoration. The healing session is a time for restoration to begin to occur. The atmosphere of hospitality is the climate that the supplicant steps into when there is a healing event. Healing prayer ministers have a pastoral calling—to guide the supplicants into the holiness of God. There should be a sense of holiness in the hospitable environment of the healing event. Holiness in the Hebrew sense means that something or someone has been "set apart." In the Greek, holiness means something is saturated with the divine life of God. We should be receiving our supplicants in a hospitable climate—a space characterized by holiness, both set apart and saturated with God's life-giving presence.

The healing event should also be a place where the kindness and the mercy of God abound. Jesus, the Good Shepherd, and the Holy Spirit, the Consoler, become real to the wounded. The supplicants should leave with a sense of God's merciful involvement in their lives, despite any brokenness. The result of hospitality in the healing event is a sense of well-being.

Psalm 23:2 declares,

He makes me lie down in green pastures,
he leads me beside quiet waters,
he restores my soul. (NIV)

STEP 2 : DISCERN THE SUPPLICANT'S SPIRITUAL BASELINE

Recently, I had a ministry engagement with two thousand leaders of the charismatic renewal in San Salvador, Central America. I was to lead worship and teach on the Anointing and its effects. At one point I sensed the inspiration to circulate among these leaders before the service started. I was overwhelmed by the sense of a firm base of surrender that I discerned in the leadership. This enabled me as the principle minister of the assembly to proceed to lead into deep worship. We went far into anointed ministry that night.

After receiving the supplicant and creating the atmosphere for healing by virtue of your hospitality, your attention must turn to the task of discernment. You need to take great caution that your discernment is not confused with a judgmental attitude that would compromise the healing environment. People in the healing ministry need to be discerning, not judgmental.

Those who are in charge of the healing event discreetly use their spiritual gifts of discernment and word of knowledge to discern where the supplicant is with respect to his or her spiritual baseline. When I go to a healing event, whether it is a healing mass or an individual healing session, I begin at once to discern the levels of faith, conversion, and adherence to the Father's will that are present. We saw how these three dispositions open an individual to an encounter with the risen Lord. We cannot automatically assume that healing prayer will lead to a great encounter with the Lord. These conditions need to be present. We must attend to the task of shepherding in order to encourage supplicants and to bring them to a level of faith, conversion, and seeking God's will. This is where a true depth of healing can occur.

Doing the Maximum

In June of 2001, I was called to a healing mass in San Jose, California. For several weeks I had been personally going through a "spiritual funk" of inner trials. The only preparation I did on the day of the mass was what I did alone with the Lord that afternoon on the side of an east San Jose hill. I had discerned deep in my spirit that this community was in bad spiritual shape. In my "flesh" that made me even more depressed and resistant to seeking Lord's will.

Finally in this struggle, I said to God, "I feel so bad. Tonight I will just do the minimum. I don't feel like doing this service and don't want to waste my time and energy anyway."

Immediately, I heard strongly and clearly, "You will do the maximum."

I was receiving that God wanted this community to know the basic fundamentals of faith and to develop a relationship with him. I asked God, "How can I talk about faith when my spiritual ground feels like it is crumbling beneath me?"

He said, "Do you really believe that?"

I thought for a moment. "Well no, not really. But that's how I feel!"

"Then just obey, and you will see what I will do."

I arrived at the church and confirmed that the community was indeed in chaos. The disorder and disorientation among the leadership was so great that it was affecting the faith of the whole community of about four hundred. Almost everything they did or said that evening was becoming a obstacle for a healing environment. No one I knew came to provide prayer support, as is my custom. Besides the disorganization of the event in general, the large music group sang and played in such a way that the songs were not recognizable. No one was worshiping! There had been no preparation by the leaders (they didn't even conceive of it) and those designated to pray with me didn't know the first thing about healing prayer or spiritual warfare. They didn't even provide a microphone for me.

Totally bewildered, I exclaimed, "God, what am I to do with this?" Surrounded by so many people, I felt alone, abandoned, sorry for myself.

"Take authority over every part of this event, step by step . . . and keep your message on the target of faith." This was the word of wisdom I received and needed. I took charge of everything, from getting a microphone to setup for the mass. I personally took over the worship from the altar (the musicians were only too glad) and led the prayer. In an instant the atmosphere changed, as I started to share the word of faith. During my message I was interrupted by one of the leaders with a demonic manifestation so strong that the person had to be physically removed from the church.

When a group or a person is not on a suitable spiritual baseline, the leader of prayer needs to deal with that issue first, before all else. This concept is simple but often overlooked. That night hundreds of people committed themselves to Jesus Christ and hundreds reported healing. When I returned to where I was staying that evening, the people remarked, "Father, it is evident that you have had a breakthrough!" And indeed I had. Both in me and in the people I served. No matter how adverse the circumstances, the Anointing is a simple matter of faith, listening and obedience. And since that time, no more "spiritual funk!"

The Supplicant's Faith

Often at healing services or masses when I discern the faith level to be palpably low I begin the mass or healing service with a simple exhortation on the role of faith based on the Word of God.

I will bring out the examples of faith in the Bible and convey that word of faith before healing prayer even starts. Why? Because people's faith level must be increased in order for deeper healing to take place. They need expectant faith. The scriptures affirm, "Faith comes from hearing the message, and the message is heard through the word of Christ" (Rom 10:17, NIV). Therefore, to speak faith into the spiritual atmosphere of a healing event has a very positive and prophetic effect.

The Supplicant's Conversion

The same is true for conversion. In this delicate matter you will have to assume a pastoral attitude. As shepherds, we take a spiritual staff (a symbol of authority) in order to lead individuals to repent from sin. We must remember that the staff is for the sheep but a club is for spiritual enemies. The pastor cannot be taking the club to the sheep! We cannot "beat people over the head" if there is sin in their lives. I acknowledge that some might be called to rebuke sin, but pastors, being called to gentle shepherding, need to resist moralizing (telling people what's right and wrong in their lives). First of all, I am a sinner and recognize the fact. But more importantly, I have found that when we get into the Lord's holy presence, the Spirit will convict of sin. The Holy Spirit will speak to us about failures in our lives when we get into his Presence. If there is a need for conversion and a letting go of sin, let's be pastorally sensitive and gentle!

The Supplicant's Adherence to the Father's Will

Many people go to healing events to try to "manipulate" God. They think they can somehow "twist his arm," or that by the force of their prayer, they will get a hearing with God. This represents a magical, fanciful approach to God. This calls for discernment concerning the supplicant's adherence to the will of God. Is there is something lacking in this area? Without being judgmental, a gentle shepherding will lead people to consent to what God wants to do in their lives. If I discern resistance, I'll often ask individuals or groups directly, "Do you consent that he would reveal his will to you and that he would change your mind about some things?" I ask if they will allow God to change their way of thinking. This has the powerful effect of breaking down strongholds that would prevent healing.

STEP 3: ENTER INTO PRAYER

Keep Good Order

Almost anything can happen in a healing event. This means that those in charge are to be prepared to deal with any eventuality. Healing prayer, just on a psychological level, can be an overwhelming experience, especially if a supplicant has never received it before or if he or she is in deep psychological pain. This can manifest itself numerous ways during healing prayer. People can express strong emotions, shake, or even become hysterical. Those inexperienced in the healing ministry sometimes mistakenly think these are manifestations of healing taking place. Some think it is a sure sign that the devil is at work. Don't be fooled. Most of the time it is the flesh! As you enter into prayer, promote a tranquil atmosphere and don't lose control of the event, whether it be a large service or just a few people.

On many occasions I have led services where people have started to "lose it." For the sake of the Body of Christ, this must be handled swiftly, charitably, yet in a decisive way. Your first assumption should be that this manifestation is not demonic (as some would presume), but rather the flesh reacting to a powerful spiritual experience. Gently and audibly encourage the person to receive the gift of the Lord's peace. If the behavior persists, gently but firmly state that the person is not here for this kind of behavior and directly ask the person to get control of himself or herself. If that fails, then it may be necessary to have the person physically removed if you are in a public gathering.

I am not referring here to what clearly is demonic. Handling demonic manifestations will be addressed in another volume. What we do need to understand is that people who manifest hysteria (losing control of themselves) are most often in the flesh. A couple of years ago at a generational healing retreat of about sixty people there was a small group of women who in worship, took turns being so overcome that they fell on the floor, rigid, in a cruciform position.

We were before the Blessed Sacrament in worship when suddenly one of these women did this. The others in her little group gathered around, according to their custom, to pray over the affected one. It was a self-induced, pseudo-mystical, trance-like state. Seeing that this was blatantly out of order and that this scene was affecting the whole assembly, I went through the process of trying to "bring her back to herself," but was too late.

Finally I insisted that the others go back to worshiping God and leave her alone. Losing her "audience," she finally rejoined the group. The next day another member of this group did the same thing, but this time there were fewer people in the room. I immediately insisted that everyone leave the room. She had lost her audience and quickly came to herself. In healing events, I make it clear that hysterical behavior is not tolerated. The gift of discernment—which distinguishes among the human, the demonic, and the divine—is necessary to keep the session in the flow of the Holy Spirit. The leadership of the event is responsible for this discernment.

A good and simple rule to follow is this: if some action or words takes the focus off of God and puts it on something or someone else, you can be pretty sure it is not from God.

Respect the Supplicant's Needs

Respect is needed for the brother or sister who seeks healing. What does it mean to "respect the need"? Jesus respected the needs of the people who came to him with brokenness. He recognized they were in pain from symptoms of disease. Anybody who is in healing ministry must never say to a supplicant, "Your pain is not important." People's felt needs were important to Jesus and, as love demands, they need to be important to us. Like Jesus, we can respect the supplicant's perceived need even if he or she is ignoring (or unable to deal with) the root cause. This respect is maintained even as we shepherd the person to a deeper level of awareness of true needs.

> As humans we all have our boundaries. This is highly important in the healing ministry.

Maintain Confidentiality

One of the best ways we can inspire confidence and promote healing is the sealing of the healing prayer in confidentiality. On the natural plane our supplicants need to know that they are in an emotionally and spiritually safe place. That includes the issue of confidentiality. From the outset when personal issues are shared let the supplicant know that what is shared stays in the room, unless it is by freely given mutual agreement that it may be shared elsewhere.[2] This may happen when you need to consult someone else about a particular issue in healing. Part of your sacred duty as God's minister is to honor that commitment to confidentiality.

Respect Boundaries

People with brokenness have the felt need of having their symptoms addressed. In addition to confidentiality, the sister or brother has the need to be treated with respect, discretion, and appropriateness. These are delicate issues. Some ministers of healing cross personal boundaries. I have been a supplicant and have experienced ministers who were invasive of my physical, psychological, or spiritual boundaries.

As humans we all have our boundaries. This is highly important in the healing ministry. It means that "personal space" is not invaded. I have seen healing sessions where ministers assume that supplicants always want to have hands laid on them. This is not necessarily true. What is appropriate is that if you sense you need to lay hands on someone, you can ask, "Would you mind if I placed my hand on your shoulder or gently on your head?" That really means *lightly*. You don't squash the person's head down or push him or her back, as has happened to me more than a few times! Healthy and holy boundaries are the way that we care of each other. Remember, one of the meanings of *paga*—intercession—is a boundary.

The reason for discussing the issues of confidentiality and boundaries is that you are ministering to people who have been wounded in some way. Most likely, they perceive much of their world through those wounds. If their boundaries are broken, this can create a deepening of their wounds and jeopardize your ministry with them.

Let's consider three kinds of boundaries in relation to the healing ministry: physical, emotional, and spiritual.

Physical Boundaries

Most people want to be touched in a safe way, and so the laying on of hands can be a wonderful gesture just on a natural plane. However, if you are praying for someone who has, for instance, been sexually abused, laying on of hands might be perceived— even if unconsciously—as an aggressive move, and it will block healing. Then there is the issue of where to touch. In general, I would recommend that if you sense that laying on of hands would be appropriate, ask the person if he or she would mind if you lay your hand on the head or shoulder while you pray. Or you might just want to hold hands during the prayer. With some, no touch at all might be the appropriate way to pray, at least at first.

Laying hands on other parts of the body *may* be appropriate, but always with discretion and respect. I would definitely avoid stroking or rubbing the supplicant: it is distracting and is often misinterpreted as a sexual overture. Also to be avoided is waving your hands over the person or an afflicted area as if you were transferring some spiritual or "psychic" energy. That is a New Age technique and gives the impression that you have some power apart from God.

Emotional Boundaries

The second kind of boundary is emotional. Violation of this boundary includes prying into people's personal lives when they are not yet ready to share. Depth of sharing depends on the trust that is generated between minister and supplicant. When emotional boundaries are crossed, people feel "violated." A minister of healing prayer is not there as a psychological therapist or counselor. When personal things are shared, make a mental note of each general issue, and bring it to prayer (something that the supplicant is often unable to do). In doing this you will show a profound respect for the felt need. Not only will the Lord work supernaturally through your prayer, but the person will feel that you respect and honor him or her before God.

Spiritual Boundaries

The third type of boundary is spiritual as it touches on spiritual issues. The spiritual part of us is where we make important decisions of conscience and is the heart of our relationship with God. I would like to share three aspects of spiritual boundaries:

a. **Respect the person's conscience.** You honor someone's emotional boundary when you respect the person's conscience. That is, you do not pressure the supplicant to divulge sin or other shameful situations. The issue may very well come up; you may even receive a word of knowledge about a sinful situation. If so, that is for you to pray as an intercessor apart from the healing event. If the person volunteers the information, then at that point you can pray and minister. If a supplicant indicates, "I don't want to talk about this," immediately and gently move on to another subject. A person will share when he or she is ready.

b. Be careful about spiritual warfare issues. During the healing event, you may discern that there are spiritual warfare issues present. That information must be used discreetly. It can do an immense amount of harm—and is indeed spiritual abuse—to reveal to someone that he or she is "demonized" and then move into deliverance prayer when the person is not ready for it. What to do? Again, intercede apart from the healing event for the person's deliverance. If you are alone with the person, deliverance ministry can quickly become harmful in a number of ways—to you and to the person if you are not solidly trained in it. In the third volume of this series we will explore times, places, and circumstances that are appropriate for deliverance ministry.

c. Be gentle with burdens of prayer and spiritual works. While doing healing prayer you are in a pastoral realm. This means in all cases that healing is a coming into a whole relationship with the Lord. Leading the supplicant to Christ is done with a great deal of wisdom. Therefore it is important not to place great burdens of prayer or spiritual works of him or her. The Holy Spirit has a wonderful way of guiding people to Christ. This boundary entails discerning where the Lord has led the person and affirming the positive. Likewise, this means that if the person is part of a denomination that doesn't agree with yours, you don't go into a mode of making the person "see the light" of your church doctrines. Healing ministry is not about trying to make converts to your church body; it is about making the Body of Christ whole. I have had much experience praying with Protestant and Orthodox brothers and sisters for healing. It is always enriching to me to see how God works in unfamiliar ways!

Shepherd into Truth

Understanding boundaries will make a minister of healing sensitive to the truth about the supplicant and in God's way help the minister to pastor the supplicant into a deeper relationship with God. Psychological and moral problems, together with people's own sinfulness, cause a great deal of distortion about who an individual is. But God's truth is at the root level of a person's being. Learning about and dealing with a supplicant's dysfunctional behavior in light of the Word of God ensures that the healing is maintained.

In the case of the paralytic discussed in an earlier chapter, the man's physical symptom was paralysis but Jesus discerned the root cause to be sin: "Child, your sins are forgiven" (Mk. 2:5, NAB). Another biblical example of getting at a deeper awareness of truth is found in the account of the Samaritan woman in the fourth chapter of John. Jesus poignantly asked the Samaritan woman to go get her husband.

She said, "I have no husband."

Jesus replied, "You are right when you say you have no husband. The fact is, you have had five husbands, and the man you now have is not your husband. What you have just said is quite true" (Jn. 4:17–18, NIV). This was a moment of truth.

We will hear a lot about people's sinfulness in the healing ministry. Sin is a falsehood, a lie. Most often it is a lie about ourselves that ends up cursing us and blocking our destiny in God. Getting to the truth with the supplicant means seeking to uncover the mystery of what God has destined for him or her. When we have an eye toward the root cause, we have a eye toward the truth. God's original purpose in Christ is to act redemptively so as to restore us to the truth. Therefore you act as a minister of the restoration in truth.

"The thief comes to rob, to kill and to destroy, but I have come that they may have life and have it in abundance" (Jn. 10:10, NJB). If we are not in line with our destiny of being in Christ's image, some part of us has been taken away, killed, or otherwise destroyed. The purpose of healing prayer is none other than to restore, to bring life, and to make whole the image of God that has been distorted by sickness.

Healing is the freedom to embrace God, his will, purpose, and destiny. This is a different idea of healing than the one to which we have been accustomed. This way of thinking turns our prayer around. The person ministering healing prayer has the mind of a profound longing, awareness, and constant questioning about God's purpose. It is crucial to understand that God wants to heal the supplicant so that the person can freely embrace his will. If we are ministering in God's Spirit, we are ministering according to God's heart. And that *paga* of intercession takes on a prophetic dimension that puts the supplicant in line with his or her destiny.

Journal Questions for Starting Healing Prayer

1. How hospitable are you capable of being?
2. Where does good order need to improve in your ministry?
3. Compose a well-rounded healing prayer for someone that you know needs God's healing.

[1] Thomas and Alkire, *Healing as a Parish Ministry*, p. 68.
[2] The exceptions to confidentiality are if someone's (including the supplicant's) life is in immediate danger, or if it becomes clear that children are being abused. In those cases, the local authorities are to be notified.

Chapter 17

To Heal as Jesus Healed

Let us join together in a prayer:

Loving Father, we come before you in the name of Jesus your Son and we ask you to send your Holy Spirit, not only to transform our hearts but the whole of our lives and especially our ministry. We pray that there would be a divine manifestation of the Anointing in all we do for you. We want to heal as your Son Jesus healed. Open us, Lord, to the full operation of your Holy Spirit. We ask for those gifts that would enable us to serve and minister in the Body of your Son. And may all we do give you the greatest honor and glory. Amen

Gathering Together as the Body of Christ

Jesus said, "Where two or three are gathered together in my name, there am I in the midst of them" (Mt. 18: 20, NAB). There are three elements of this scripture for those who would gather that are of central importance in the ministry of healing.

1. The Gathering of God's People

Whether a gathering consists of two or three or several thousand, what is important is that there is a coming together. The word "church" comes from *ekklesia* (Greek) or *qahal-Yahweh* (Hebrew), meaning a gathering of God's people. To be the Church of Jesus Christ means we come together as a body, the Body of Christ. St. Paul calls the Church the Body of Christ consisting of many members, indispensable to each other, coming as many parts to co-work with the Holy Spirit (1 Cor. 12:12–17). The ministry of healing is expressed not apart from, not independently of, but centrally in the Body of Christ. It is not, as some in the extreme have said, a fringe ministry, but an integral part of the Church.

2. Prayer in the Name of Jesus

The power of the name of Jesus heals, lifts up, delivers and restores: "It is the name of Jesus that fully manifests the supreme power of the "name which is above every name" (Phil. 2:9–10). "The evil spirits fear his name; in his name his disciples perform miracles, for the Father grants all they ask in this name."[1] Jesus promised that those who pray in his name would have power to do immense things. As we have seen, those who *truly* pray in the name of Jesus are not praying their own desires; they pray, according to the biblical sense, in the person of Jesus. Praying in the person of Jesus means that one assumes full measure of being a member of the Body of Christ. Gathering together for healing prayer is a profound way of being Church.

How then shall we pray in the healing event? Begin with praise and thanksgiving for God's goodness and mercy and with a confident affirmation of his healing power. In your own words present the supplicant to the Father or Jesus and focus on the specific healing you are asking for. As much as possible, present to God the pain or symptom the supplicant has articulated. If you sense it is appropriate, move in petitionary prayer to the root cause of the illness. Francis MacNutt puts it this way:

> In praying for the sick person—with or without the laying on of hands—we can be spontaneous and improvise prayer for healing . . . We can assume any posture that is most comfortable for us—sitting, kneeling, or standing—where we can best forget ourselves and relax and concentrate on the presence of God.[2]

Once we get started in this fashion, we can let the Spirit take hold of the prayer and carry us to a deeper place of ministry.

All healing prayer, therefore, is based on gathering as the Body of Christ, the use of his name and the power of his Presence.

3. The Presence of Jesus

Jesus assures us of his Presence when he says that when two or three are gathered in his name, "I am there among them." When we gather in Jesus' name he gives us the honor of the divine Presence, the Presence that heals through the power of the Holy Spirit.

All healing prayer, therefore, is based on gathering as the Body of Christ, the use of his name and the power of his Presence. The manifestation of the Anointing to heal, which is the power of the Holy Spirit, is essential for the healing event. In Chapter 2 we looked at the aspects of the Anointing in Jesus' life. Now let's look at how it works in a healing event. It is here that this special power is put into operation. Above all techniques, methods, or styles, the Anointing is manifested to destroy unholy yokes and lift burdens, heal and bring into relationship with God.

WHAT TO DO IN HEALING PRAYER

In the Gospel of Mark a deaf man with a speech impediment is brought to Jesus. Jesus took him away from the crowds. Then he put his fingers into the man's ears and touched his tongue with his spit. "Then he looked up to heaven and groaned, and said to him, 'Ephphatha!' (that is, 'Be opened!') And [immediately] the man's ears were opened, his speech impediment was removed, and he spoke plainly" (Mk. 7:34–35, NAB).

In this passage three elements come together that normally are included in healing ministry: gestures, a prayer in the Spirit, and the use of words. It is probably not a great idea that you should put your fingers into people's ears and touch their tongues with spittle. Culturally, you would be violating some boundaries. Beyond this, though, we can draw important principles for the healing ministry from the process Jesus used.

Jesus receives a public request to lay hands on a deaf man with a speech impediment. He includes the *gesture* of laying on of hands. It is a symbolic gesture that speaks of being chosen. In the tradition of the Jewish and Christian faiths when hands are laid on someone there is a *choosing*, a singling out and a setting aside for God's special purpose. In the healing ministry the gesture says this person has been chosen so that the works of God can be shown forth in him. But there is another message that is conveyed personally to the person with brokenness: You are special, cared for, and loved by the Church and by God. It is a symbolic point of contact, but be careful not to claim that it is an "energy transfer" point. That would be biblically and theologically questionable.

If possible, lay your hands gently and directly on the person seeking healing, according to the guidelines set forth above concerning boundaries. Laying on of hands is itself a boundary, a *paga* of intercession because it is "a place of meeting." You might notice that the palms of your hands become hot as you pray. That can be a physical manifestation of the Anointing of the Holy Spirit, but don't get distracted by it. Rather, keep your focus on that which the Lord wants to do.

WHAT TO FEEL IN HEALING PRAYER

The passage in Luke indicates that Jesus looked up and sighed. This action of looking up and sighing evidently was a prayer. It didn't have to be a prayer of words. Many times in healing ministry our prayer is the action of simply lifting up of human heart, spirit, and mind to God in favor of the supplicant without words. This is a basic aspect of intercession. I am personally not one for groaning in prayer. However, St. Paul says that "the Spirit personally makes our petitions for us in groans that cannot be put into words" (Rom 8:26, NJB).

A very special sister in the Lord with whom I often have the privilege of praying reports that when she is burdened by the Spirit she often finds herself grunting as spiritual ministry takes place. (She's very discreet about it.) Another friend, who is an evangelical pastor with whom I have prayed several times, tends to groan in deep sighs. The point is that our prayer be taken over by the Spirit of God. You will often be called to be an intercessor while someone else is taking the lead in the verbal prayer. Besides "being in agreement" with that person's prayer, you can sense the deep movement of the Spirit as you support the healing prayer. If you have a "prayer language" you can use it without being distracting by praying "under your breath" in tongues, unless it would be evident that this kind of prayer would be appropriate to be louder.

WHAT TO SAY IN HEALING PRAYER

Jesus says "*Ephphatha!*" which is the Aramaic word for "be opened." Jesus pronounces a word over the man and that word conveys an element of faith and expectation. The word is put into the "spiritual atmosphere." It was only one word! (What a lesson for me in my prayer!) Jesus' prayer was not a rambling on, but a get-to-the-point piercing of the heavenly places. He was not interested in impressing himself, others, or God with eloquence or flashy concepts. That's how you can heal as Jesus did—simply!

If you are leading the prayer or are going to contribute to it, you might consider this simple pattern:

- *Acknowledge* who God is and what he can do in praise and thanksgiving.
- *Summarize* briefly what the supplicant has asked to be prayed for, respecting the felt-need.
- *Focus in your prayer* to ask Jesus to touch that area or need with his healing power.
- *Be open to pray* discreetly for whatever you sense God is moving you to pray in Spirit-led intercession.
- *Use the gifts of the Spirit.* If it is in good order, they can be expressed outwardly.
- *Ask that his plan* be released and that he be glorified through this.
- *Pray in the Name of Jesus*, as he has commanded us to do.

One of the ways that God works powerfully in healing prayer is when we use the Bible—the Word of God—as a "sword." By that I mean using the phrases and concepts contained in the word to formulate the words of our prayers. Those who know the scriptures are also used more by the Spirit of God in manifesting the charisms. It adds a deep dimension to what we say in prayer.

The more we are acquainted with it and know the Bible, the more the Holy Spirit can bring to our minds the wonderful principles and images that are contained in it. "All scripture is inspired by God and useful for refuting error, for guiding people's lives and teaching them to be upright" (2 Tim. 3:16, NJB). We can use the scriptures as a tool to build people up and point them to their destiny in Christ Jesus.

MANIFESTATIONS OF THE SPIRIT

The greatest expression of being in the Body of Christ is when the different members are functioning together. This working together is the context of the *charismata*, or spiritual gifts, that are enumerated in chapters 12, 13 and 14 of Paul's first letter to the Corinthians. There is a list of nine "charismatic" gifts. While acknowledging the importance of other gifts enumerated elsewhere, for the sake of the healing prayer session we will pay special attention to this list of gifts and discuss their application in the healing ministry.

> When God gathers us together as Christians, his purpose is to unveil himself both through the sacraments and through the charismatic gifts.

Now to each one the manifestation of the Spirit is given for the common good. To one there is given through the Spirit the *message of wisdom*, to another the *message of knowledge* by means of the same Spirit, to another *faith* by the same Spirit, to another *gifts of healing* by that one Spirit, to another *miraculous powers*, to another *prophecy*, to another *distinguishing between spirits*, to another *speaking in different kinds of tongues*, and to still another the *interpretation of tongues*. All these are the work of one and the same Spirit, and he gives them to each one, just as he determines. (1 Cor. 12:7–11, NIV, italics added)

St. Paul first affirms, "Now to each one the *manifestation* of the Spirit is given for the common good" (italics added). Let's focus on the word "manifestation." The Greek word used is *phanerosis*, meaning to "make visible" or "show forth." It conveys a similar idea to the Greek word, *epiphania*, or epiphany, meaning a showing forth or a revealing of what is hidden—somewhat akin to *revelation*—taking away the "veil." When God gathers us together as Christians, his purpose is to unveil himself both through the sacraments and through the charismatic gifts.

There is something that happens when people are gathered together as the anointed Body of Christ that takes away the veil that is over our eyes with respect to the Spirit. It is never possible to do this completely without coming together as his Body, in holy communion with each other. This is true no matter how fulfilling individual devotions might be. Our gathering provides the atmosphere for the showing forth of the Spirit of God in the charisms. A healing service, mass, or session unveils a God who delights in healing, lifting up his people, and manifesting in greater measure the destiny to which they are called. Leanne Payne writes, "Failure to move in the gifts of the Spirit is rooted in the failure to understand Epiphany, the Presence of God dawning upon us, making Jesus manifest in our midst."[3]

There are particular expressions and ways in which God unveils himself when people are under the Anointing of the Holy Spirit. These become evident when God is at work for the common good to edify and build the Body of his Son. These expressions are the gifts of the Spirit. When we exercise our spiritual gifts, we show forth the character of God and therefore make the Body of Christ look more like Christ himself. That is why the heart and mind of anyone in a healing ministry or regularly doing healing prayer must be to build up the Body of Christ. When this is in action, the multiplicity of gifts is readily visible.

How wonderful are the works of the Spirit,
revealed in so any gifts!
Yet how marvelous is the unity
the Spirit creates from their diversity,
as he dwells in the hearts of your children,
filling the whole Church with his presence
and guiding it with his wisdom![4]

For a Catholic believer the healing session in some way parallels the celebration of the sacraments, especially the Eucharist, as a normal expression of communion in the Body of Christ. The Second Vatican Council stated that the clearest expression of the Church takes place in worship, especially the Eucharist.[5] That is to say that in the Eucharistic celebration there is a wonderful harmony—all the participants taking their own places and ministering to God in their own proper way. We see God unveiled in the Eucharistic assembly! So also in the gathering in Jesus' name for healing there is a reflection of the Body of Christ: God's beauty, greatness, and almighty power show forth.

The charisms are ultimately works, or energies, of the Father. They are manifestations, or a showing forth, of the Holy Spirit. Spiritual gifts are also manifestations of the Body of Christ, so our prayer is perfectly trinitarian. That is, opening ourselves to the works of the Father, showing his Spirit in the Body of Christ. Our gathering is a reflection of the Holy Trinity himself. The Russians have a wonderful way of putting this in their concept of *sobornost*. It means that the Church strives to be a manifestation of the Holy Trinity.

When the Spirit is manifested, God is unveiled:

- The face of God is uncovered as Father in all his works.
- God is revealed as Jesus, the eternal Word of God made flesh.
- God is revealed as the Spirit when we see the energy of the manifestations in the charisms.

This is at the heart of trinitarian theology, a trinitarian way of praying and a trinitarian way of being Church.

Is Every Mass a Healing Mass?

Several months ago, a lay evangelist who often works with a well-known priest came to our area, preaching and bringing people to Christ. When he was told that there would be a healing mass in the same place the following month he became coarse and argumentative, insisting the there was no such thing as a "healing mass." Mimicking the priest with whom he works, he began to ridicule the idea of a special healing mass with the slogan, "Every mass is a healing mass."

True enough! Being so close to the death and resurrection of Jesus Christ in the Eucharist provides the power for the believer to be healed (and God always desires to heal). But aside from the fact that the Roman Catholic Church officially provides for special masses for healing in the *Roman Missal*, there is in the Body of Christ a particular manifestation that is related to healing: this is another dimension exercised in the healing ministry under the special Anointing of God's Spirit. And this charism can very well be used in connection with a special celebration of the Eucharist, as has been abundantly demonstrated over the past twenty-five years.

---

[1] *Catechism of the Catholic Church*, #434.
[2] Francis MacNutt, *Healing*, Notre Dame, Ave Maria Press, 1999, p. 162.
[3] Leanne Payne, *The Healing Presence: Curing the Soul through Union with Christ*. Grand Rapids, MI, Baker Books, 1997, p. 114.
[4] Preface for the Mass of Christian Unity (#76), Roman Missal, p. 525.
[5] Vatican Council II, *Constitution on the Sacred Liturgy*, #41.

Chapter 18

THE ANOINTING TO HEAL: MOVING IN THE GIFTS OF THE HOLY SPIRIT

The charisms of the Holy Spirit are essential for a fullness in healing ministry. Leanne Payne,[1] David Ireland,[2] and others have given us some useful ways at looking at nine spiritual gifts enumerated in 1 Corinthians 12:7–11.

The Purposeful Use of the Gifts of the Spirit

Please understand that all charisms have a purpose in God and are meant to be used with purpose. It has often been the case that these charisms have been exercised without any awareness of purpose; that is, where they are leading the individual, group, or community. They were manifested just for the sake of using them or, even worse, for the sake of "showing off." This has often exposed the charismatic renewal to ridicule and futility. God *does* have a purpose in the expressions of the charisms and this purpose can be at least partially known. When this is the case, the manifestation of the charisms is much more readily accepted and recognized as godly and it takes on great power in the Body of Christ. We need to strive earnestly for a purposeful use of these gifts.

One useful way of looking at the gifts of the Spirit is by dividing them into three categories.

Power to *know*
    Gifts of *revelation:*
- discernment of spirits
- word of knowledge
- word of wisdom

Power to *do*
    Gifts of *power:*
- healing
- miracles
- faith

Power to *say*
    Gifts of *inspiration:*
- tongues
- interpretation of tongues
- prophecy

THE POWER TO KNOW

The power to know includes the charisms of discernment of spirits, word of knowledge, and word of wisdom. They are charisms of revelation, so called because through them something is being revealed supernaturally that was not easily known in the natural realm.

The Discernment of Spirits

The charism of discernment of spirits is the ability to know in the supernatural whether something comes from the Spirit of God, from the human spirit, or from demonic spirits. The topic of discernment in the Christian tradition is vast. Many books are written about it. *Both* natural knowledge and the supernatural charism have to be taken into account in discerning issues, movements, charisms, and prayer. This is to say that the person with this charism uses knowledge and reason in harmony with what is received from the Spirit of God.

The charism of discernment wants to get at the real origin of whatever is being considered. A typical example of when discernment of spirits is needed is when someone "feels" oppressed and becomes agitated. I have seen many instances when people "lose it" and become hysterical. As we saw in the previous chapter, individuals and groups often conclude that this is the work of demonic powers. However, these same physical symptoms may be caused by a hormonal imbalance or mental instability. Or the person may be under a large degree of psychological stress due to difficulties in relationships. I have found that this latter cause is by far the most common. When clarity and acceptance come in relationship problems, symptoms seem to get dramatically better. It is fundamental within the Christian teaching of discernment that before concluding that some manifestation is demonic, in which case deliverance prayer would be indicated, it needs to be determined whether there is a natural cause. Otherwise, the prayer can turn into spiritual abuse. The important key in this balance is experience.

When in doubt, a person with the confirmed, known, and experienced gift of discernment should be consulted. People who have the tested charism of discernment know intuitively through the Spirit of God what is coming from God, what is the human spirit or the demonic. These individuals use sound teaching and reason before expressing that discernment and concluding the source of the manifestation.

In Spirit-led healing prayer, we need certain knowledge to recognize whether a manifestation of a gift is indeed from God. This is essential both in evaluating the problems that are taken to prayer, and also to know whether the charisms being expressed are real, authentically from the Spirit.

It is important to know with whom you are ministering. Once when I was presiding over a healing mass in northern California, at the end I was led to ask for three (and only three) testimonies. Several brothers and sisters who were gifted in healing prayed with me. I knew that one sister, Cheryl, was very gifted with healing charisms. I also knew that one thing Cheryl didn't have was discernment. During the mass we saw dramatic healings take place and the testimonies were having a faith-building impact. At the end of the time for testimonies, Cheryl motioned to me vigorously that there was still another testimony. Putting aside the word of wisdom I had received, and also the fact of Cheryl's lack of discernment, I accepted her suggestion and asked the young lady whose testimony Cheryl was excited about to come forward.

The poor young woman was psychologically ill and began to testify how that day she had lost her job and started to feel desperate. The testimony went from bad to worse. I was interviewing her before a full church, now feeling "dis-edified" and straining to find something positive in the woman's "testimony." I managed to salvage something, but it was a lesson for me about the importance of knowing who can exercise the gift of discernment in the healing ministry.

The charism of discernment is manifested in the healing ministry as an indication or a confirmation regarding the origin of brokenness as a confirmation or check of the other gifts and procedures in healing prayer.

It is important not to confuse discernment with other gifts, such as the word of knowledge or wisdom. It is commonplace to hear in charismatic circles something like the following: "I received the discernment that this person has a damaged kidney." That is not "a discernment," but a word of knowledge. Or someone might say, "I have the discernment that we need to pray about this supplicant's relationship with his mother." Again, that is not discernment but rather a word of wisdom. Discernment would be manifest if it were discovered, for example, that there was a demonic spirit of rage present. (In a later volume the issue of discernment of malignant spirits will be extensively discussed.)

The Word of Knowledge

In the above example of a member of a healing team receiving a "word" about the damaged kidney, there is a statement about a situation that is supernaturally revealed and not otherwise easily known. Something was revealed or manifested with regard to the problem that God wants to deal with in some way. A second in this set of revelation gifts is *the power to know,* or *the word of knowledge.*

Notice the gift is called the *word* of knowledge. The Greek word used in 1 Corinthians 12:8 is *logos*—a word uttered, that is, manifested publicly, that imparts knowledge and a necessary focus that cannot easily be known in the natural. What is the point of such a knowledge? Why do we need such a gift? In spiritual ministry our natural abilities to know are generally not sufficient, and they can often miss the mark. That is not to downplay the natural realm. It is of vital importance. We will return to this point later.

But the *word of knowledge* is a charism, beyond the natural. It is a manifestation by God himself, worked through human cooperation as to what he is presently doing or about to do in the exercise of ministry. Dom Benedict Heron gives us helpful overview:

> Some Christians with gifts of healing are given these "words"—
> we usually call them "words of knowledge"—in healing services.
> They will feel that God is healing or wanting to heal someone
> present with a particular complaint, such as a sick right knee, or
> lung trouble, or deafness in the left ear, or a bad back, or depression. When or if it is appropriate the person who receives the
> "word" will announce it publicly, and frequently these "words"

are confirmed as the sick person in question makes him or herself known and if necessary comes forward to be prayed with for healing.[3]

Why is there such a charism? The word of knowledge is manifested

- So that you as a minister can direct your prayer appropriately
- So that supplicants who are "stuck" in their prayer can be awakened to the fact that God wants to heal them
- So that people can be edified by it so that there will be a manifestation of the Spirit of God such that he will be glorified.

The Word of Wisdom

The word of wisdom is a revelatory gift because it tends to be "procedural" in nature. It informs and projects us to where God wants us to go in the event, session, or prayer. It is a practical guide given by the Holy Spirit as to the *way God would have us to proceed*. When someone receives a firm spiritual conviction and says, "I sense that we need to move in this direction" or "We should pray in such an such way," that is the word of wisdom. The word will always be toward and in harmony with the destiny of that community or person. The word of wisdom in healing prayer offers practical steps taken in ministry to reach that destiny.

The word of wisdom is also used to identify the next steps following on a word of knowledge. In the above example in which the word of wisdom revealed a damaged kidney, the word of wisdom would identify a course of action, even with respect to everyday practical matters such as drinking water. This gift can reveal God's direction both for the prayer and also to identify a course of action.

In a healing assembly we need wisdom to know what God's agenda is for the gathering:

- How should we proceed
- What kind of prayer should be taking place and when
- Who should be praying
- What is good order for that particular group

I am often insecure concerning how to proceed in events and in healing prayer. That is an uncomfortable position to be in, especially when one is leading events, as I do. On the other hand, such a position allows God to manifest himself without so much meddling of the flesh. I believe that people who are dependent on the Lord for wisdom and who earnestly and actively seek it from him will enjoy a greater manifestation of the Anointing. The letter of James declares this consoling word:

> If any of you lacks wisdom, he should ask God who gives to all generously and ungrudgingly, and he will be given it. But he should ask in faith, not doubting, for the one who doubts is like a wave of the sea that is driven and tossed about by the wind. (Jas. 1:5–6, NAB)

Once, at a healing event in Pleasanton, California, having done everything to prepare well, I began to be concerned about not sensing any direction for this mass. Usually, when I get into deeper prayer, direction starts to surface. This time there was nothing. On arrival I was told that the mass would not be in the church but in a gym, and there were a variety of circumstances present that I had never experienced before, including a new music group, a makeshift worship space, and many other factors, both practical and spiritual. Having previously received no inspiration from the Spirit, my mind took over and I developed a plan of action that would enable the event to proceed smoothly. But I felt the bottom had fallen out from under me.

Finally, during the immediate preparation on the stage behind the curtain with trustworthy brothers and sisters, I was led not only to "release" the gathering into the Lord's hands but I began to pray earnestly and directly for the manifestation of the charism of the word of wisdom. I prayed in front of the team, "Father, I don't trust myself; you are the Lord of this mass and it is for your purpose that we are here. I confess that I lack wisdom for this assembly and now solemnly ask you in the name of your Son, according to your word, to manifest the way you want us to proceed."

We purpose in our heart to lay aside our own agendas and let God come forth with a fresh word and a new way of working. It is done through the word of wisdom.

The prayer began to be strong. Inspired words and direction began to come forth through the prayer of the brothers and sisters as we all agreed in prayer for this. The intercession soon became prophetic in nature as they began to pray that I would be used during my time with them. I turned my spiritual ear toward the prophetic and heard the words and direction in their prayer that were on God's heart for that night. It all "gelled" and in confidence I was able to start. But the whole procedure had been turned around. Not only was there immediately a sense of saturation of the gym with the presence of God, but there emerged a way of conducting the service, followed by the mass, that was to become a regular pattern for future healing events. As it turned out, that pattern respected all the forthcoming protocol that would be sent by the pastors of the Catholic Church.

I have found that every healing event or session is different from the others: the needs of God's people in different places vary, and he gives a fresh word. When healing events are "routine" and ritualized, they become stale, tasteless, and fruitless. The human element takes over and eventually quenches the Holy Spirit. This is due to a lack of seeking and being open to—actively and earnestly—God's wisdom for his people. Before every assembly we pray specifically for this charism. We purpose in our heart to lay aside our own agendas and let God come forth with a fresh word and a new way of working. It is done through the word of wisdom.

In praying for healing for an individual the same is true. We often do not know how to pray. We hear the individual's circumstances and have the temptation to pray from our mind in line with the circumstances. We need to seek the Father's wisdom: "Father, we do not know how to pray for our sister. Show us your way, your will." Wisdom on how to proceed will follow.

The revelation gifts of discernment, knowledge, and wisdom work together to minister healing and wholeness to the Body of Christ. Think of it this way: If the word of knowledge is a *diagnosis*, the word of wisdom is the *prescription*.

> Healing as a charism involves more than one gift. It is a cluster, or series, of interrelated and interlocking manifestations of the power of God.

THE POWER TO DO

The second category is gifts that manifest God's power. They include the interrelated gifts of healing, miracles, and faith. I've heard it said, "I don't need to witness this kind of thing because my faith is not based on miracles. In any case," they argue, "Christ emptied himself of all power and went to the cross, therefore we don't need manifestations of God's power." To maintain an attitude of not accepting the charisms is not to see the whole picture. For the believer, it is not a matter of generating faith (although there are many Christians who could use that). There is something about demonstrating the power of God that *humbles* the human being to know powerlessness in the face of God. Why is this needed? The Kingdom of God is blocked if I am full of myself and think that I have the power to carry out God's designs.

The Gifts of Healing

The apostle Paul in 1 Corinthians 12:9 lists as a manifestation the "gifts of healing." Notice the plural word, gifts. Christian experience confirms that there are indeed gifts of healing. Healing as a charism involves more than one gift. It is a cluster, or series, of interrelated and interlocking manifestations of the power of God. Leanne Payne argues that all the gifts of the Spirit are healing gifts, "because wherever God's people are free to move in them, God uses them all in various combinations in the healing of His people."[4]

As we have seen above, the charisms of the "power to know" all come into play in the healing ministry. So do the other charisms. What God seeks when he heals us is that level of wholeness that will enable us to walk in his will and purpose for our lives. This involves the use of all the gifts he has disposed to his Church. I have seldom seen an individual Christian who has opened him or herself to this dimension of service with only one gift. A number of gifts are usually manifested in different and varying degrees— they come in clusters. But no one has all the gifts in fullness. That is why healing ministry far and away is best exercised corporately, as with the use of a healing team.

What happens, then, when the charisms of healing are at work? What distinguishes a *healing* from a *miracle*?

The charisms of healing are at work

- When ministers who have them *exercise that ministry in prayer*

- When the result is that the *restorative processes in the human being are engaged* and are to a greater or lesser degree accelerated; it is most often manifested over time, sometimes dramatically
- When this charism is *applied to any level* of human existence, bodily, emotional, or spiritual

The Gift of Miracles

T.G. Pater in *The New Catholic Encyclopedia* provides a very useful definition of miracles: "A miracle is an extraordinary event, perceptible to the senses, produced by God in a religious context as a sign of the supernatural."[5] To this, we would have to add that these signs are instantaneous more often than not. The power gifts include the gift of wonder working. There are some saints in the Church who have been given the title "wonder worker"—the recognition that this miraculous power of God was at work through them. For instance, in the early centuries of the Church there lived St. Anthony the Wonder Worker and St. Gregory the Wonder Worker. This means they were endowed with a special charism so that when they prayed things happened instantaneously. In the middle ages St. Anthony of Padua moved in the miraculous. In our own age, St. Padre Pio worked an abundance of miraculous signs— always with the goal of putting people into relationship with Jesus Christ. On the Protestant side, there are many people through whom the gift of miracles was manifested, including Amy Semple McPherson, Smith Wigglesworth, and Kathryn Kuhlman, who I had the memorable opportunity to see when I was a seminarian.

The exercise of the charism of miracles, or wonder working, ultimately is to build up God's Kingdom. We must realize that the presence of the gift of miracles or any other gift is not a sign of the holiness of the person through whom they are worked, but of the holiness of God.

Within the context of healing ministry, miracles are sudden, positive, and remarkable changes in the health of an individual, such that the bodily function is considerably relieved or restored. In many instances, natural laws are overridden or suspended in favor of God's intervention. These occurrences cannot be explained by empirical science.

Healing miracles are purposed by God in two ways:

1. They confirm in a manifestation of the power of God the message that was delivered.
2. They provide the basis for testimonies that glorify God and his character; "seal" the healing work of God in the person and the community; draw others to seek God's intervention in their lives; provide a foundation that can turn into faith, for those who need it.

The Gift of Faith

St. Paul in his list of gifts is not talking about the gift of faith as a belief or a creed. Nor does faith here refer to the faith a person needs just to be in an atmosphere of healing—the spiritual baseline spoken of earlier. The gift of faith is an unshakable knowing that is bestowed as a gift of ministry. It is the faith that Jesus exhorted believers to when he said:

> I tell you the truth, if anyone says to this mountain, "Go, throw yourself into the sea," and does not doubt in his heart but believes that what he says will happen, it will be done for him. Therefore I tell you, whatever you ask for in prayer, believe that you have received it, and it will be yours. (Mk. 11:23–24, NIV)

There are some people who, because of a special gift from God have an unshakable faith that habitually moves mountains! Brokenness is often like a mountain that needs to be moved. Paul interprets the use of the charism of faith in 1 Corinthians 13:2:

"Though I have all the faith necessary to move mountains—if I am without love, I am nothing" (NIV). When the gift of faith is in operation, circumstances are of no consequence. There exists a supernatural knowing that the power of God can and will bring about healing. It is as the faith of Abraham, which calls into existence that which was not before (Rom 4:17).

When the gift of faith is in operation, wonderful and powerful things happen. Faith, when operating as a healing charism,

- Is used as a weapon on God's side
- Perforates walls of unbelief and breaks barriers that arise
- Pulls down strongholds and, persevering, puts the enemy to flight
- Is the agent of enormous change

THE POWER TO SAY

The next category of gifts includes the charisms of inspiration or the "power to say." Here again, three gifts are operative: the gift of tongues, interpretation of tongues, and prophecy.

The Gift of Tongues

Chapter 14 included a more extensive treatment of the "gift of tongues," which is expressed in various ways as a manifestation of "prayer in the Spirit." Two dimensions of tongues are used in healing ministry:

1. Tongues as a Threshold Gift

The charism of tongues is a "spirit-to-Spirit" communication with God that allows us to get into the spiritual "door" and flow in other gifts. Some people say that the gift of tongues is not important, that we should be seeking the more important gifts. My response is that it is good to start first with the lesser, then go forward into the more important gifts. But in any case, no gift of God can rightly be looked upon as diminished in any way.

I have found that the gift of tongues—or in this particular usage the "prayer language"—puts our spirit in contact with the Spirit of God and leads us to a *paga*-intercessory meeting—with God. We then become aware of when prophetic gifts are coming forth or when the gift of faith is called for or other healing gifts are being brought into play.

Dutch Sheets descriptively terms such prayer "The Butterfly Anointing":

> At times when I'm praying in the Spirit I feel like a butterfly looks. Have you ever observed a butterfly flying from one location to another? They flutter this way and that, up and down, "herky-jerky." It appears they do not have the slightest idea where they are going. They almost look drunk. When I begin to pray in the Spirit, not knowing what I'm saying, sometimes with my mind wondering this way and that, I feel as though I'm trying to move in the butterfly anointing.
>
> *Where am I going?*
> *What am I doing?*
> *Will I land in the right place, on the right person?*
> *Is this really accomplishing anything?*
>
> But just as surely as that butterfly knows exactly where it's going, so the Holy Spirit directs my prayers precisely! They WILL "light upon" correctly.[6]

I often see this in the concrete when people begin praying in tongues, then they intercede in their understanding and then go back to tongues. Or they speak a word of wisdom, then go back to tongues. Or they may speak prophetically, then go back to tongues. I don't object to this; it may seem somewhat awkward, but I recognize that what they are doing is relying on a spiritual threshold of their prayer language in order to receive more of what the Spirit is doing at that particular time. Often I have the sensation that while they are praying in tongues, something is being prayerfully "enabled," or "worked through," in the spiritual realm.

2. Tongues as Directly Ministerial

In groups or teams that are more mature in charismatic ministry, the gift of tongues goes way beyond the threshold of a "prayer language." It can, according to inspiration, be a particular intercessory movement in prayer to resolve something in the spirit realm. It can also be used together with the charism of interpreting tongues.

A word of caution about the gift of tongues. Even after being commonplace in the Church for many years, some people still find this charism to be controversial. The purpose here is not to resolve an argument about whether these people accept the gift or not. It needs to be said, however, that the purpose of healing ministry is to focus the supplicants in order that they receive the wholeness that is in Christ Jesus. If they do not understand this charism, audibly speaking or praying in tongues *can* be a distraction: instead of opening up to Jesus' healing power, a supplicant can shut down.

The same can also be true at a healing mass or other larger event, if there are a number of people who have not experienced this before. Tongues or other gifts must not become a spectacle or show and therefore subject to ridicule. Such a gathering can quickly turn into a circus-like atmosphere and thus work against the grace of God. On the other hand, if there is a basic understanding and acceptance of this charism as authentic, or real, it can be used to great profit for the Kingdom of God. Remember that the exercise of the charisms is unto a *purpose.*

The Gift of Interpretation of Tongues

Many years ago I came into a deeper understanding of this gift when someone stated that to give an interpretation is *not* to give a translation. There is a difference. In the present work we are interested in the charisms as they pertain to the healing ministry. The interpretation of someone who has just spoken forth in tongues at a healing session can work in several ways:

- The interpretation is received as a strong interior intuition of what was just said or prayed for.
- It may be expressed in a prophetic-type form, but not always.
- It may be a vague reflection or indirect impression of what is going on in the spiritual realm.
- It may be directly understood as an utterance in a language known by someone present.

If a message in tongues is spoken in the gathering, needless to say, there should be an interpretation. If there is no one recognized as being able to interpret, the person should not speak forth in tongues, as St. Paul instructs in 1 Corinthians 14:28.

The Gift of Prophecy

Finally, a gift often used in the ministry of healing is the charism of prophecy. St. Paul included this gift among the higher charisms. He mentions, "someone who prophesies speaks to other people, building them up, and giving them encouragement and reassurance" (1 Cor. 14:3, NJB). We should not confuse individual prophecies or prophetic utterances with the realm of prophetic *ministry*, which is a vast topic. However, because in healing prayer we are not seeking a remedy from God for it's own sake, it is fitting that those with the gift of prophecy among the team be enabled, using prudence, to express the gift. I say, "using prudence" because when people are broken and hurting, it is often difficult for them to comprehend the wider picture of their life in God.

Prophecy must be exercised pastorally, in the measure of that which the supplicant can grasp. Jesus said to his disciples, "I have much more to say to you, more than you can now bear. But when he, the Spirit of truth, comes, he will guide you into all truth" (Jn. 16:12–13, NIV). As we walk in increasingly greater healing, we have the capacity for a greater measure of the Holy Spirit who brings us into the truth. That puts us in the realm of the prophetic.

As has been emphasized repeatedly in the book, it is vital that ministers of healing prayer seek to point their supplicants to that which is in harmony with God's purpose and destiny. Healing as such is most often remedial: it is a *getting back* to where we *should have been*. The prophetic is that which projects us toward what God has purposed for lives. Healing *disposes* the person for that. Experience in healing ministry has often seen the exercise of the charism of prophecy, but rarely actually brings the person into a full prophetic experience. Without being absolute, in healing prayer prophecies are most often related to the particular healing needs of the supplicant, whereas the realm of the prophetic concerns more the whole of life and the Church. The latter is exercised by those who are recognized with prophetic ministry.

I have seen many times that when healing and deliverance take place and a person has become "unblocked," he or she is enabled to enter much more freely into the prophetic realm. And that is as it should be: it makes perfect sense spiritually and theologically.

EXERCISING THE CHARISMS

Respect Your Charisms

The apostle Paul writes to the Christians living in Rome concerning the exercise of the gifts of the Spirit from another point of view:

For by the grace given me I say to every one of you: Do not think of yourself more highly than you ought, but rather think of yourself with sober judgment, in accordance with the measure of faith God has given you. Just as each of us has one body with many members, and these members do not all have the same function, so in Christ we who are many form one body, and each member belongs to all the others. We have different gifts, according to the grace given us. If a man's gift is prophesying, let him use it in proportion to his faith. If it is serving, let him serve; if it is teaching, let him teach. (Rom. 12:3–7, NIV)

In this passage, we have a further exhortation to exercise the ministries and charisms that are in the Body of Christ. We should be exercising, first of all, those gifts that God has given us, not pretending to exercise gifts we do not have. Most of us have the capacity for more than one charism, but experience demonstrates that in spiritually mature people, the Spirit seems to focus on one or two charisms even though the people use others. This focus will project them toward their ministry.

I think our churches suffer from a vast spiritual immaturity when it comes to the exercise of the gifts. Many people rush to do things in the church that do not correspond with the pattern of gifts God wants to manifest in them. They have been taught to "sign up" for ministries that strike their fancy, without knowing the first thing about discernment or being sensitive to the gifts God has purposed for them, let alone discipleship. Once discerned, a Christian needs to *respect* the way that God has manifested himself in him or her through the charisms. That means we do with a full heart that which he has called us to do. If it is teaching, healing, encouraging, exhorting, or almsgiving, we should respect the work that the Holy Spirit has done in us and not seek to do other things.

Some may be reading this book because healing has intrigued you. This does not necessarily mean that God has called you and endowed you with the ministry of healing. Everyone will be called to practice healing prayer from time to time and healing may take place by virtue of a charism, but that doesn't mean that healing is going to be the focus of your ministry. Paul is exhorting us to discern our ministry and work generously within our giftedness.

Paul says, "If it is a gift of prophecy we should prophecy as much as our faith tells us" (Rom. 12:6). In other words, as we grow in our faith and relationship with Christ, the exercise of the gifts is released and becomes free-flowing. This is a vital principal because when God manifests a gift in us we

> The wonderful thing about healing ministry is that you can do it at any time, as long as it is fitting and prudent.

can call on that gift at any time in cooperation with the Holy Spirit and it will be operative. In other words, it does not turn "on" or "off" depending on the particular moment. You have been *given* the gifts; they can be called on and exercised as the occasion and the inspiration requires—and in a variety of ways and forms, according to the protocols of the place, time, people, and circumstances.

The wonderful thing about healing ministry is that you can do it at any time, as long as it is fitting and prudent. Even if the external environment doesn't permit laying on of hands and audible prayer, when you intercede the gift of healing is in operation. The principle is the same as with any action of grace. It *abides* in us and we can choose to cooperate with it at any point. *Blessed is the person who habitually makes present the healing power of God!*

NATURAL AND SUPERNATURAL KNOWLEDGE

The Natural Realm

Lisa is a medical doctor who studied, through the Institute for Healing Ministry, the same spiritual principles that have been presented in this book. She is the kind of doctor who, in her quiet and compassionate manner, inspires confidence because of her extensive training in medicine. She manifests a vast knowledge of the natural when it comes to treating the body. When ministering in healing prayer under the Anointing of the Spirit of God, Lisa becomes as another woman; her healing prayer turns powerful, authoritative, and bold.

One of the outstanding features of Lisa's healing prayer is that it is so focused; it is like a laser light targeted on the particular need of the supplicant. I'm convinced that the reason her ministry is so powerful is that she has a keen natural knowledge of the human body and the way it functions. The Holy Spirit, through her base of natural knowledge, works supernaturally as she flows in the gifts of the word of wisdom, the word of knowledge, and healing.

It is here that natural knowledge is essential for a healing ministry. Anyone contemplating beginning or growing in the healing ministry should have a basic and ongoing growth in correctly understanding how the human body works. The same is true for the human mind with regard to inner healing prayer and the human spirit for spiritual healing and deliverance.

Becoming abusive is a constant danger in the area of healing prayer. If you come to it with erroneous information or even superstitious notions about how the body works, prayer will be erroneous and soon misdirected-abuse *will* take place. Good and accurate natural knowledge will give you confidence as you seek to lead supplicants into wholeness in Christ. I am not suggesting that you as a minister of healing prayer, become a medical expert, just that you become reasonably informed about what you are doing.

A good natural knowledge of how the body works will enable your prayer to focus on root causes and avoid going astray by chasing symptoms. You might say, That is not important because God knows the problem anyway. While it is true that he knows, and will hopefully have mercy on any erroneous prayer, that does not excuse ignorance that works at cross-purposes with the truth about the way he created us. The same applies to learning more about the way the mind works and about basic and solid psychological truths, along with solid principles of inner healing and deliverance. Used in harmony with solid spiritual principles, natural knowledge expands your human capacity and gives room for the Holy Spirit to flow even more powerfully.

If you are in, or contemplating becoming involved with healing prayer, I urge you to get on the road to being reasonably informed from solid sources concerning the realm of knowledge in the natural (coupled with formation in healing prayer) in the following areas:

- *Human anatomy* and the functions and processes of the human body
- *Christian psychology* and how the human mind works
- *Christian teaching about what the human person* is before God (this includes the *spiritual dimension* of a human person)
- *Principles and application of healing prayer*

Ongoing progress in these dimensions of natural knowledge, together with the call to healing ministry, will produce enormously powerful manifestations of healing in the Spirit of Jesus.

Alicia is immensely successful in her healing ministry. People from all over California seek her out. She has one of the most powerful prophetic gifts I have ever seen, combined with discernment that is trustworthy. I always love to be ministered to by her for my own brokenness, both because of her trustworthiness and also because I know she will minister God's Spirit to me. Years ago she used to pray just out of what she received from the Spirit of God, but there was something lacking in her prayer—her capacity in the natural. In order to give more room to the Spirit of God, she enrolled as an auditor at a local junior college in some courses in human psychology and physiology (without having to take tests, prepare reports, etc.). As a result, her ministry became dramatically richer and more focused. She knows what she is praying for and she knows how to direct that prayer.

The Supernatural

The gifts of God's Spirit are meant to function co-naturally with a person who is surrendered to God. Great theologians, from Augustine through Albert the Great and Thomas Aquinas, all define the supernatural as exactly that—super-nature, or built upon what God created in the natural. And God's Spirit respects the nature he created. He works with it and builds upon it. The manifestation of the Holy Spirit through the charisms is flowing in the supernatural.

On the other hand, it is important to realize that we can rely too much on our own human resources and reasoning. The mind often gets in the way of the Spirit's work. This is especially true when we move into analyzing the gifts of God's Spirit and subjecting them to human criteria. For instance, when a word of knowledge is manifested, it would be erroneous to "discern" it by applying our own limited natural associations of concepts and reasoning as to why it is or isn't from the Lord. The supernatural dimension of God's work is best received with simplicity, devotion, and the heart.

If you are an evangelical Christian, this principle is not far from evangelical theology that maintains that the principles demonstrated in the natural order are reflections of God's supernatural principles. For instance the principle of "sowing and reaping" in the natural reflects how God works in the supernatural. Catholic and evangelical teaching have a delightful convergence in this area.

The goal of this chapter is to encourage you to become an open, transparent, and capable vessel of the Anointing of God's love for his Church. In the healing ministry you will be able to say with St. Paul,

> For by the grace given me I say to every one of you: Do not think of yourself more highly than you ought, but rather think of yourself with sober judgment, in accordance with the measure of faith God has given you. Just as each of us has one body with many members, and these members do not all have the same function, so in Christ we who are many form one body, and each member belongs to all the others. We have different gifts, according to the grace given us. If a man's gift is prophesying, let him use it in proportion to his faith. If it is serving, let him serve; if it is teaching, let him teach. (2 Cor. 4:5–7, NIV)

Let us agree in prayer:

Father, I ask for an increase and deepening of my spiritual gifts. Teach me to be simple and transparent, yet wise and prudent in their use. Free me to move in the gifts you have given, as I bind my exercise of them to your highest and best purpose. Amen

Journal Questions for the Gifts of the Spirit

1. Which of the nine service gifts of the Holy Spirit have you seen at work in yourself?
2. What gifts do you feel you are open to receive? Why?
3. What gifts are you most afraid of or resistant to? Why?
4. In what areas touching on healing ministry does your natural knowledge need development?

[1] Payne, Leanne, *The Healing Presence: Curing the Soul through Union with Christ,* Grand Rapids, MI, Baker Books, 1995, see pp. 113–116.

[2] Ireland, David, *Activating the Gifts of the Holy Spirit,* Whitaker House, 1997, pp. 95–116.

[3] Benedict Heron, *Channels of Healing Prayer,* Notre Dame, Ave Maria Press, 1989, p. 48.

[4] Payne, Leanne, *op. cit.,* p. 115.

[5] See "Miracles (theology of)," *New Catholic Encyclopedia,* Catholic University Press, 1967, p. 890.

[6] Dutch Sheets, *Intercessory Prayer,* Ventura, CA, Regal Books, 1996, p. 100.

LISTENING TO THE VOICE OF THE SPIRIT

One of the most crucial questions a minister of healing prayer is continually confronted with is, How do I know when or if God is speaking to me? This chapter will be concerned primarily with the charism of the word of knowledge. Some of the same principles apply to all the word gifts. In the particular context of healing prayer and ministry, it is critical to consider a series of questions:

- How do I know God's agenda for this session?
- How can I be sure that my discernment is correct?
- How do I know that a particular word of knowledge is true?
- How do words of knowledge come to me?

We individually need to learn how to be attentive to the voice of the Spirit. In this section we will discuss how God speaks to us in words, images and bodily sensations.

A Stretch in Los Angeles

Several years ago I attended a conference in Los Angeles with the late Fr. Emiliano Tardiff, Bishop Onesimo Cepeda, Fr. Inocencio

Llamas, and teacher Salvador Gomez. During the masses I was on stage with these giants of the Hispanic charismatic renewal. After communion during the first mass, Fr. Llamas and Fr. Tardiff were speaking words of knowledge from the altar for the five thousand people attending the conference.

At certain moments I sensed within me two specific words of knowledge. Unsure of myself, I approached Fr. Llamas and whispered in his ear that I sensed God was healing a woman with a leg problem who was using crutches. The "word" was really an image impressed on my spirit that she would be able to take the crutches away and walk normally. Suddenly, Fr. Llamas took the microphone from Fr. Tardiff's hand and passed it to me. Here I was with these gifted men, having to deliver a word of knowledge before five thousand people!

Later that night a priest friend from the Diocese of Monterey with whom I was sharing a hotel room asked me, "How did you receive that word? How did it come to you?" Frankly, I had never given it much thought. After reflecting, I finally said, "It came to me as an image of someone extending her crutches and walking." I had seen it as an image in my spirit. Going further I told my priest friend that at other times, the word of knowledge comes as a very firm conviction or intuition that something is happening.

The healing of the woman using crutches was not manifested at that time. Sunday, there was another mass with the same crowd. I received a word of knowledge that someone was being healed in his or her heart and that several people would receive a spiritual heart healing. This time, I did not deliver the word of knowledge as I was still feeling rather intimidated. I shrank from delivering the word because I didn't feel I belonged. Besides, it was apparent to me that Friday's word had not come to pass. This attitude made me disobedient.

I later told Fr. Llamas what I had received. He replied, "You should have obeyed and that word should have been spoken." It *should* have been spoken because at the end of that Sunday mass a woman walked down the main aisle extending two crutches in victory over her leg problem!

St. Paul says in Romans 12:7 that we should prophesy as much as our faith tells us. He was encouraging the Roman Christians to exercise the gift of prophecy in the measure that their faith allowed them. God has a way of stretching our faith so that the flow of his power in the gifts can increase. He sure stretched me when I was in Los Angeles with the gifted men of God. This gave me confidence and supported me so that I would have a greater measure of confidence in expressing the word of knowledge in the future.

Listening to the Lord

The English Benedictine monk, Dom Benedict Heron zeroes in on the importance of listening during ministry:

> Listening to God is especially important in praying for healing. If we do not learn to listen to God, we shall often not know what to pray for. We should listen not only to what the sick person has to say but also to what God is telling us—and the two do not always coincide. We should pray for the gift of discernment, for without it we shall sometimes misunderstand both the person and the situation, give unhelpful advice, and prayer partly for the wrong things.[1]

Let us be attentive to the voice of the Spirit! Francis MacNutt relates that his friend, "Rev. Tommy Tyson, who is one of the best listeners I know, says that he gives only one ear to the sick person. The other ear he gives to God. In this way the Spirit comes to enlighten us when we are in the dark about what to pray for."[2] In

1998 I experienced these "ears" of Tommy Tyson as Chip Sundstrom and I shared prayer with him and Linda Schubert for guidance for our ministry. It was a live model of ministry as Tommy, through prayer, seemed to connect everything we shared to the Spirit of God. God's power overflowed as we prayed together. I suggest that all of us use the two ears or eyes model: one to the supplicant or group and the other to the Lord.

How does that voice come? Two common ways are *words* and *images*. The voice of the Spirit comes also in bodily sensations or even in other ways that are intuitive or mysterious and cannot be put into words. There is one overriding principle: the way God speaks is still a mystery of the way the divine presence touches our humanity. There is always wonder and awe in God's communication with humanity. His speaking to us is a mercy that can be only adequately responded to in some measure by praise, gratitude and obedience.

1. HE SPEAKS IN WORDS

As a Word of Prayer

The voice of the Spirit comes to us in words that are often associated with what God wants to do or is doing in the gathering for healing prayer. This word or words may come forth almost inadvertently as a petitionary prayer for healing. This is a simple and most basic way to pray for healing. Ministers of healing prayer experience a desire to pray when someone has a need. This desire is often placed in them by the Spirit of God. When the need and the desire for prayer coincide, the ministers pray with words that express the desire that is on their hearts. A more advanced expression of the word in prayer is when the prayer is taken hold of by the Holy Spirit, according to Romans 8:27, as we saw in Chapter 6. The desires of the Spirit are brought to expression by human prayer.

As Pure Charism

The voice of the Spirit may come in a word of knowledge or prophetic word, as we discussed in the last chapter. Sometimes, particularly in more spiritually attuned environments, the prophetic word can be *declared* to the supplicant, which may elicit a response from the supplicant. Here are a few random examples:

- "I am receiving the word fire" (possibly a symbolic word, indicating a purification was underway).
- "I am receiving the word bicycle" (possibly referring to an accident on a bicycle that later had indirect effects).
- "I hear in my spirit that we should pray with regard to your mother" (possibly indicating that a lack of forgiveness is preventing physical healing).

A more mature prophetic utterance might declare, "You are being called to a fuller healing because at this point of your life God has done some new things and has positioned people in your life that you will be able to minister to."

Difficulties arise with proceeding in the above way when the level of receptivity of the person for whom you are praying or the place where you are ministering does not lend itself to this kind of declared word. Abuse happens when we are not sensitive to this. Ministers, in mistaken or misguided zeal, sometimes give words on behalf of God, declaring things for which people have no context in which to put them or for people who have no knowledge about this form of prayer.

It is always opportune to *pray* the words we receive. This will help put the supplicant at ease and avoid feeling threatened when the words are declared as a "message from God." For this reason I suggest that most often, people in healing ministry turn words they receive into a prayer.

For example, if you are praying for a person who is having problems with the emotion of anger and you received the word *fire*, you could turn that word into a prayer. Instead of saying, "God is bringing fire upon you," which can sound terribly threatening, you might pray, "Lord, I pray that any fire that is not of you be extinguished in the heart of this brother and that the fire of your Holy Spirit would grow; may his heart burn for you." A person can readily accept this type of word placed in the context of a gentle prayer. In this way the word is not only received, but confusion is avoided. The word of knowledge is immediately taken to prayer and constructively used for the supplicant's healing.

> It is important to give the word or biblical text without editorializing.

Biblical Words

God speaks his word through biblical texts. Often when we pray for a supplicant, a biblical text will come to the mind of one or more members of the team. For example, let's use John 10:10 where Jesus says, "I have come that they may have life and have it in abundance" (NJB). The text can be given to the person by saying, "I am receiving this biblical text . . ." This is naturally followed by a prayer concerning the bestowal of more abundant life. Or you can simply pray the text by saying something like, "Lord, I pray that just as you have come to give abundant life, that this sister will be healed so as to be able to walk in more abundant life." *Praying* the scripture lets the Word of God penetrate the human spirit.

It is important to give the word or biblical text without editorializing. Some people give a word by also giving information that is not relevant and which may derail the focus of the prayer. They say something like, "My mind was on something else when suddenly this came into my mind, so it must be from the Lord." True as these circumstances may have been, these kind of commentaries distract from what God wants to do, are of the flesh, and should be totally eliminated from any kind of healing prayer. Forget about how you received the word. Forget about your inner workings and reactions; just give the word and pray! At the Institute for Healing Ministry we often helped each other in prayer teams with the manifestation of the gifts in a kind of "laboratory" experience. I often stood next to sisters or brothers who were delivering words, gently coaching them to be bold. At the same time, if I heard them go into extraneous commentary, I would whisper in their ear, "The pure word, just say the pure word."

2. HE SPEAKS IN IMAGES

The word I received at the conference in Los Angeles concerning the woman who would be able to walk without crutches, was really an image. It was an image of a woman carrying her crutches. This was *not just a mental picture*; it seemed to be coming from the deepest part of me—something that had been "deposited" in my spirit. The moment I spoke it, the image became a word of knowledge. Receiving images like this is a normal experience for ministers of healing prayer.

Along similar lines, Francis MacNutt reflects on the positive results when ministers use images in prayer:

> Most ministers of healing suggest that we be specific in our prayer, that we visualize as clearly as possible what we are asking God to heal. For instance, if we are praying for the healing of a broken bone we can ask the Father (or Jesus) to take away every infection, to stimulate the growth of the cells needed to restore the bone, and to fill in any breaks. Such a specific request seems to enliven our own faith, as we see in our imagination what we are praying for. It also stimulates the faith of the

sick person as he listens and pictures in his own mind what we are asking God to accomplish in reality. This helps him become more actively involved in the prayer, even if he says nothing.[3]

The Holy Spirit uses images in the working of several of the gifts as they are manifested in healing prayer—the prophetic, word of knowledge, word of wisdom, and discernment. This manifestation follows a process:

- *An image forms in the spiritual self of the minister*. It may be an image of a body part, a symbolic image such as those which were used above as words (fire and bicycle), or it can be an image of someone performing an action, etc.
- The minister then *puts this image to the test or challenges it* by not concentrating on it but by focusing on what is currently happening in the session;
- If the image persists, then it can be *delivered and it turns into a manifestation of one of the gifts* and is used as a basis for healing prayer.

If it is delivered, that is usually the end of the minister's responsibility for that word. If it is not picked up by the team or by the supplicant, let it go: God will take care of it and bring it to fruition if it is really from him.

When I receive an image that is meant as a word of knowledge, I will often turn it into a prayer. Some people in ministry may say, "I see a liver," or "Your liver is being healed," or "Something is not right in your liver." They then go into a discussion with the supplicant about the person's liver, which may or may not be helpful to what God wants to do. Instead, I suggest that turning an image into a prayer brings the Spirit's power directly to the affliction: "Lord, I pray for this sister's liver, that there would be a healing presence, a healing light placed in the liver and all its functions; that it would begin to work in accord with the purpose for which you created it." If you don't know how to pray concerning the image you receive, if it is appropriate, you might pray softly, even inaudibly in tongues.

Obviously, there are some images that might not be appropriate or prudent to share. If they are from the Lord, they can simply be prayed for in Spirit-led intercession. It is always wise to err on the side of prudence.

Sometimes people who are praying receive symbolic images, such as animals, light and darkness, scenes in nature, or objects. Once I was praying in a team when one of the members received the images of a tricycle and shoes. This represented for the supplicant, not one specific event, but a period of life during which the person used those particular types of shoes and a tricycle. God was indicating that he wanted to heal the time in the person's life that was represented by those images.

The Spirit Flourishes Where the Gifts Operate

A few years back I went to a Benny Hinn Crusade in Anaheim, California. For me, the worship was the most special part of the crusade. Long before the service began, Pastor Benny's assistants were already praying and receiving testimonies of healing.

I was in the pastors' section, sitting next to a youth pastor who had a skin disease, for which I started to pray silently. I received in a word of knowledge that not only God was healing him of this particular disease but of several other afflictions. As the service began, one of the assistants zeroed in on the two of us, saying that she had received a word that there was healing taking place. I discreetly pointed to the youth pastor, whom she called to the aisle. As it turned out, the young man was not only healed of the skin affliction but was delivered from oppression and other physical problems. He was one of the people called up on stage and was prayed for by Pastor Benny.

I mentioned that for me, the worship was the most special part of the service. At the crusade a solemn exhortation was given before an offering was taken. Immediately after the offering, a song of profound worship was sung. During this time, I began to sense in me an uneasiness, almost a fear. Then I saw in my spirit a flood, as if it were pouring into the auditorium through the principle doors behind us. For a brief moment, I thought there was a danger entering. But before I could think this through, I saw in my spirit and sensed that the "water" had already entered and the thousands of people were in a crystal-clear, beautiful lake of the Anointing of the Holy Spirit. At that point, Pastor Benny invited anyone who had been healed to step into the aisle. Literally thousands lined up to give testimonies.

Imaging according to the Spirit of God unleashes the mighty power of God's anointing and therefore abundant living, as Jesus promised us.

This episode showed me the importance of financial sowing as part of worship. I learned a spiritual principal that has forever affected me. Worship and sowing draw down a powerful manifestation of the Anointing. The act of sowing is an act of profound worship. The revelation I received through the image was that of the flood-gates of God's Anointing opening by virtue of listening and obeying God's direction in the act of sowing, or giving, into an offering. This principal has become a key part of my life and my ministry of healing.

That day, through the word of knowledge, God impressed on me what he was doing in the assembly in the spirit realm. Through images, I not only saw the power of God at work in the young man but was brought into a revelation of God's principles for the flow of the Anointing.

Recently, in Argentina, I attended a Catholic worship service that operated according to the same openness and respect for God's principles of worship. It was a poor parish, with the offering taken in the midst of a severe economic crisis in the country. But I sensed the same Anointing that I learned about in Los Angeles.

In anointed prayer, the Spirit speaks though symbolic images unto revelation (the prophetic realm) and healing (the demonstration of the power of God).

Changing the Images for a New Way of Thinking

The Spirit uses inspired images to guide the imagination of the supplicant to God's purpose and destiny. This is of utmost importance, because people who come for healing prayer often have distorted and broken images of themselves and of their reality. The world and Satan, with his minions, promote images of negativity, despair, oppression, and ill-health. People become trapped, obsessed, and diseased by those images. Imaging according to the Spirit of God unleashes the mighty power of God's Anointing and therefore abundant living, as Jesus promised us. The Word of God in the Bible, together with discerned imagery in the Judeo-Christian tradition go a long way to provide for God's healing power to be released in healing. But it is imperative that the new imagery be matched to the supplicant's need. Exactly because of this reason, we need the gifts of the Spirit.

Great spiritual teachers like Ignatius of Loyola, Teresa the Great, and John Eudes have bequeathed to the Body of Christ ways in which we can literally put ourselves into the gospel scenes. That way, the Bible becomes an all-important part of the healed way in which we view the world and progress in our healing. Robert DeGrandis counsels us to use the powerful tradition of meditative prayer over the scriptures for healing. He reflects,

I have used visualization with children and have been utterly amazed at the way the Lord speaks to children though visualization. We encourage you when you read the scripture to read it not so much from a historical viewpoint, but a personal one.[4]

Later, he says,

> In general visualizations you may want to take a Gospel scene.
> For example in Mark 2:1,2 you can visualize yourself being let
> down on a stretcher in front of Jesus. We can all experience that
> as we see our four best friends dropping us down through a roof
> in front of Jesus and hearing Jesus say, "Your sins are forgiven; I
> have forgiven you. Now forgive yourself." Put yourself into the
> Gospel scene.[5]

Whatever images God's Spirit inspires, be it the figure of the
Good Shepherd, the bright light of God's love, the transforming
fire of the Spirit himself, or a thousand others, God's Spirit brings
a new way of looking at life and relationships. These images have
the power to bring wholeness and holiness to brokenness and alienation. They provide a new way of looking at life and, together with
God's word, guide our journey of healing. Changing the images to
those of God is healing prayer at its best.

3. HE SPEAKS IN BODILY SENSATIONS

Several years ago I had the opportunity to minister at a healing
mass in San Miguel, El Salvador. My friend and co-worker Nicolas
Hernandez was ministering with me. During Holy Communion
the Spirit led him to focus in and pray for a particular lady in at-
tendance at the mass. She later gave testimony that she had been
healed of a stomach condition. I asked Nicolas to tell me how he
was led to pray. He said that the lady had been pointed out to him
by the Holy Spirit. While he was praying for her in the Spirit, he
said he felt, as it were, an "electrical" current go through his
stomach and later asked her if she had a stomach condition
(Nicolas doesn't have stomach problems). She reported that she

had experienced the same "current" followed by the first relief from stomach pain in months.

The third way that God indicates to us a "word" is through bodily sensations. I must admit to a personal hesitation in this area. First of all, to date, I have never personally experienced any kind of bodily sensations that would indicate God's healing intervention. Second, it seems to me that of all ways that words can be indicated, this is most open to the possibility of misinterpretation, falsification, or psychological phenomenon. Having said this, however, I cannot discount its validity when I have seen the most balanced of people, who are solid and trustworthy, receive a word of knowledge by this means.

Sometimes ministers experience some of the same bodily symptoms as the people they are praying for. When the prayer is concluded, there is no more pain and all symptoms are gone. One who has no qualms about this way of receiving words of knowledge is Dom Benedict Heron. He puts it this way:

> How do people with this gift receive a "word of knowledge" for physical healing? There are several ways. For physical sickness the most common way is probably that of feeling a pain or sensation in one's own body when God wants to heal someone else with a sickness in the same part of their body. So receiving a pain or sensation in one's left hand could indicate that God is wanting to heal or is healing someone's left hand.[6]

Discerning the word of God in bodily sensations can be a delicate issue. A dear sister in the Lord once told me that she used to receive the word of knowledge through bodily sensations but since then had begged the Lord to take it away from her! The reason it is so delicate is the relationship between the human body and the human psyche. These things can be easily feigned or psychologically produced in a phenomenon known as "transference." They

285

can also be quite disconcerting. I was once in a gathering doing preparatory work for a healing conference. The person responsible for the prayer ministry declared, "All of a sudden I feel a chill; I know the devil is here." She started to go into deliverance prayer on the basis of her "chill." This was totally subjective and was not confirmed by the other members of the prayer team.

Bodily sensations can not only indicate knowledge of what is to be prayed for but are also an indication that the healing Anointing is present. Carlos is a close friend near La Plata, Argentina. For some years now he has seen the manifestation of God's healing as a result of his prayer. Recently, I was in a family gathering where his grown son complained of a headache. After several minutes I asked about the headache and Ezequiel said it was gone. I had not realized that Carlos immediately prayed under his breath for his son. Later Carlos shared that before his son spoke, Carlos had a sensation all over his body and especially on his hands that he regularly receives that he takes as a sign that he should pray for healing. He described it as a "metallic" heat that he can feel all over. Although Carlos is a spiritual man and radically Christian, he's had no instruction in this area and frankly didn't know what to make of his bodily sensations.

Was it the Holy Spirit who produced this strange sensation in Carlos so that he would minister healing? My best answer is yes and no. When the Anointing is manifested for healing, God is working in the human spirit of the minister to inspire prayer. There is a connection among spirit, mind, and body. When God is at work in a special way like this, there is bound to be a reaction on the bodily level. So in a real way we can say the person produces the sensation, but as a reaction to the Anointing. The reaction will

With an attitude of submission, a willingness to be corrected, and the exercise of our gifts in faith, we can be confident that God will perfect our gifts.

be different for each individual, according to the condition of each one.

Issues to Consider in the Use of Gifts

a. Discernment of "Words" and Gifts

Words, images, and bodily sensations all must be used together with the gifts of wisdom and discernment. We must be open to submit whatever we receive to the Lord's agenda and use these with prudence. We must also be attentive to the *protocol* of the place and the event, submitting to those who are in a position to discern our gifts. Without the exercise of discernment, a meeting will quickly go astray. God is a God of order and not of confusion. Think of it this way:

> Discernment of charisms is always necessary. No charism is exempt from being referred and submitted to the Church's shepherds. "Their office [is] not indeed to extinguish the Spirit, but to test all things and hold fast to what is good," so that all the diverse and complementary charisms work together "for the common good."[7]

When I was beginning in the healing ministry, I would receive many words of knowledge concerning healings. I wasn't sure what to do with them or how to use them coupled with the word of wisdom. I would come home from healing events feeling distressed and fearful that I had delivered false words or that I had made these things up in my mind. Sometimes I even felt I had been a disservice to the Body of Christ. In my insecurity I was afraid of becoming a charlatan. Since then I have learned through experience that these fears are a part of the walk of anybody involved in healing ministry. It is part of the purification and growth process.

There is room for a "healthy mistrust" of oneself so that you can rely on God and on the discernment of others in the Body of Christ. One thing is for sure: we cannot in the end discern our own gifts. At the same time, we need to give ourselves room to make mistakes, feel secure in admitting to them, learn, and move on with serenity. As long as we are seeking the true common good with a sincere heart and are seeking the more perfect manifestation of God's Spirit, God will take our imperfections and contaminated words and purify them.

With an attitude of submission, a willingness to be corrected, and the exercise of our gifts in faith, we can be confident that God will perfect our gifts. They will be shaped and conformed according to the way that he wants to develop them. And for sure it is not the way *we* think they should be developed.

Insisting that a word that does not resonate with those for whom it was directed must be accepted or acted on indicates the need for growth and maturity in the Spirit. Submit your words and then let them go. God will do the rest!

What our hearts are seeking is the authenticity of our gifts; that is, that they are genuinely from the Spirit of God and not from us. This means that we subject them to the Word of God. Compatibility with the Bible and with basic Christian teaching is the first measure of authenticity. Second, we are accountable to those people and pastors who are in our lives to discern and test our gifts. This attitude will lead to authenticity. Also, we must remember that the use of the gifts is for the building up of God's church, its edification, and not our exaltation.

b. Spiritual Protocol

Recently at an important conference of the charismatic renewal, the director of the conference asked Linda Schubert and me to lead an extended worship segment. Seeking God's wisdom about this time, we sensed that all prophetic utterances or other word gifts would be received from anyone in the assembly, provided they were discerned by some designated mature folks who were introduced for that purpose. This session turned out to be one of the powerful moments of the conference as we ministered in healing prayer, coupled with words that were coming from the whole assembly.

At one point a lady approached the platform with what she said was a word. One of our fellow ministers, Nora Merlo, intercepted her, asking her to share the word first with her so it could be discerned. The lady refused, saying it was not to be shared before being given to the whole group. Nora conveyed that it would not be possible to share the word publicly without it first being discerned. The lady, now angry, tried to force herself onto the stage. Nora had to physically take her elsewhere. The woman insisted that the Spirit was being quenched (because she was required to submit her word to discernment).

Just the opposite was true! There was a free operation of the gifts. Dynamic individual and corporate healing was flowing. The protocol established was just the vehicle that enabled the Spirit to flow freely without turning into a chaotic situation. I maintain that an event or assembly without good order can become a venue for abuse, confusion, and even diabolic intervention. St. Paul often wrestled with this issue as the fourteenth chapter of 1 Corinthians makes clear. I have found over and over again that, coupled with an explicit respect for the manifestation of the charisms, an established protocol for healing events frees the Holy Spirit to act in power. Following established protocol is part of the discipline of the Anointing.

The Oxford dictionary defines protocol as, "the accepted code of behavior in a particular situation." That makes it one of the first and most vital issues to be considered in organizing a healing event. On September 14, 2000 the Vatican issued a document precisely about the issue of protocol during Catholic healing ministry; it was occasioned by a prominent church official acting outside of good church order. The document was widely interpreted as restricting healing ministry. Though there are some restrictions (for example, exorcisms are not permitted during public masses), there is a positive aspect in that the Catholic Church's highest pastors call for order and discernment when the charisms of healing are operating.[8]

In her book, *The Voice of God*, Cindy Jacobs devotes a large chapter to spiritual protocol in the context of the prophetic. She asks,

> Why a chapter of spiritual protocol? Many churches lack an understanding of how prophecy should be handled both corporately and individually within their midst. Done properly, and having correct scriptural protocol, the prophetic word is a catalytic, powerful influence on the church. Ministered incorrectly, it can cause enormous confusion and church splits. Through the years, I've seen many mistakes made through giving and receiving prophetic words that could have been cleared up simply by understanding protocol.[9]

Cindy speaks here about prophecy. I wish to state emphatically that the same principles apply to the healing ministry, especially since the prophetic is often incorporated into healing prayer. Like Cindy, through the years I have seen many errors that have more to do with protocol than with not correctly hearing the voice of God. I want to quickly add that I too have made a good deal of those mistakes!

c. Timing

Closely connected to discernment and protocol is the issue of timing. A minister of healing prayer needs to be attentive to *when God wants it delivered*. Words of knowledge about the person or the assembly need to be delivered or prayed for at the time that they will have maximum receptivity. You can pray, "Lord, how do you want me to use this word and when?" That is essentially a prayer for wisdom. I believe in accord with James 1:5 that God, who is anxious to prosper his work will see the word through by bestowing wisdom about how to use it.

If you sense a "check" in your spirit about the word, it is best to wait or, given the opportunity, share it for discernment with a fellow minister. It may very well be that the word is for you personally and not meant to be said aloud. You may have been given the word so that you can intercede about the issue. Always ask for wisdom.

d. Avoiding Spiritual and Psychological Abuse

Several years ago an experienced minister in generational healing came to a prominent parish in northern California. Local people, including a priest, were organized to assist her in individual ministry after her presentations. During the ministry to a supplicant whom I know, the minister announced that the supplicant had been raped by her father before she was three years old and that she was repressing the memory and thus unable to be healed. This was a false word, undiscerned and given imprudently to a supplicant she had never met. As a result of that "word," the woman had to spend years in therapy, in part being healed from the sowing of a false word given that day by this "spiritual healer." This is an example of both spiritual and psychological abuse.

Avoiding spiritual and psychological abuse means being aware that potentially dangerous ministerial situations can occur in which manipulation, imposition of your own spirituality, opinions, or even spiritual gifts can be given to other people when they are not ready for it. Imprudent, undiscerned, or untimely words are forms of such abuse.

For example, if someone was sexually abused in his or her childhood but he or she is not fully aware of it, it would be imprudent and abusive to tell the supplicant of this word and force the person to "face the issue." Even if the sexual abuse did occur, a word of knowledge or even explicit prayer concerning this issue may still be out of order. The reason is because such delicate and deep issues not in the supplicant's awareness can produce psychological shock and resistance to healing. I have found that they are given to healing ministers for the sake of giving direction to intercession. Such knowledge being properly handled, I have seen numerous examples of supplicants coming to awareness or recalling traumatic memories themselves when God sees they are ready to receive healing. Our healing intercession before God can bring this about.

Let me give you another example. At a healing conference in northern California a woman went to a prayer team for healing ministry. One person on the team thought of herself as a prophet of God. This "prophet" kept praying for the supplicant's son. But the supplicant said, "I don't have a son." The prophet said, "But I need to pray for your son." The supplicant kept repeating, "I have no son," as she had never been married nor had ever had a child. The minister kept insisting because she felt she was a special envoy from God, and said so. This was spiritually abusive if for no other reason than the minister became argumentative and was not respecting the supplicant.

A Person of Discernment

Being a minister of the Lord's healing means you are a person of discernment. Words, images, and sensations turned into prayer are the substance of healing ministry and this ministry embraces life. Everything in our ministry is up for ongoing discernment by the appropriate people God has indicated for this task, whether it be a fellow team member, spiritual head, pastor, or bishop. It is both a mind-set and lifestyle renewed each day as we enter into prayer asking for excellence in our ministry.

I invite you to open yourself even more to the way God would move in your healing prayer. He has a voice and longs to speak to his people, to heal and to build them up. Although mistakes sometimes happen in hearing his voice, we should not become discouraged. We are the Body of Christ and as the Church we believe in his word and strive to obey it. We are his sheep and the sheep know his voice. We must trust in an ever merciful God who is able to make his voice heard and will make it known to us. Trust not in your ability to hear and follow him but in his ability to lead and direct you.

I invite you to pray with me:

Lord Jesus, I long to hear your voice and do your will. I am in awe that you should speak to me—not only about your love for me, but also about the way you wish to use me for others. I give you my consent to be used for their healing in whatever way you desire. Let your Spirit flow in me, yielding the word of knowledge, the word of wisdom, the prophetic and healing gifts. Please convict me of and forgive any time I have misused your gifts or abused your people.

I give you permission to change me, my way of thinking, and my way of doing things. Lord, purify my ministry and conform it to your Spirit. Send people into my life to give discernment, wisdom and correction and give me a teachable spirit. I ask this in your precious name, Lord Jesus. Amen

Journal Questions for Listening to the Voice of the Spirit

1. Have you ever received words, images, or sensations with regard to people for whom you were praying or ministering to? Describe how they came to you. What is the usual way God speaks to you regarding concrete ministerial situations?
2. Have you ever made mistakes concerning what you have felt God saying? What did you learn from them?
3. Have you ever made mistakes regarding protocol? How did you grow from them?
4. Were you ever psychologically or spiritually abused in receiving ministry? Have you been able to deal with that in God's healing way?
5. Who in your life / ministry can you count on for discernment of your gifts?

[1] Benedict Heron, *Channels of Healing Prayer*, Notre Dame, Ave Maria Press, 1989, p. 47.

[2] Francis MacNutt, *Healing*, Notre Dame, Ave Maria Press, 1999, p. 157.

[3] Ibid., pp. 162–163.

[4] Robert DeGrandis, *Layperson's Manual for The Healing Ministry*, privately printed, 1985, p. 78.

[5] Ibid., p. 80.

[6] Heron, *op. cit.*, p. 49.

[7] *Catechism of the Catholic Church*, #801.

[8] *Instruction on Prayers for Healing*, Vatican Congregation for the Doctrine of the Faith, September 14, 2000.

[9] Cindy Jacobs, *The Voice of God*, Regal Books, Ventura, CA, 1995, p. 143.

Chapter 20

Glory to God! Essential Work after Healing Prayer

The Disciplined Anointing

An important part of every healing event is what takes place immediately afterward. It is part of the "disciplined anointing." Many people leave healing events knowing that God worked mightily, only to face falling into illness again. Also, I have frequently observed a phenomenon in which ministers who have done healing intercession during the event are affected negatively in one way or another by what took place. One could say, What harm could come from prayer? Of course there is no harm in prayer, but sometimes our flesh gets involved with it, and because of the deep spiritual work an opening can be produced through which the flesh, or even a malignant spiritual power, can gain an influence. This leaves room for what is not from God to be transmitted—yes, transmitted even while praying. Being a minister of healing prayer requires that, as far as possible, we follow through with our spiritual work. Taking a few minutes to "seal" a spiritual work after an engagement in healing prayer is a discipline that will provide both excellence in ministry and protection from negative repercussions.

Chris is a powerhouse of prayer, sought out by many people for his strong gifts in healing, discernment and the word of knowledge. On several occasions I have ministered in small groups with him. One night several years ago, we had ministered as a team for several hours with a woman who had deep generational wounding, which we later found out involved family members having been tortured by soldiers a generation ago in Eastern Europe.

After the woman left, Chris began to experience chest pains and shortness of breath. He is a skilled athlete, so this seemed all rather strange. I repeatedly was on the verge of calling the paramedics, but he insisted it was something spiritual manifesting in his flesh and almost immobilizing him. After a half hour of intense prayer, the pain lifted, but he was left with a strange sensation in his upper chest. We then realized that Chris had hooked into that brokenness and created an unclean, unholy bond through his vulnerability and her wound. Thank God it wasn't his heart, but he learned to "put on his armor," especially around his weaknesses.

Not too long after that I was presiding over a healing mass in Santa Cruz, California. A woman rather inexperienced in healing prayer was ministering with teams I often use at healing masses. She had come late to the mass and not participated in the preparation. During the prayer after mass, she began to experience a spiritual and emotional oppression accompanied by cramps in her stomach. As we prayed with her, it became evident that she had let her flesh become so involved in the prayer that she was receiving into herself some of the things that were going on with the people she had prayed for. It was quickly dealt with, but this is a scene often repeated in healing events. There was an inadequate preparation on her part and she was left vulnerable. It goes to show the importance of being there for both the preparation and the spiritual work afterwards.

To attend to the after-work, I suggest the following steps in sealing what God has done.

1. Acknowledge the Work of the Father

The first thing we should do is acknowledge that the Father has done work in the Holy Spirit and that this is part of the mercies of God, which have been manifested during the healing event. We need to glorify the Lord Jesus for what he has done in his Body. Beforehand, make sure the team knows that they will meet after the event has concluded. Include the participation of music ministers or their leaders and anyone else who helped significantly at the healing event.

We have experienced powerful manifestations of the Spirit during these prayer sessions. They have become a very special and necessary opportunity for me and for the ministry teams that work with me. On many occasions God has worked with the team in much deeper ways than would be possible during the event itself. This is exactly as it should be because there has been a dying to self and to the flesh while ministry was taking place. God often does anointed work among the team members who listened and were obedient during the event. If the team is Catholic, going before the Blessed Sacrament will be a special blessing.

This is the time to acknowledge God's work done at the event and thank him for it. It is a time for spontaneous praise. This is very scriptural, for St. Paul exhorts us to offer ourselves "remembering the mercies of God" (Rom 12:1, NJB). The psalmist declares, "We thank you, God, we give thanks; we call upon your name, declare your wonderful deeds" (Ps. 75:2, NAB). One of the pillars of the whole Jewish/Christian tradition is of giving thanks. Thanksgiving gives glory and credit to God; it reminds us that we are but servants. Thanksgiving for what God has done is also the hallmark of living in covenant with God. You will find that in spite of being tired, the praise and thanksgiving will have an unusual sweetness to it. At one event in a poor parish in East Palo Alto, California, the work that God did as we entered into this prayer was so strong, becoming prophetic, that it surpassed the wonderful healings we had seen at the mass.

2. Pray that God's Work is Brought to Completion

Paul writes, "I am confident of this, that the one who began a good work in you will continue to complete it until the day of Christ Jesus" (Phil. 1:6, NAB). A spiritual work is begun during healing events. Intercession is needed that this work will come to fulfillment and completion, and that those who were healed stay healed.

Not only the prayer team needs spiritual "after-work." You as a minister were connected spiritually, if only for a moment, with the people for whom you prayed. They were loved, ministered to and protected by the intercession the Lord had you do. I believe it is important that this work continue actively for a great deal of healing takes place after the event—even for days or weeks. We acknowledge that after healing events God continues to work. Intercede that God will continue to bless those people and heal them even on their way home, as they sleep, and in the coming days.

3. Recognize Your Part in the Work and Return it to God

The Holy Spirit works through human cooperation. The word "work" in Greek is *ergon* from which we get the word "energy." The Holy Spirit has his energies at work in a prayer event and we have ours. When the Anointing is manifest, both work in harmony. After the event we, in adoration and humility, recognize that we have worked in common with the Holy Spirit. The part we have done we explicitly give back to God so that he should be glorified.

Someone asked me, "Why is this so necessary?" St. Paul says that we glory only in the cross of our Lord Jesus Christ (Gal 6:14). We cannot glory in ourselves. This is the way to excellence in ministry. The Catholic liturgy recognizes that the only glory the saints enjoy is that which is bestowed as gift:

> My job is only to help the broken get to the presence of God. He does the rest! Neither you nor I can attribute this work to ourselves.

You are glorified in your saints,
for their glory is the crowning of your gifts.[1]

If we neglect this spiritual work of giving God all the glory for manifesting his healing, we run into danger of getting into pride and vanity that has led so many to self-deception. People often approach me with testimonies, saying, "You healed me." Or they wish to receive prayer with the petition, "Would you heal me?" I'm careful to correct this: I have never healed anyone. Only Jesus Christ is the Healer. My job is only to help the broken get to the presence of God. He does the rest! Neither you nor I can attribute this work to ourselves.

In the prayer after the healing event I recommend that you explicitly come before God and pray, "Lord we recognize that we have done a work in common with your Holy Spirit. We give back to you our part in this work for the glory of your Son, Jesus Christ." If we have truly worked with the Holy Spirit, we will glorify Jesus. This prayer must not be a false "lip service" or an empty ritual we go through. It needs to be a heart-felt, humble realization that God is the one who pours out his grace and that Jesus is the true Healer.

4. Cut Unholy and Unclean Bonds

Ephesians 6:17 indicates that we have as part of the armor of God, the "sword of the Spirit," that is the Word of God. This refers to the knowledge of the Word that we should have to counteract Satan's work, just as Jesus did when he was tested in the desert. We can symbolically take that sword and we can cut unholy bonds with it. The bonds I am referring to are bonds that are of the flesh and therefore are unholy bonds. While some traditions call these "soul-ties," I prefer the word bonds, but it amounts to the same. Because of fleshly vulnerabilities that we bring, these unclean bonds may have been established even during the healing ministry.

Many things can bond persons together in both holy and unholy ways. In God's covenant we are meant to have holy bonds, bonds of mutual love, bonds in our covenant relationships. It is in holy bonds that true communion is formed through the Holy Spirit. We saw the different ways of being in communion in Chapter 6.

God's covenant grace flows through holy bonds and creates holy communion. A negative or unholy bond can be formed during a healing session. Let's say, for example, the supplicant said or did something that made the healing minister angry. Until this is dealt with, a bond is then established that is emotional and fleshly. The enemy can take advantage of this spiritual weakness and wreak havoc. In the prayer minister's home, community, or work there might arise out-of-the-ordinary situations which cause God's work to be nullified through rancor and discord. Besides anger, there are other kinds of bonds as there are other kinds of emotions and works of the flesh.

There can be a heart bond. For instance, if a young man comes for prayer and the minister of healing is a woman who has a son with problems or a life similar to the supplicant's, a heart bond of pity may be formed. In psychological terms this is known as a form of "transference." If her heart-felt emotions start to speak to her more than the Spirit, then she is creating a bond with the young man which is not holy, but of the flesh.

The concept of unholy bonds is hard to grasp because many people think, "My heart goes out to him," or "I feel so sorry for her." People in ministry are often moved with such compassion as to cry for that person. Is this not good? After all, Jesus was moved with compassion and pity for those he healed. We want to affirm that compassion for suffering people is essential in the healing ministry. Yet there is a kind of "compassion" that may become obsessive and "co-dependent," based more on raw emotion than on true need. We must be wary, lest this cloud our seeing reality the way it is. We cannot attempt to drive God's agenda by our emotions. I propose that these distorted types of human emotions may actually get in the way of God's Spirit acting. The bond that gets solidified is a "bond of pity." This kind of bond has an unholy residue and must be cut.

There are many kinds of bonds. There could be a bond of a sexual attraction that was formed during the prayer session. This may occur when person who is praying feels carnally attracted and subsequently can't get the supplicant out of his or her mind. This is an unholy bond. Inexperienced ministers of healing often mistake this for something godly. If it persists, it can lead to perilous consequences, both for the supplicant and also for the minister and his or her ministry.

Even deeper spiritual bonds can also be formed. These are often occult bonds where the supplicant has been involved in witchcraft and has bonded with spiritual powers that are diabolic. With unattended weakness, that spiritual bond can flow through to the minister of healing, as can any curses that are on the supplicant. Knowing this, we take the "Sword of the Spirit" and we deliberately cut every unholy and unclean bond that may have formed.

The prayer goes simply: "In Jesus' name I take the sword of the Spirit, which is the Word of God, and I loose, cut, and sever every unclean and unholy bond that may have tried to impose itself during this ministry and I destroy it."

5. Seal the Work God Has Done

The healing environment lends itself to a spiritual openness that must be sealed in God. Wounds can be opened during a healing session. When God has worked in someone, that work can sometimes dissipate if it is not sealed. Part of the after-work of prayer ministry is to intercede that God *seals* the work he has done in the supplicants. This sealing is done not only over the person who is prayed for, but also over the person who has prayed. God often does work in the person who prays while he or she is ministering.

The Oxford dictionary defines a "seal" as a substance that is applied in order to isolate or set apart what is underneath by preventing entrance to and exit from it: to make it impervious. A seal can also be defined as a guarantee of authenticity, concluding or establishing something definitively.

In healing prayer, we can seal in God's work, thus protecting it and establishing it definitively. It is always part of my "after-work" of healing events and it is done in prayer. In the Christian revelation, there are two types of seals. Throughout our rich tradition there is the doctrine regarding the two "hands" of God—Christ and the Holy Spirit. Through these divine Persons the Father works in the world: the blood of Christ and through the Holy Spirit. Both of these are scriptural.

Look with me briefly at two interesting figures of these seals from the Bible. In Jesus' story of the Good Samaritan, the assaulted and hurting man had wine and oil poured onto his wounds (Lk. 10:34). Scripturally, wine is a figure of blood, in this case, the blood of Christ whereas the oil is a figure of the Holy Spirit. Both were poured on the wounds, representing the double way that the Father always works in us, in the Church, and in the world to heal and restore—through his Son and through his Spirit.

There is another figure that comes from the Old Testament, in Leviticus 14:1–32. Jesus makes reference to this when he told lepers to go and present themselves to the priests (Mt. 8:4; Mk. 1:44; Lk. 17:14). In Leviticus 14 we read about the two elements necessary for a leper who had received healing to be restored to the community and ultimately admitted to the temple for worship. He had to be anointed on various parts of his body with the blood of sacrifice. After that over the same places, the special anointing oil was applied. This is called the "lepers' anointing." Again, we see prefigured the blood of Christ (redemption) and the oil representing the Holy Spirit (purpose and destiny).

Seal with the Blood of Christ

The blood of Christ is a purifying, redeeming seal. It protects, making sure that what is holy remains intact, and that which is unholy cannot enter. The blood of Christ is *remedial* and *restorative*; that is, it makes up for what is deficient by drawing the power of Christ's sacrificial death upon it. When we, in the name of Jesus, declare something sealed in the blood of the Cross, we call down that protection and establish the people we ministered to in true freedom from bondage and sin. Therefore it is applied to the healing of what was broken.

Seal with the Holy Spirit

There is also the seal of the Holy Spirit. The Holy Spirit seals unto the day of redemption, as Paul writes,

> Now you too, in him have heard the message of the truth and the gospel of your salvation, and having put your trust in it you have been stamped with the seal of the Holy Spirit of the Promise, who is the pledge of our inheritance, for the freedom of the people whom God has taken for his own, for the praise of his glory. (Eph. 1:13–14, NJB)

Later he repeats, "Do not grieve the holy Spirit of God, with which you were sealed for the day of redemption" (Eph 4:30, NAB). Being sealed with the Holy Spirit is a "claiming" of a guarantee of destiny; the third Person of the Holy Trinity is the One who brings us completely into Jesus the Anointed One and his Anointing. The Holy Spirit forms us into the image and subsequently the likeness of Christ. This places our ministry in line with its eternal goal of complete healing in the resurrection. When we seal in the Holy Spirit, it is more than remedial; it is a seal that safeguards us unto the fullness of the work of God.

The beauty of working for the Kingdom of God in the healing ministry is that the broken Body of Christ is brought into restoration and redemption through his blood. We work in that Body in order for broken people to be healed and empowered for that which God has purposed for their lives. The healing ministry prophetically points people to their destiny in the Father saying, "You *can* walk there, your brokenness has been conquered by the resurrection of Jesus Christ. The Holy Spirit is upon you! In Jesus' name, stand and walk!"

---

[1] Preface for Holy Men and Women, *Roman Missal.*

ABOUT THE AUTHOR

Fr. Peter Sanders, C.O. is a member of the Congregation of the Oratory of St. Philip Neri located in Monterey, California. His teaching and healing ministry extends beyond Catholic circles into inter-faith dimensions, directing retreats, seminars and speaking at conferences. His ministry takes him to communities in North America, Mexico, Central and South America, as well as Europe and the Middle East.

Fr Peter is a worship leader and musician who believes that the exercise of ministry—including that of teaching and healing—is most life-transforming when it takes place in the atmosphere of God-centered, anointed worship. No matter what the venue, that truth is brought to life when he ministers in person.

Fr. Peter presents the deep biblical truths of faith in ways that they can be directly applied to everyday life and in the case of leaders, to ministerial situations. Over 500 people in Northern California have been trained through the *Institute for Healing Ministry* directed by Fr. Peter. The material covered in that *Institute* together with other teachings forms the first of a series of books entitled *Healing in the Spirit of*

Jesus: a hands-on guide to the ministry. In addition, he developed a series of in-depth courses on the *Catechism of the Catholic Church.*

Besides his priestly studies, Fr. Peter holds graduate degrees in Religious Education, Counseling Psychology, and Sacred Theology. For information on Fr. Peter's teaching schedule, tapes, books and retreats, contact:

New Pentecost Catholic Ministries
P.O. Box 1688
Monterey, CA 93942

INDEX

Note: "f" indicates that the reference is in a footnote.

C

Cantalamessa, Raniero, 67, 75f

Catechism of the Catholic Church, 11, 43f, 59, 60f, 92f, 101, 104f, 120f, 129f, 142f, 146, 159f, 178f, 179, 196f, 212f, 248f, 294f,

Catholic Church, 38, 40, 41, 65, 75, 78, 99, 108, 112, 123, 143, 179, 186, 189, 190, 191, 194, 206, 248, 256, 290

Charismatic, 9, 10, 38, 63, 66, 125 154, 179, 191, 205, 208, 227, 245, 246, 249, 263, 274, 288

Charisms, 47, 61, 85, 86, 87, 112, 178f, 190, 191, 192, 206, 210, 223, 244, 246, 247, 248, 249, 250, 251, 252, 253, 254, 256, 257, 258, 259, 260, 261, 263, 264, 265, 266, 267, 270, 273, 287, 289, 290,

Communion, 25, 26, 34, 55, 80, 81, 82, 83, 116, 117, 135, 136, 139, 140, 192, 194, 207, 226, 246, 247, 274, 284, 300

Conversion, 48, 63, 84, 97, 101, 105, 115, 116, 117, 120, 142, 227, 228, 230,

Covenant, 28, 70, 73, 81, 82, 83, 95, 96, 113, 135, 140, 164, 173, 177, 187, 220, 297, 300

D

Dawson, Joy, 157, 159f

DeGrandis, Robert, 1, 23, 32f, 283, 294f

Discernment, 12,47, 49, 51, 52, 53, 54, 61, 62, 63, 70, 73, 75, 78, 79, 84, 90, 96, 132, 156, 186, 205, 210, 218, 227, 230, 232, 250, 251, 252, 253, 257, 266, 270, 275, 280, 287, 288, 289, 290, 291, 292, 296

Discipleship, 55, 56, 59, 63, 64, 74, 100, 106, 118, 124, 125, 126, 127, 132, 134, 138, 190, 202, 203, 204, 213, 266,

E

Encouragement, 7, 12, 166, 174, 175, 176, 264

Eucharist, 25, 55, 81, 82, 83, 140, 148, 182, 192, 203, 204

Eusebius, 22

Evangelical churches, 38, 53, 139, 271

Evangelization, 26

F

Faith, 21, 22, 23, 27, 35, 38, 56, 59, 65, 66, 81, 82, 83, 84, 90, 97, 98, 99, 101, 103, 105, 106, 107, 108, 109, 110, 112, 112, 113, 114, 116, 117, 121, 122, 123, 138, 141, 144, 150, 157, 158, 167, 168, 169, 170, 173, 177, 182, 183, 184, 185, 188, 189, 192, 201, 202, 210, 217, 227, 228, 229, 230, 243, 245, 250, 255, 257, 260, 261, 262, 266, 267, 271, 275, 279, 286, 288, 305

Francis de Sales, 87, 92f, 118, 120f, 136, 142f

Friendship, 25, 26, 35, 68, 166, 167, 169

Index

W

To order additional copies of

SPIRITof
JESUS

Have your credit card ready and call
Toll free: (877) 421-READ (7323)
Or send $15.95* each plus $5.95 S&H** to

WinePress Publishing
PO Box 428
Enumclaw, WA 98022

Or order online at: www.winepresspub.com

*Washington residents, add 8.4% sales tax
**add $1.50 S&H for each additional book ordered